D1506739

THE ANTIQUE
COLLECTOR'S GUIDES

CLOCKS AND WATCHES

GENERAL EDITOR
David Coombs

THE ANTIQUE COLLECTOR'S GUIDES

CLOCKS AND WATCHES

ALAN SMITH

Drawings by Peter Fitzjohn

CRESCENT BOOKS
NEW YORK

Published by Ebury Press
Division of The National Magazine Company Ltd
Colquhoun House
27-37 Broadwick Street
London W1V 1FR

First impression 1975
Reprinted 1989
Copyright © 1975 The National Magazine Company Ltd

This 1989 edition published by Crescent Books
distributed by Crown Publishers, Inc., 225 Park Avenue South,
New York, New York 10003

Printed and bound in Yugoslavia
by Mladinska Knjiga, Ljubljana

ISBN 0 517 68478 0
hgfedcba

For Deirdre

Introduction

To attempt to produce a book about the clocks and watches of the past five hundred years, taking English clock and watchmaking as the most important part of it but also devoting a considerable amount of space to the products of other European countries and America, has meant looking at the whole problem from a bird's eye view, bearing in mind what has already been written and trying to decide what would be most useful for the students and collectors of today. At the outset it has meant accepting the fact that many important aspects have to be left out altogether, such as the water clocks of the Middle Ages which are now only known through documents, or the great astronomical clocks of ancient China such as Su Sung's water clock of the late 11th century. It has meant accepting that if the reader can afford to purchase a Knibb, an East or a Tompion he can certainly afford to buy one of the very fine specialist publications on the 'golden age' of English horology, which are far more detailed and informative on clocks of that period than a broadly-based book of this kind could possibly be. It has meant accepting that the average collector of modest means today will want to have information about clocks and watches of the 19th and early 20th centuries, where there is still a world of unexplored territory which in its own way, and seen against the circumstances of the period concerned, is just as important and relevant as the great periods of earlier clockmaking which have already been written about at very great length. Finally it has been necessary to accept that there is a growing interest not only in clocks and watches as pieces of furniture or personal jewellery, but also in the ways in which they work and in which they were made.

In recent years there have been several sales of clock and watchmaking tools, and so keen has the competition become to obtain them that it is certain that they are being acquired as historical evidence, rather than for use at the bench. In our complex technological age this is understandable as we look back with something of perhaps misplaced nostalgia to an age which, whatever its shortcomings and insecurity might be, made use of the skills of hand and eye, in which the craftsman was identifiable as a human being and not merely as a cog in a vast machine. To begin to appreciate, therefore, something of the role of the craftsman and the tools he used is the justification of the final part of Chapter 2, however brief and inevitably limited this section must be due to shortage of space. In the same way the rest of Chapter 2 attempts to analyse some of the major technological problems in the working of clocks and watches, partly to avoid constant repetition in later sections, partly to give some idea of the development of watches and clocks as specialised machines, irrespective of the age or country in which they were made. To understand the principles involved in clock and watchwork, even though an owner may not personally feel competent to undertake repairs or even straightforward dismantling and cleaning, will give a pleasure and satisfaction much greater than that of simple ownership.

To study clocks and watches is to study our world in microcosm and to learn something of the development of technology and metallurgy, the evolution of design, the course of economic and social history, astronomy, physics, mathematics and even philosophy. It is perhaps not readily realised that the knowledge which was to be harnessed at the time of the Industrial Revolution was already waiting to be exploited at least a century earlier, discovered by the clock, watch and instrument makers who, having solved complex mechanical problems had provided answers which would eventually make possible the use of new sources of power. The expansion of the world in terms of transport and communications owes an untold debt to the watch and clockmakers who devised the instruments to make exploration possible. In the 19th century it is to the United States that we must turn to examine how new methods of manufacture were devised to meet the needs of a newly industrialised world and not to those older, conservative nations of western Europe. In America the early craftsmen at first quietly used the principles of clockmaking which had been brought from Europe, in a country short of both raw materials and skills, but by developing with energy and determination new and devastatingly original ideas in their manufacturing techniques, they provided the world with timepieces in vast numbers and at prices which even the humblest of men and women could afford. A study of the making of clocks and watches in the United States is possibly more important for an understanding of the world of today than the study of the work of those great horological masters of 17th and 18th century England and France. What is more the products of that country and period are still available outside museum collections, a useful point to remember when few of us can afford a Graham or an Ellicott, even supposing that there were sufficient to go round. A Chauncey Jerome or an Ingraham clock we might still acquire with relative ease, and there are many American machine-made watches which are worthy of study and a pleasure to own.

In English clockmaking there has been all too little written about the contributions to the trade of the northern makers, particularly those of Lancashire and Yorkshire where many fine pieces were made in the late 18th and 19th centuries. In the world of watchmaking it is becoming increasingly clear that south west Lancashire provided the London makers with rough movements and specialised tools and parts from the 17th century onwards, often working in conditions approaching abject poverty. The names of the Lancashire workers are not remembered, and even in the days in which they were working they were generally as unknown as they are today. It is only the names of the notable figures who finished the work in London and elsewhere which have come down to us as the really eminent men of the craft. Like much else in this book there has been no room to explore this field fully, but at least the matter has been mentioned to give the story something of a true perspective.

Electrical horology is very much part of our lives today and the serious study of the origins of electrical timekeeping is beginning in earnest, and deserves its place in a book of this sort, even at the expense of such old favourites as the inclined plane clock, the Congreve rolling ball clock and many others which will be found missing from these pages. As our ways of life are changing, those fine old turret clocks, hidden from most people's eyes in church or town hall towers, are one by one disappearing to be replaced by modern electric synchronous motors, though fortunately many are being preserved in museum collections or are being shipped abroad, in reconditioned state, to countries whose electrical supplies are still uncertain. Too large and awkward for all but the most enthusiastic collectors, turret clocks form an important part of our story and have therefore been included, if only briefly.

Whether we think of clocks as furniture and part of the evolving styles of interior decoration, or whether we think of watches as useful articles of personal adornment following the dictates of fashion, or whether we think of clocks and watches as mechanisms which have faithfully worked on our behalf over many years, and sometimes failed in the process, there are many lessons quite separate from the world of horology itself which we can learn from a study of the ways in which they work, the ways in which they were made and the countries and periods which originally produced them.

THE ANTIQUE
COLLECTOR'S GUIDES

Clocks & Watches

1
Time

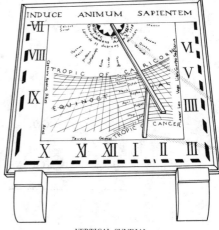

VERTICAL SUNDIAL
Eyam Parish Church, Derbyshire, 1775

The rotation of the earth in its daily round is the basic clock which regulates our lives, our times of waking, working, eating, relaxation and sleep. This is the fundamental cycle which has governed human life throughout the ages, and the annual rotation of the earth round the sun, with its consequent change in the length of days and nights and in the seasons, has also governed and shaped the way in which we live. The desirability of measuring the daily progress of the sun across the sky and of dividing the day into measurable parts, combined with the human 'clock' of hunger and tiredness, was clearly recognised in the Near Eastern cradle of our civilisation probably as long ago as four thousand years, and the use of the sun stick amongst primitive peoples seems to indicate a knowledge of how this could be done in the remotest antiquity. In ancient times the study of astronomy, on which our time-keeping system is based, and the calculation of the calendar was intimately connected with religion.

As man has developed he has devised various types of *dial* which could be used to measure the daily movement of the sun, and there are many *sundials* still in existence which are fascinating both in their design and ingenuity. Perhaps the most widely known are those placed on pillars in churchyards or on the walls of the church tower or porch and used to regulate the times of divine service. A famous one at Kirkdale Church in Yorkshire still survives, dating from Saxon times, but most remain from the 18th or 19th centuries such as the example shown here of 1775 when the sundial was the only means the ordinary man had of checking his clock or watch. This sundial from Eyam in Derbyshire not only shows the time at that place but also the time at noon of various cities throughout the world such as Quebec, Rome, Constantinople and Jerusalem. A separate inscription also gives the position of the sun north and south of the equator in the different months of the year.

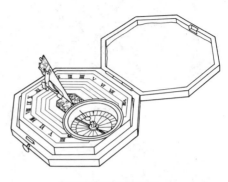

PORTABLE TABLET SUNDIAL
late 18th century

PORTABLE SILVER SUNDIAL
Butterfield à Paris, c.1700

Fixed sundials such as those on church walls were obviously limited in their use by the availability of sunshine and the fact that they were situated in one place. From the 17th century, *portable dials* were devised which could be used at any convenient time and place. Like the fixed sundials, however, the *style*—derived from the Greek word *stulos* meaning a pillar—or *gnomon* which is the pointer used to cast the shadow on the dial, must be adjusted to an angle of slope equal to the angle of latitude where the dial is being used and must be pointing south in the northern hemisphere. By placing it at this angle the sloping gnomon is parallel to the axis of the earth. For this reason therefore, both the portable dials shown here are provided with a *magnetic compass* so that the owner could orientate the dial after placing it on a horizontal surface, and being made for use in Europe they have adjustment for latitudes north of the equator.

The *tablet dial*, made of wood with a printed paper dial pasted on, is a cheaper and later form of a type made in southern Germany in the 17th century. On it the gnomon, which in this case is a thin silk cord, could be altered for latitude at its upper end by fixing it in different holes on a printed vertical scale. There are *two* dials on it so that when the sun was high the *horizontal* dial was used, but in the morning and evening when the sun was low the *vertical* dial worked better. On the silver portable dial the gnomon could be altered to the correct latitude by raising or lowering the slope according to an engraved scale, the precise position being shown by the beak of the decorative 'bird' support. The latitudes of thirty-three European cities are conveniently engraved for reference on the underneath side of the instrument. Such beautifully made dials were provided with a velvet lined, leather covered case for carrying.

CUBICAL SUNDIAL
D. Beringer, late 18th century

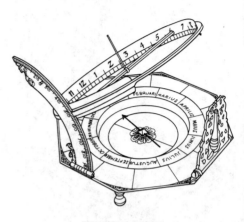

EQUATORIAL SUNDIAL
Johann Villebrand, Augsburg *c*.1690

The tablet sundial (p. 15) utilised two dials, one horizontal and the other vertical. Other portable sundials were designed with several pointers and hour scales working on the same principle in a slightly more complex way. The *cubical sundial* made with printed paper dials and thin brass gnomon plates has five reading surfaces, each of which indicates the time more or less conveniently according to the position of the sun. Like the tablet dial it has a compass for direction and can be adjusted for latitude through a swivel hinge on its supporting pillar. Some multi-dial instruments of this kind had different dials for indicating different ways of dividing the day. The early Italian system, for example, divided the daily cycle into twenty-four equal hours starting at sunset, while the similar Babylonian system started at sunrise. Some large stone sundials with several faces made it possible to read the time in different places, and this idea has continued to be used in clocks, particularly those of service to travellers.

A very beautiful example in silver and gilded brass is the *equatorial sundial* of the late 17th century. It is known as equatorial because the circular scale marked with the hours lies in a plane parallel to the plane of the earth's equator. The fine pointed gnomon in the centre can be swivelled on its axis either above or below the equatorial ring according to the elevation of the sun, and it is parallel to the axis of the earth. A *plumb bob* on the right assists in setting the dial in a correctly horizontal position and the compass is adjustable for variations of the magnetic north pole. All the various parts fold flat for convenience in carrying. This equatorial dial was made about 1690 in Augsburg, Bavaria, the source of many fine dials of this kind and also of many fine clocks (pp. 78, 80). There were many variations in the principle of the equatorial dial of which the *ring dial* (p. 18) is an interesting version.

SUNDIAL IN A WATCH CASE
Abraham Gribelin, Blois c.1630

PILLAR OR COLUMN SUNDIAL
French, 17th century

The watch illustrated here by *Abraham Gribelin* of Blois has a sundial set in the case. The gnomon is shown folded flat and it is not adjustable for latitude, which pre-supposes that it was intended to be used in the vicinity of Blois in northern France (47°35′N), and a small compass is enclosed to orientate it when taking a reading. This type of watch will be discussed later (p. 87) and other examples are known of clocks fitted with sundials such as the *tambour cased clock* on p. 73 which has a sundial on the underneath cover plate. Many pocket sundials of the 17th century were elaborately engraved with formalised floral and leaf designs in the same way as the watches of the period. Early sundials were generally only divided into hours, sometimes with half hours and quarters added like the dials of contemporary watches and clocks, but later 18th century dials, although plainer in style, were more scientifically and accurately divided into five minute intervals, or even into minutes.

The *pillar dial* shows another type which was used in Europe until the 19th century, often amongst country people and of more primitive construction than the fine 17th century example here. It is not fitted with a compass but is adjusted with reference to the date. The *gnomon* is a dragon's tail which is revolved until it corresponds with one of the signs of the Zodiac below, according to the month. The whole dial is then turned until the gnomon points to the sun and the vertical shadow of it is read off against the dots on the pillar. These dots are arranged with six spaces for six hours of the sun's elevation in the morning until noon, the same dots indicating the six hours of declination after noon. There is no indication whether or not the hour shown is before or after noon. Thus the shortest divisions on the right correspond with Sagittarius and Capricorn (winter) and the long spaces on the left with Gemini and Cancer (summer).

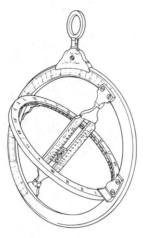

UNIVERSAL RING DIAL
English, late 18th century

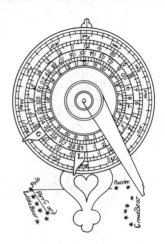

NOCTURNAL
drawing from The Mariner's New
Calendar, 1761

The sundials previously described would be of no use on a ship unless the sea was very calm. The *universal ring dial*, suspended from a finger or convenient hook, provided the mariner with a dial which, in large sizes at least, could be used with considerable accuracy. The *pendant* at the top was made to slide round the vertical ring until the correct latitude, *either north or south* of the equator, was indicated on the appropriate engraved scale, and the *sliding index* with a small hole in it on the central bar was moved to set the instrument for the date. Once set, the dial was turned until a spot of sunlight shining through the hole in the index fell upon the inner edge of the *equatorial ring*, which was graduated in hours and minutes. As with other sundials, many ring dials are engraved with the different latitudes of important cities. Other versions for land use are mounted on *pedestal plinths* in place of the pendant and loop.

The obvious shortcoming of the sundial is its uselessness at night. *Nocturnals* were made from the 16th century onwards to overcome this problem and they all work on the principle of regarding the stars as a huge clock dial, slowly revolving round the fixed North Star. The nocturnal is held vertically by the handle until the North Star is seen through the central hole and then the long pointer is turned until it is in line with the Little or Great Bear constellation. The instrument must first be set according to the date of the month on the outer scale with the pointer G if the Great Bear is to be used, or with the pointer L if the Little Bear is used. Once set against the night sky the nocturnal could be taken indoors to read off the time on the innermost scale. The nocturnal illustrated shows a *lunar scale* of $29\frac{1}{2}$ days on the outer part of the inner ring.

OIL LAMP CLOCK
German, 18th century

SAND GLASS CLOCK
Italian, 17th century

All sundials indicate *solar time* which is different from *mean time* and only coincides with it on four dates each year—about April 16th, June 14th, September 1st and December 25th. This was not a serious matter until the introduction in the 17th century of the *pendulum* and the *balance spring*, which made clocks and watches very much more accurate than they had been (pp. 90, 102). From about 1670 the best clocks were set to correct time by reference to a printed table showing the *equation of time*, that is the number of minutes and seconds the clock should be faster or slower than the time indicated on the sundial. From these complications it is not surprising that instruments for measuring *known periods of time* in each day were frequently used—for gauging the length of a given task, for marking the changes of watch at sea, or for timing the vicar's sermon. *Interval timers*, as they are called, were devised in different ways and two are illustrated.

The *oil clock* and the *sand glass* come at the end of a long tradition which includes *clepsydra* or *water clocks* and other no longer surviving devices. The oil clock, with divisions on the pewter mount, shows the passage of the hours as the lamp burns and the oil level falls in the glass. The advantage of this 'clock' is that it also serves to provide light. In the sand glass illustrated the running sand measures the four quarters of an hour by means of four glass containers made of two separate glass bulbs containing measured quantities of dry sand, bound together with cord and wax to join their narrow apertures. Pocket sand glasses of one minute or half minute duration were frequently carried by medical men until the 19th century to time the pulses of their patients, while the egg-timer sand glass is still to be found as an ephemeral tourist trinket. Clockwork interval timers have now entirely replaced the sand glass for domestic use (p. 211).

2
Clocks, Watches and Tools

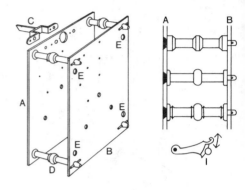

LONG CASE CLOCK FRAME IN BRASS AND SELECTION
OF PILLARS
English, 18th century

Mechanical clocks driven by weights or springs, recording the passage of time by means of trains of wheels and pinions and controlled or regulated by various types of escapement, have a long and varied history. To understand a clock or watch it is necessary to know more than just what it looks like from the outside; indeed much of the pleasure of ownership consists of understanding and caring for a clock or watch as a mechanical instrument. Aesthetic pleasure cannot be confined to outward casework alone, for the movements of many clocks and watches are works of art themselves. The desire to understand the way in which a movement works leads naturally to a wish to know how it was made, the tools and workshops that were used and the conditions under which the work was done. The quality, precision and sheer functional beauty of many clock and watchmaking tools are as pleasing as the clocks which they were used to make.

Although various types of *frame* have been made to accommodate the wheel trains of clocks (pp. 68, 71, 89, 107), most consist of two flat brass plates containing the *pivot holes*, held firmly in relation to each other by sets of *pillars* (D), usually four but sometimes more. The plate known as the *top* or *front* plate (B) is removable, being held on to the pillars by steel pins, the pillars being riveted to the *back* plate (A). In more recent times screws or nuts have been used instead and on some fine 17th century clocks *latches* (I) were provided for ease of dismantling and quality of finish. The dial of the clock is often fitted to the top or front plate which has special holes provided to take the ends of the dial pillars (E). In pendulum clocks a *suspension cock* is mostly provided at the back (C), though in American and some Continental clocks it is found at the front instead, occasionally in front of the dial.

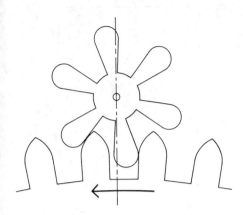

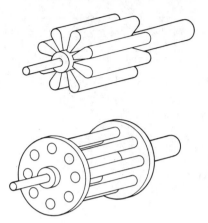

ENGAGEMENT OF WHEEL TEETH AND PINION LEAVES

EIGHT LEAF PINION AND LANTERN PINION

The wheels and pinions of clock trains were at first made of iron or steel, but from the late 16th century it became universal, in domestic clocks, for the pinions to be of steel but the wheels of brass. In conventional clock movements the *wheels drive the pinions*, providing a highly geared mechanism which can be controlled by a comparatively small resistance. The *teeth* of wheels and the *leaves* of pinions are so shaped that motion is transferred as smoothly as possible, care being taken that they do not lock or rub while revolving. In old clocks wear can be severe on the pinion leaves, which are worn more quickly than the brass wheel teeth. The softer metal more readily absorbs the hard, microscopic fragments of abrasive dust and dirt and provides a cutting surface which wears away the steel. For this reason oil should never be used on the teeth of wheels in clocks, for it attracts and holds the dirt and forms an abrasive paste.

The relative sizes of wheel teeth and pinions were calculated according to the 'count' of the particular wheel train required and by the use of a *sector*, a tool which gives the correct diameter of the pinion according to the number of leaves required and the size of the engaging wheel. In many German and American clocks (Ch. 8, 9) wheels, pinions and *arbors* were made of wood. Another form of pinion was the *lantern* type, improved though not widely adopted as a *roller* pinion by Joseph Ives in America (p. 156). Lantern pinions were often used in turret clocks and here they had two major advantages compared with the conventional form. First the steel pins could be replaced easily when worn, unlike the leaves of an ordinary pinion which are integral with the arbor, and second in turret clocks, which are often housed in dirty, exposed towers, the accumulated deposits of dirt fall through the pins and escape, instead of becoming trapped and packed between solid leaves.

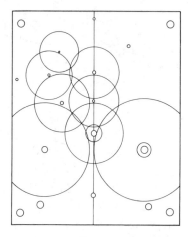

TOP PLATE OF AN 8-DAY LONG CASE CLOCK

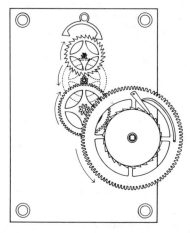

8-DAY WHEEL TRAIN OF AN ENGLISH LONG CASE CLOCK

Brass plates for movements in the 18th century and earlier were cast in moulds and had to be hammered or *planished* to harden the metal before use. Although fine quality clocks had the hammer marks stoned away and the surfaces polished, many cheaper or country clocks bear the marks of this process, and reveal their age by pitting of the surface as a result of slightly faulty casting. When a clock was being made the two plates, front and back, were secured closely together and all the pivot and other holes common to both were drilled together. The positioning of the pivot holes was determined by the size and tooth numbers of the trains of wheels, and the *pitch circles* or lines of intersection of wheel teeth and pinion leaves were *scribed* on to the front plate to set out the work, as can be seen in the above example. To economise on time and labour many makers kept *templates* of the positioning of pivot holes for standard sized movements.

There are many different 'counts' of wheel trains according to various factors—the length of running of the clock at each winding, the type of escapement used, the length or 'beat' of the pendulum and the particular preference of the maker. The diagram here shows a typical wheel train of the 'going' part of an 8-day English long case clock. Starting with the *great wheel* from which the weight-driven power is derived, its 96 teeth drive an 8-leaved pinion on the *centre wheel* of 60 teeth, driving an 8-leaved pinion on the *third wheel* of 48 teeth which drives a 6-leaved pinion on the *escape wheel* arbor. The escape wheel has 30 teeth, one of which is allowed to 'escape' by the *anchor* at every other swing of the *Royal* or *seconds* pendulum (p. 25). The centre wheel, which carries the *minute hand*, therefore revolves once every hour:

centre wheel   third   escape
one revolution wheel   wheel

$$\frac{60}{1} \times \frac{48}{8} \times \frac{30(\times 2)}{6}$$

$= 3{,}600$ seconds $= 60$ minutes $= 1$ hour

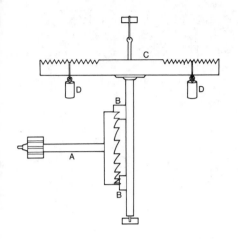

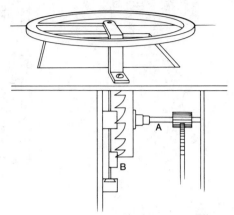

VERGE AND FOLIOT ESCAPEMENT

VERGE AND BALANCE ESCAPEMENT

The *anchor* on the opposite page was a type of *escapement* invented in the late 17th century. The earliest escapement known was the *verge and foliot* and this was certainly applied to clockwork by the beginning of the 14th century (p. 68). Possibly the oscillating motion of the foliot was suggested by the similar action of an alarm hammer ringing a bell when set in motion by a toothed wheel acting on pallets on the vertical hammer rod (p. 69). In the drawing above the pinion, arbor and wheel (A) being the last in a wheel train, are prevented from turning by the *pallets* (B, B) on a vertical rod or *verge* suspended above. The pallets are set at an angle of about 95° relative to each other and as one tooth of the escape wheel (A) passes one pallet it is locked by the other. The locking pallet is pushed out of the way causing the foliot to swing, and in so doing the first pallet locks it again.

As the pallets lock and unlock the escape wheel teeth they are moved by the 'impulse' of the escape wheel as it tries to revolve. The speed at which this is done is regulated by the crossbar or foliot (C) which in turn is regulated by placing small weights (D, D) on its ends. When nearer to the centre these allow faster oscillation than when placed near the ends. When the *balance* was introduced in early lantern clocks, the vibrations were controlled by fixing a hog's bristle in the top plate to limit the action of the swing and to provide a more or less resilient 'buffer' against the balance arm. Regulation was controlled by either changing the *depthing* of the verge pallets into the teeth of the escape wheel, or by altering the driving weight and thus the power supplied. In both forms, either verge and foliot or verge and balance, the action was inaccurate and subject to the cleanliness and lubrication of the wheel train and the quality of the parts.

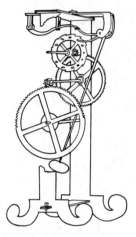

GALILEO'S PENDULUM ESCAPEMENT

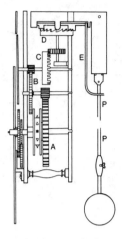

HUYGHENS VERGE ESCAPEMENT
WITH PENDULUM

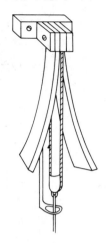

CYCLOIDAL CHEEKS AND
PENDULUM SUSPENSION

The erratic behaviour of the early verge escapement was not overcome until the introduction of the *pendulum* in the 1650s (p. 90). The drawing of Galileo's escapement shows his idea of controlling a wheel train by a pendulum fitted with two arms, in a forked position, near the point from which the pendulum swings. In the drawing the last wheel of the train (escape wheel) moves clockwise and is on the point of *impulsing* the pendulum, prior to its right-hand swing, by a pin which engages the lower forked arm. When this swing takes place the pivoted lever at the top left falls to lock the wheel on a ratchet tooth on its edge, and as the pendulum returns the wheel is again unlocked to repeat the action. Thus we have *locking, unlocking* and *impulse*, the basis of all types of escapement. Though Galileo never made this escapement for an actual clock, one at least is known to have been started by his son Vicenzio, though it was not apparently completed.

Christiaan Huyghens controlled an escape wheel and verge by a pendulum. In his early clocks the *great wheel* (A) drives a *second wheel* (B) which in turn drives a *contrate wheel* (C) geared to an *escape wheel* (D) turning in a horizontal plane on a vertical arbor. Across the top the verge staff and pallets are pivoted horizontally and the oscillation of the verge is controlled by the pendulum (P) through a wire *crutch* (E). The pendulum was regulated by lowering the bob to make it go slower and raising it to cause it to gain. Huyghens attempted to make his pendulum truly *isochronous*, i.e. to make it keep equal time when vibrating through varying arcs, by suspending it on threads between metal *cycloidal cheeks*, but the system was early abandoned. The action of these cheeks was to make the pendulum swing in a *cycloidal curve*, the theoretical ideal, this curve being the one traced by a fixed point on the circumference of a circle rolling along a straight line.

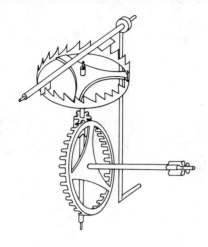

VERGE ESCAPEMENT WITH CRUTCH   THE ANCHOR ESCAPEMENT

The action of Huyghens' pendulum and verge escapement can perhaps better be understood by reference to the drawing above in which the 'tail' of the verge, or *crutch*, engages with the pendulum which is not shown here. Once the idea of using cycloidal cheeks had been given up a crutch was no longer necessary, for the 'tail' of the verge staff became the pendulum itself, with a weight or *bob* screwed on to its lower end (p. 90). Although these pendulums were not truly isochronous in that the arc of swing varied according to the power of the impulse transmitted by the movement, and other mechanical factors, the improvement over the verge and foliot or balance was so remarkable that this invention remains as the first really great horological advance—a breakthrough of the first magnitude. In many later bracket clocks the verge staff was pivoted at one end only, the end near the pendulum having a *knife edge suspension* riding in a V slot in the suspension cock.

The short bob, or half-second pendulum, although persisting right through the 18th century in bracket clocks, gave way to the long or *Royal* pendulum of one second beat soon after 1670. This was possible through the invention of the *anchor escapement* (pp. 90, 91) in which the teeth of the escape wheel were cut in the *edge* of the wheel instead of at right-angles to it, and so that they could be locked, unlocked and impulsed by pallets arranged in the form of an anchor, in the same plane. With a clockwise rotating escape wheel each pallet in turn locks its following tooth and impulse to keep the pendulum swinging is given as the pallet moves away. By using this escapement the locking and unlocking is achieved with a much smaller pendulum swing than that necessary for the verge, and thus the pendulum could be very much longer. In the action of locking the pallets tend to push the teeth of the escape wheel slightly backwards, causing an action known as *recoil*.

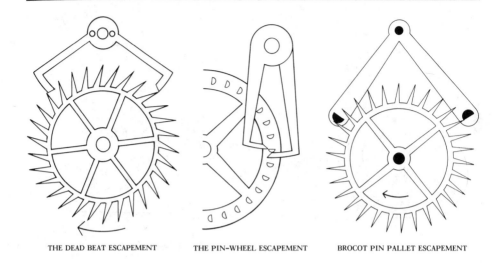

THE DEAD BEAT ESCAPEMENT   THE PIN-WHEEL ESCAPEMENT   BROCOT PIN PALLET ESCAPEMENT

A type of anchor escapement known as the *dead beat* was devised by George Graham in the 18th century (p. 100) and this escapement remained the standard type for many precision clocks until the introduction of electrical principles in the late 19th century. The dead beat escapement has *no recoil* and the pallet surfaces, which receive impulse from the pointed escape wheel teeth, are often jewelled, i.e. fitted on their working surfaces with hard, polished stones such as sapphire or garnet, to resist wear. It is necessary to make the dead beat escapement with much greater precision than the ordinary anchor, and it was mostly used with temperature compensated pendulums for regulator clocks (p. 28). As the escape wheel teeth are very fine with sharp points they can be easily damaged by misuse, and regulator clocks are invariably fitted with *maintaining power* (p. 30) to keep the clock going forwards while it is being wound, which in precision work also avoids the loss of time required for winding.

Two other escapements involving a type of anchor are the *pin wheel* and the *pin pallet* escapements. The pin wheel escapement consists of an escape wheel without teeth, but with semi-circular faced *pins* projecting from one side, which lock and give impulse to the pallet faces of a narrow, two-armed anchor. Though occasionally used in English clocks and more often on French ones, it found particular application on turret clock movements. Unlike the anchor or dead beat, each pallet *in turn* is used to lock and impulse the two pallet surfaces consecutively. The pin pallet escapement is much more like a normal anchor, but here the pallets are in the form of pins with semi-circular acting faces engaging with the escape wheel teeth. The escapement was devised by Achille Brocot (p. 182) and is often seen in 19th century clocks in front of the dial, with the pin pallets made of carnelian. This hard stone, which wears well, overcame the problem of keeping a supply of oil on the acting surfaces of the pallets.

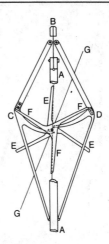

THE TIC–TAC OR DRUM ESCAPEMENT   DOUBLE THREE–LEGGED GRAVITY ESCAPEMENT

Another form of escapement allied to the anchor is the *tic-tac* or *drum* escapement which was often used in French clocks, though may occasionally be found in English bracket clocks. Embracing only two teeth of the escape wheel impulse is given only every alternate swing of the pendulum on the *curved* pallet surface, the other pallet merely acting as a locking pallet. A number of escapements were constructed in 18th and 19th century clocks which embrace only three or four teeth of the escape wheel, which may be classed as being half way between the tic-tac and the true anchor, which normally embraces seven or eight teeth. Sometimes anchors are made of a hardened steel *strip* for cheapness of manufacture, and these may be seen in many American clocks acting *underneath* the escape wheel instead of above. The difficulty of all anchor escapements is that to a greater or lesser extent they interfere with the natural vibration of the pendulum.

To overcome this interference and to make the pendulum as 'free' as possible, a type of *gravity* escapement was devised by Lord Grimthorpe and was much used in turret clocks and some precision time-pieces (p. 146). Its action can best be understood by concentrated observation, but the basic principle is that the *pendulum* (A) suspended from the point (B) is impulsed by two *gravity arms* (C, D) pivoted above and acting alternately, one on each side and giving impulse by their gravitational weight. Two *three-legged armed plates* (E, F) alternately lock on the gravity arms as they rotate clockwise, and pins at the centre act on the sloping faces of two curved brackets on the inside of the gravity arms to set each arm ready for impulse. The *fly* (G) simply controls the speed of revolution of the three-legged plates and absorbs inertia as the arms are locked. The virtue of this system is that the arms convey constant gravitational impulse and the pendulum is almost entirely free from interference.

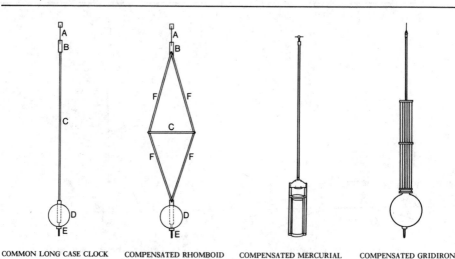

COMMON LONG CASE CLOCK PENDULUM   COMPENSATED RHOMBOID PENDULUM   COMPENSATED MERCURIAL PENDULUM   COMPENSATED GRIDIRON PENDULUM

The pendulum of a clock swinging from a fixed point vibrates at a *natural* rate and therefore controls the progress of the clock according to that rate. Various types of pendulum have been devised to overcome the effects of changes of temperature which lengthen or shorten its effective length and therefore its rate, of which three are shown here. The first pendulum is illustrated to show the most common long case clock type, uncompensated and consisting only of a thin wire (C) suspended on a thin metal spring (A) with a lead-filled brass bob (D) adjustable by the *rating screw* (E). *Wooden* pendulum rods react less to changes of temperature and were sometimes used. The *rhomboid* pendulum, found very occasionally in domestic clocks (p. 127) but mostly in turret clocks, is temperature compensated by its construction of brass and steel strips. As the pendulum lengthens in higher temperatures the brass strip (C) expands *outwards*, causing the steel strips (F) to hinge outwards also and effectively shorten the pendulum.

Similar but more sophisticated compensation is provided by the *mercurial* and *gridiron* pendulums, the former invented by George Graham and the latter by John Harrison (p. 100). The mercurial pendulum has a glass bottle of mercury as its bob. In higher temperatures the column of mercury increases in height to raise the effective *centre of oscillation* in compensation for the lengthening of the rod, the reverse action taking place when it is cold. The gridiron pendulum is composed of five, seven or nine rods of steel and brass (five=3 steel, 2 brass; seven=4 steel, 3 brass; nine=5 steel, 4 brass). These rods, attached to or passing loosely through horizontal plates, keep the pendulum bob at a constant distance from the point of suspension by the fact that the coefficient of expansion of brass is greater than that of steel in the ratio of 5 to 3. The rod lengths are arranged so that any expansion of the steel downwards is balanced by the upward expansion of the brass.

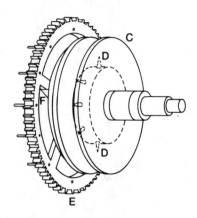

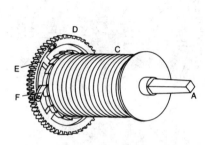

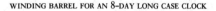

WINDING BARREL FOR AN 8-DAY LONG CASE CLOCK

WINDING PULLEY FOR A 30-HOUR LONG CASE CLOCK

In English long case clocks the power supplied by the weight or weights will allow the clock to run for 8 days or for about 30 hours according to the wheel train design. Eight-day winding takes place on a hollow brass *barrel* (C) which is turned by the winding key on the *square* (A), the *click* or *pawl* (F) and the *click spring* (E) being used to transmit the power to the great wheel (D) either for going or striking trains. The 8-day barrel normally has a continuous groove of sixteen turns round which a *gut line* is wrapped as the clock is wound, two turns for each day. The gut lines, made of sheep or ox intestines cured and twisted, may last twenty years. In this type of winding the weight is hung on a *pulley*, the other end of the line being attached to the seat board of the clock. Thus the weights are *compounded*, only delivering half their actual weight to the winding barrels of the great wheels.

Thirty-hour clocks were driven either by two weights on two ropes, one for going and one for striking, or with one weight and a small counter-weight on an endless rope or chain (p. 30). The power is transmitted by a *pulley* (C), the inside of the pulley groove having *spikes* (D) to grip the rope. A *spring click* (F) engages with the spokes of the great wheel (E) in a primitive form of ratchet mechanism, and when the *endless* cord or chain is used this is necessary only on the striking train great wheel, though with separate weights for the going and striking two such pulleys are required. Fraying of the rope caused fluff and dust to foul the movement, and many clocks were either made or converted to use chain instead. In this case the bottom of the pulley groove is cut in such a way that the alternate links of the chain lie in a narrow groove between the spikes, the latter being spaced to engage accurately with the intervening links.

HUYGHENS ENDLESS ROPE OR CHAIN WINDING

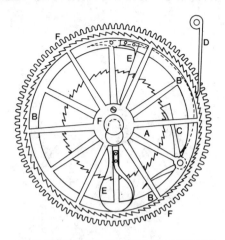

HARRISON'S MAINTAINING POWER FOR A WINDING
BARREL

In winding a weight-driven clock the length of time required for winding will disturb the time indicated by the clock. In many cases winding actually causes the clock to go *backwards*. This problem was overcome by providing *maintaining power*, an early type being the *bolt and shutter* used on clocks in the late 17th century (p. 91). The clock on p. 93 has shutters in front of the winding holes; before the clock can be wound a cord is pulled which temporarily removes the shutters and brings a leaf spring into contact with the teeth of the third wheel to keep the clock going in a forward direction during winding. A similar device may be seen in the weighted maintaining power arm of the turret clock on p. 145, though in this case the maintaining power is applied through a simple lever system directly on to one of the train wheels, the weighted arm slowly falling back in front of the winding square a few minutes later as the clock continues to run.

The maintaining power invented by John Harrison was much used in precision clocks and later in watch fusees and chronometers. Alongside the *great wheel* (F) a *secondary wheel* with a *ratchet edge* (B) holds the *click* (C) which engages with the *winding barrel* (A). The two *springs* (E) which lie between the spokes of F and B are thus in *compression* when the clock is under power. As power is removed during winding the wheel (B) cannot go backwards because of the *detent* (D) which is pivoted to the frame of the clock, therefore the expansion of the compressed springs (E) keeps the great wheel going *forwards* until winding is complete. The *endless rope* or *chain* devised by Christiaan Huyghens was applied to 30-hour clocks only. The ratchet wheel of the striking train allows the clock to be wound by pulling the small weight downwards, and as half the power of the large weight continues undisturbed to keep the going train in motion, maintaining power is automatically provided.

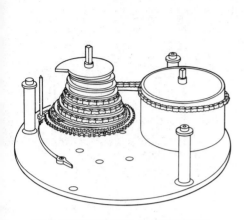

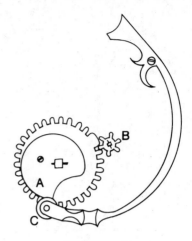

FUSEE AND SPRING BARREL IN A CLOCK FRAME

THE STACKFREED

The power of a coiled spring attempting to unwind itself inside its brass barrel is by no means constant. This was a serious problem in applying spring power to early clocks, for the verge varied its rate according to the power supplied to the escape wheel. The problem was early overcome by the use of the *fusee* (pp. 72, 73), shown here with its spring barrel in position on the pillar plate of a clock. The clock is wound by the fusee *square*, and in winding the spring is coiled tightly in its barrel by a chain which is wound on to the spiral groove of the conical fusee. As the clock runs the mainspring, hooked on to its central arbor inside the barrel, turns the barrel itself thus pulling the fusee round, at the narrow end at first, but finally, when nearly run down, at the wide part near the great wheel. Thus the fusee acts as an equalising continuous gear, compensating for the unequal torque of the mainspring throughout its run.

To enable the fusee to be wound, the conically shaped part of the fusee is separate from its great wheel, which it drives through å ratchet and clicks, the toothed fusee wheel engaging the centre wheel and thence to the rest of the train. A much cruder system known as the *stackfreed* was used in many German clocks and watches during the 16th century (p. 76). In this device winding is done on the pinion (B) while a *cam* on the spring barrel (A) rides against the roller on a strong spring (C). In the drawing the spring is fully wound. When first wound the extra force of the newly wound mainspring has to force spring C outwards, which therefore acts as a kind of brake. From this point onwards the gently sloping edge of the cam is *aided* by spring C and thus the mainspring receives help as it gradually declines in power. The winding is 'locked' by a blind tooth which prevents the pinion (B) from being turned any further.

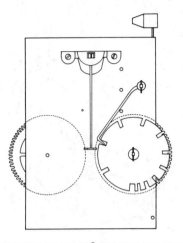

LOCKING PLATE FOR AN 8-DAY LONG CASE CLOCK

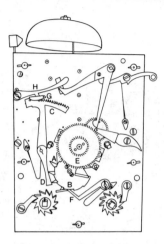

RACK STRIKING FOR AN 8-DAY BRACKET CLOCK

In striking clocks, two basic systems for *counting* the blows of the hammer were used, the earliest being the *count plate* or *locking plate* which continued for various types of clock until well into the 19th century. Count plate striking is shown above, on the back of an 8-day clock frame. The *detent* or *lifting piece* is raised from a slot in the edge of the plate as the striking train unlocks; the train locks again when the next slot comes into line with the detent and the falling detent allows a ¹ocking piece to stop the striking train inside the clock. The count plate on an 8-day clock is attached to the striking great wheel arbor, and sometimes it is found between the great wheel and its winding barrel, known as *internal* count plate locking. Locking plate striking provides a form of *progressive* striking which, if it should once get out of phase with the time indicated by the clock, will continue to strike wrongly during the succeeding hours.

Rack striking, introduced by Edward Barlow, always strikes the *right* number of strokes on the bell according to the position of the hour hand. Below the *hour wheel* (E) a *star wheel* (A) is seen carrying a *stepped cam* or *snail* (B), each step corresponding with one of the twelve hours. As the striking train is unlocked the *rack* (C) on the left falls to the left until stopped by its *tail* (D) against the snail, the distance it falls determining the number of strokes to be delivered by the bell hammer. The position of the snail is changed each hour by a pin on the hour wheel, and held in place by the *jumper* (F) on the star wheel. As the striking runs the rack returns to its normal position for at each stroke of the hammer the rack is 'gathered' by the *gathering pallet* (G) which finally locks the train when the *lifting piece* (H) falls into the last slot in the rack.

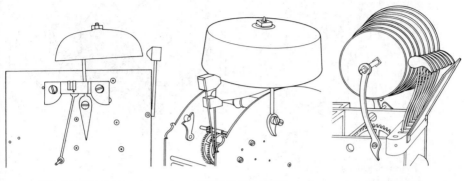

BELL AND BELL STAND
From an early 19th century clock

BELL AND BELL STAND
From a late 17th century clock

NEST OF BELLS
From an 18th century quarter
striking clock

The bells of clocks were mounted on *bell stands* over the movement. Many long case clock bells are left in the condition in which they were cast, i.e. with a slightly rough surface left by the casting sand, but better quality bells were turned in the lathe to produce a fine smooth finish on the outside. Tuning of bells is done by turning away a thin layer of metal from the outer edge and the *bell metal* itself is an alloy of copper and tin, with more tin than is used for making bronze. The pitch of bells depends on their size except for fine tuning, smaller bells producing a higher note. Bells were cast for clocks in different shapes, the early ones for lantern clocks often being rather deep with a steep rim; early 18th century bells were often more flat on the top while bells of the late 18th and early 19th century tend to be hemispherical in form. As bells can be easily cracked many are found not original to their movements.

Quarter striking clocks used many different permutations according to the number of bells used. *Grande sonnerie* refers to that type of striking in which the *hours and the quarters* are struck at each quarter. More complicated striking systems are usually associated with turret clock work where the ordinary church bells could also be used for the clock. In domestic clocks quarter striking could vary from a simple arrangement on two bells to quite complicated work on a *nest of bells* up to eight in number, while some musical clocks played simple tunes on eight, ten or twelve bells, sometimes with two hammers for each bell. In such cases the bell hammers are raised by pins on a revolving barrel in the manner of a musical box. In the 19th century a very popular striking sequence was the *Westminster four bell chime*, as used by the great clock of that name (p. 146), a tune first used at St. Mary's Church, Cambridge in 1793.

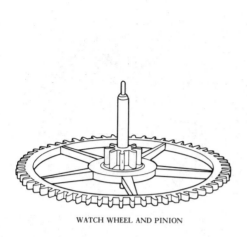

WATCH WHEEL AND PINION

WHEEL TRAIN FROM A VERGE WATCH
Early 19th century

In general terms the lay-out of a watch and the principles of its construction are those of a miniaturised clock, its *train* mounted between two flat plates held together by four pillars. In verge escapement watches the basic train consists of *spring barrel, fusee*—including *fusee stop work*—*centre wheel, third wheel, fourth wheel* of contrate form, *escape* or *crown wheel* at right angles to the main train, engaging the *pallets* of the *verge staff*, and the *balance* outside the top plate at the back of the watch. Beneath the dial the *motion work* is fitted, as in clocks, and the movement is *hinged* into its case, a fashion which persisted to the very end of the 19th century. Unlike clock movements most of the parts of watches are gilded to prevent the brass from tarnishing, the gold being applied with an amalgam of gold and mercury until the advent of electro-gilding in the 19th century. The steel parts of watches were either left plain and brightly polished, or heat-blued where the parts showed, such as screw heads and springs.

Because of the restricted space in watches, particularly those of the late 18th and 19th centuries when watches were made as thin as possible, it is usual to find the pinions with the wheels mounted directly on them, instead of at each end of the arbors. Watch pinions, being of small size, were made by drawing wire through a *pinion plate*, the progressively shaped holes in the plate gradually bringing the wire to the desired section with longitudinal 'leaves'. The resulting wire is called *pinion wire*. It is thought that pinion wire drawing was first carried out by William Houghton who is first recorded as a 'watch pillar maker' in 1777. Houghton carried out this work at Hale Bank near Prescot, Lancashire in the late 17th century and later pinion and other wire drawing continued at Warrington, and is still done there today. Watch wheels were normally cut in small 'stacks', several wheels at a time, and when cut by machine methods twenty or more could be completed at once (p. 52).

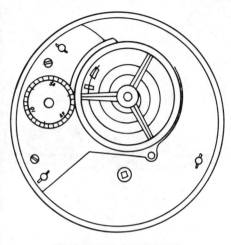

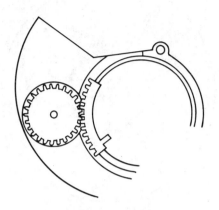

TOP PLATE FROM A VERGE WATCH
Early 19th century

REGULATOR FROM A VERGE WATCH
Early 19th century

The back or top plate of a watch varied in design over the years, but the one shown here is typical of thousands made during the late 18th and early 19th centuries. The polished steel balance is *outside* the plate, its three arms bevelled to present less resistance to the air as it vibrates, and as the balance cock has been removed we see the three turns of the balance spring (p. 45). With this kind of watch the whole movement had to be dismantled to give access to the spring barrel in case of breakage, but later 19th century watches were fitted with a separate bridge or bar, known as the *barrel bar*, so that the spring barrel could be taken out independently. Until the advent of jewelling (p. 115) the pivot holes were pierced directly in the plate, and jewelling was only gradually applied in the pivot holes of the last wheels in the train and at the escapement, the number depending largely on the overall quality of the work.

The 'rate' of a watch depends largely on the balance spring, the final adjustment being determined by the *regulator*. The regulator shown here appears as a small dial set to one side of the balance cock (pp. 115, 122). A squared pin in the centre permits this dial to be turned with a watch key; as this is done a pinion below engages with a curved rack which can move backwards and forwards on a segment of a circle concentric with the balance wheel. A small projection on this rack has a slot cut into it in which the outer coil of the balance spring lies, the sides of the slot providing 'curbs'. By moving the regulator, therefore, the *acting* length of the balance spring can be adjusted; turning the dial clockwise shortens the spring causing the watch to gain. Numerals on the small dial provide points of reference, while later forms of regulator employ a pointed arm with *curb pins*, reading on an engraved scale (pp. 123, 141, 143).

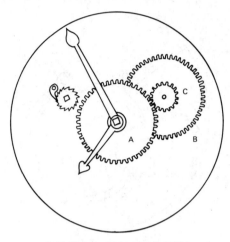

MOTION WORK FROM A VERGE WATCH
Early 19th century

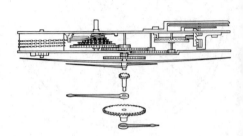

SIDE ELEVATION OF A VERGE WATCH
Early 19th century

The *motion work* for watches is very similar to that for most clocks, both being situated between the dial and the movement plate. In a clock the minute hand is held firmly against the *cannon pinion* by a pin through the *centre arbor*, a thin springy plate maintaining a clutch action between the centre arbor and the cannon pinion or cannon wheel as it is sometimes called, so that the hands can be turned on the dial to set the clock to time. In a watch the cannon pinion, also carrying the minute hand, is friction tight on the centre arbor, though later designs allowed for the pinion to 'snap on'. In the diagram the cannon pinion, unseen behind the *hour wheel* (A) engages with the *minute wheel* (B) in the centre of which a *pinion* (C) engages with the hour wheel, the reduction gearing being arranged so that the hour wheel revolves once while the minute hand revolves twelve times.

The view of the watch movement from the side shows the arrangement of the wheels and pinions from the spring barrel on the left to the verge, or crown wheel escapement on the right. Above the narrow end of the fusee a lever which is raised by the last turn of the fusee chain locks the fusee to prevent overwinding. This is *fusee stopwork* and it prevents breakage of the fusee chain. Chains for watches were extremely fine; those used for small or thin watches often appear like a piece of very fine thread. The chains were made of separate links rivetted together, and A. White (see bibliography) has described how children from the workhouse, with good eyesight, were employed in making these chains in the area round Christchurch in Hampshire after about 1790. This industry may have grown as supplies from Switzerland declined through the Napoleonic wars; in 1795 chains for movements were made in the Liverpool area, though they had not been made there in earlier times.

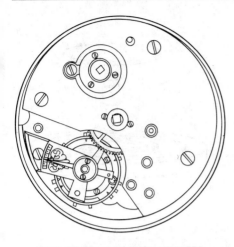

THREE-QUARTER PLATE WATCH MOVEMENT
Late 19th century

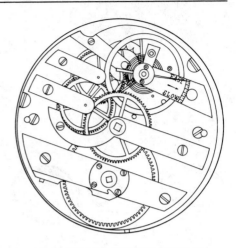

LÉPINE CALIBRE OR BAR MOVEMENT WATCH
Late 19th century

Soon after the beginning of the 19th century the verge escapement began to decline as various forms of *lever* escapement took its place, but the *full plate* movement with external balance and fusee continued in basic form until the end of the century, allowances being made for variations in proportion and decorative style. During the second half of the 19th century, however, mainly inspired by new ideas evolved in America (pp. 164 to 167) and the desire to make watches thinner and more cheaply, the fusee was gradually dispensed with, the watch being powered by a *going barrel*, i.e. a spring barrel with teeth in its outer edge to drive the train either directly on the centre wheel or through a *reversing pinion*, and wound by turning the *barrel arbor* instead of the barrel. With later watches the balance wheel and cock were recessed below the top plate as in the drawing above. This movement, with a *straight-line escapement* (p. 43) has a cutaway top plate known as a *three-quarter plate*.

About 1770 Jean Antoine Lépine (p. 177) introduced a form of watch frame in which there is no top plate at all, but just a series of bars screwed to the main movement plate, each bar holding the upper pivot of one wheel of the movement. The example illustrated is from the Swiss firm of J.-M. Badollet of Geneva, a manufacturer who produced many high grade movements. It is of going barrel type, the spring barrel directly driving the pinion of the centre wheel, and the escapement is of the *cylinder* type (p. 40) much used by Continental makers. English watch makers, more conservative in their methods, did not readily accept the Lépine calibre but continued with full-plate watches until a very late date, also continuing to make the fusee and chain even after 1900, a conservatism which caused the decline of the English trade in the 19th century when facing competition from Switzerland and America, where new ideas were readily adopted (p. 165).

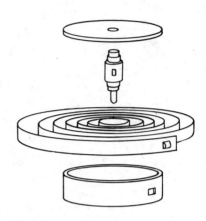

SPRING BARREL, BARREL ARBOR AND FUSEE FROM A
WATCH

SPRING AND SPRING BARREL FROM A WATCH

The drawing above shows a watch *spring barrel, spring barrel arbor, barrel cap* and *fusee*, dismantled from an English movement of about 1850. The thin steel spring of thirteen turns is less than $\frac{1}{8}$ in. deep; tightly coiled in its barrel of $\frac{5}{8}$ in. internal diameter it measures 20 in. long when fully extended. The spring is hooked at its outer end on to the barrel and the inner end is hooked on the *stationary* barrel arbor, the spring being wound by turning the barrel by means of the fine chain which connects it to the fusee (p. 36). The locking plate of the fusee is at its top or short end, while the ratchet teeth of the *Harrison maintaining power* (p. 30) is at the wide end of the fusee, inside the teeth of the great wheel. In 1858 in the Lancashire area one worker is recorded as a *fusee top maker* and another as a *fusee bottom maker* at Rainhill, near Prescot, illustrating the intense specialisation of this trade.

The drawing on the right clearly shows the arrangement of the spring, barrel arbor, barrel and cap. Little is known about the makers of the fine tempered and blued steel springs of the past and it is likely that very many were made in Switzerland, the English and American trades depending very heavily on Swiss mainsprings and balance springs in the last century. There is some evidence that Swiss springs were made from English steel wire, drawn through plates (p. 65) and processed in Switzerland, and this was certainly the case for the balance springs of watches (p. 45). The ideal arrangement for mainsprings is that the inner diameter of the spring when unwound should be the same as the outer diameter when it is wound. The arbor on which the inner end is hooked has a 'square' to take the *ratchet wheel* which was used for 'setting up' the spring, i.e. to give it some initial tension before being wound (p. 87).

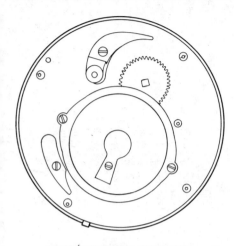

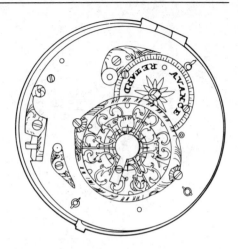

ROUGH ÉBAUCHE FOR A SWISS WATCH
18th century

FINISHED MOVEMENT OF A SWISS WATCH
18th century

To understand the way in which watches were made in the 18th century it is necessary to recognise that the trade even then was split up into the work of many specialists. In 18th century Switzerland individual wheels of watches were the product of five separate craftsmen—the *blanker* who turned the disc of brass to size, the *wheel cutter* who spaced out the teeth, the *finisher* who filed up the crossings, the *tooth maker* who gave the teeth their final shape and the *polisher*. The same principle applied to all parts of the watch and as each man specialised in his own single skill he became extremely adept at it. The two drawings above, taken from an original rough *ébauche* and *finished movement*, illustrate one of the intermediary stages in the making of a Swiss watch towards the end of the 18th century (p. 184). The ébauche consists of roughly finished plates, unfinished spring barrel and fusee, unfinished potence and balance cock and no wheelwork or pivot holes at all.

The ébauche, which was the work of many craftsmen, was sent to the finisher whose various workmen looked after the completion and fitting of all the parts. The solid balance cock was sent for piercing and engraving to the engraver, often female labour, and the finisher made sure that everything was in order while the watch was 'in the grey', that is before it was gilded. Final adjustment was done by the *timer*, who fitted the balance spring and adjusted the escapement. Some large Swiss manufacturers depended on 'outside' work and in this respect the Swiss methods of those days resembled the English practice, where ébauches were made in Lancashire and sent to London for finishing, or to Coventry by the 19th century. When the movements were complete they had to be fitted to their cases and the cases were the product of another series of trades such as the silversmith, the hinge maker, the engraver, the 'boxer-in' who fitted the pendant in keyless work, and the dial makers and hand makers.

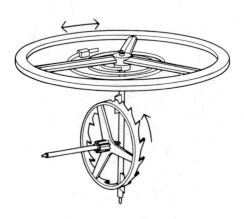

VERGE ESCAPEMENT FOR A WATCH

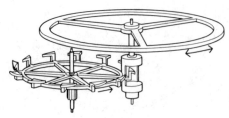

CYLINDER ESCAPEMENT FOR A WATCH

The verge escapement in clocks has already been described in conjunction with a balance (p. 23), but there are a few essential differences when the verge is used in a watch. After the introduction of the *balance spring* about 1675 (p. 102), the hog's bristle regulator was no longer necessary and it became common to have three arms to the balance, as in the drawing. The confined space between the movement plates of a watch also gave less room for the *crown* or *escape wheel* which consequently had far fewer teeth than in a clock—fifteen teeth being quite usual for the escape wheels of early watches, reducing to thirteen or even less in later, thinner watches. Balances during the 18th century were commonly of polished steel, though the effects of changes of temperature were realised by the precision makers and as early as 1773 John Arnold was experimenting with *bi-metallic compensation balances* (p. 44), as were Le Roy and Berthoud in France (pp. 174, 177).

The cylinder escapement, first perfected by George Graham (p. 122), is sometimes called the horizontal escapement because the escape wheel lies in a horizontal plane instead of a vertical plane as with the verge. Below the balance a cut-away cylinder interacts with the escape wheel teeth which are raised above the level of the wheel itself. As a tooth escapes from inside the cylinder an impulse is given to the balance in one direction, the following tooth falling on to the outside of the cylinder shell. When the balance has completed its vibration and returns, this tooth then gives impulse as it falls inside the cylinder, but this time in the opposite direction. Once inside it 'rides' on the inner surface, ready to escape like the first one, and the sequence continues. Between impulses the escape wheel remains stationary as the teeth ride either inside or outside the cylinder; this escapement is known as *frictional rest*. Steel cylinders wore quickly but Breguet made *ruby* cylinders after about 1790 to remedy this defect (p. 180).

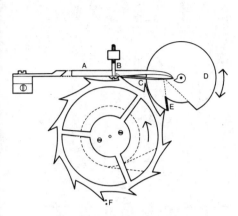

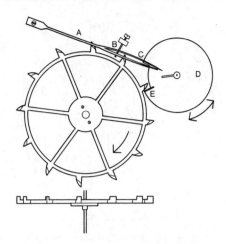

EARNSHAW'S SPRING DETENT ESCAPEMENT

ARNOLD'S SPRING DETENT ESCAPEMENT

Though the verge escapement remained universal for ordinary watches until well into the 19th century, in its standard form it was quite useless for precision work such as chronometers and deck watches. With the verge the balance is never entirely *free* and, just as efforts were constantly made to free the pendulum from interference by the escapement, so in balance-controlled watches the same problem had to be overcome. Two famous names are concerned with these efforts, Thomas Earnshaw and John Arnold (p. 116), though of course there were many others struggling with the problem. Two *detached detent* escapements were made by them, similar in principle but differing in their details of construction. The main point about both is that for a large part of their oscillations the balances are free of interference from the escape wheel which is locked by the action of a thin steel spring known as the *detent* (A), the only interference being when the balance unlocks the train and is given impulse and when it pushes aside the *passing spring* (C).

The left hand drawing shows Earnshaw's version, the other being by Arnold. On the balance staff of Earnshaw's design a large *roller* (D) carries a *pallet* (E) through which impulse is given from one of the escape wheel teeth. A *smaller pallet* in the centre of the roller is just about to strike the *passing spring* (C) to lift the *spring detent* (A) and release the escape wheel at B (here shown diagrammatically at F since the locking stone on the detent is obscured). Once unlocked the escape wheel moves anti-clockwise and imparts impulse with the following tooth to E, the balance then revolving clockwise to its full vibration; in returning the small pallet *passes* the passing spring, completes its vibration and in returning once more begins the cycle again. The balance is thus impulsed only *once* every two vibrations. In Arnold's version the detent is *drawn towards the centre* of the escape wheel to unlock, this being possible by using teeth which are raised above the level of the wheel.

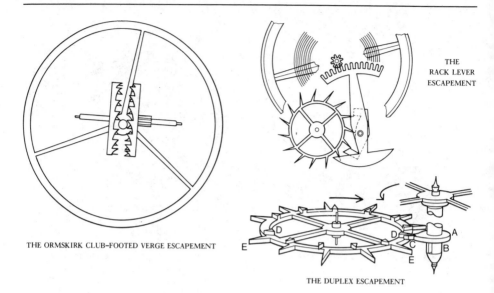

THE ORMSKIRK CLUB–FOOTED VERGE ESCAPEMENT

THE RACK LEVER ESCAPEMENT

THE DUPLEX ESCAPEMENT

Spring detent escapements were used only for high performance work, but other escapements were devised though they were never used as often as the verge. The *Debaufre* is an escapement with one pallet on the balance staff acting between a *pair* of crown-shaped escape wheels facing each other on a common arbor. It is sometimes known as a *club-footed verge* from the shape of the pallet, or the *Ormskirk verge* as many were made in Ormskirk, Lancashire, early in the 19th century (p. 135). The pallet locks and is impulsed by alternate teeth on the facing escape wheels. The *rack lever*, first patented by Peter Litherland of Liverpool (p. 141) consists of a lever with pallets acting on the escape wheel teeth not unlike the pallets of a dead beat escapement (p. 26) though thicker in proportion. On the other end of the lever a *rack* is in continuous engagement with a pinion on the balance staff; when the balance oscillates the rack moves to and fro, locking and unlocking the pallets and receiving impulse.

With a rack lever the rack is in constant engagement with the balance staff pinion, so the balance is never 'free'. The escapement was often used in conjunction with a very large escape wheel of 30 teeth, dispensing with one wheel in the train. Another escapement called the *duplex*, evolved from 18th century experiments (pp. 141, 166), was used in the form shown here for high quality watches. This escapement, like the cylinder, is a *frictional rest* type, and like the spring detent it only receives impulse once every double vibration. The escape wheel has two sets of teeth (D) and (E). As the tooth (D) impulses the pallet (C) on the roller (A) and escapes, a tooth (E) rests on the ruby cylinder (B) until the gap in that cylinder allows it to pass; once passed the following tooth (E) drops on to the cylinder (B), the balance completes its vibration and returns in a clockwise direction bringing the pallet (C) in front of the next tooth (D) to receive impulse again.

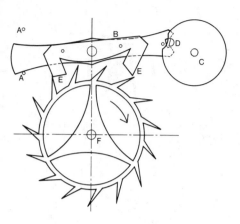

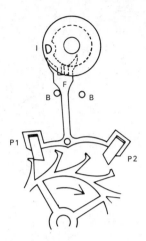

THE ENGLISH LEVER ESCAPEMENT   THE STRAIGHT-LINE LEVER ESCAPEMENT

The *detached lever escapement* gradually displaced the verge and became universal for pocket watches; it is used to this day in the straight-line form. Shown here are the *English lever*, with the lever placed at a tangent to the teeth of the escape wheel, and the *straight-line lever* at right-angles to it. The former has *pointed* escape wheel teeth, while the latter has teeth of *club-foot* shape. In the diagram of the English lever the *right* pallet (E) has just received impulse from a tooth on the escape wheel (F) and the *left* pallet (E) has locked it. As the balance vibrates anticlockwise the *impulse pin* (D) on the *roller* (C) engages the lever and the left pallet then receives impulse and the right pallet locks. Two *banking pins* (A, A) restrict the movement of the lever and a notch in the roller (C), below the impulse pin (D), engages with a vertical pin on the lever to ensure that the impulse pin *always* enters the *fork* at precisely the right time.

In the *straight-line lever* the shape of the *pallets* (P1, P2) is such that as each tooth locks it is *drawn in* towards the centre of the escape wheel, bringing the lever firmly to the *banking pin* (B). This is called *draw* and prevents unlocking through a shock or jolt while the balance is travelling in its supplementary arc (p. 44). The shape of the teeth *divides the impulse* equally between the teeth and the pallets and this is called *divided lift*; in the English lever the lift is entirely on the pallets. Another difference is that a horizontal pin called the *safety dart* above the *fork* (F) passes a crescent-shaped notch in a smaller roller above the larger one carrying the impulse pin (I). This, like the vertical pin of the English lever, ensures the safety of the ruby impulse pin during the vibration of the balance; in many cases the *English type* of vertical pin entering a notch in the *single* roller is also used with the straight-line lever.

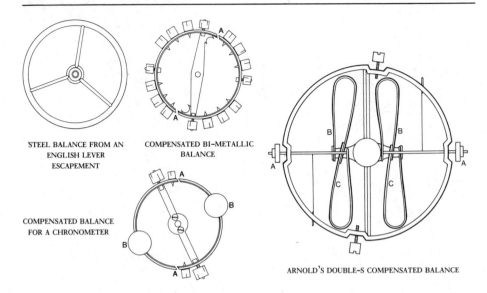

STEEL BALANCE FROM AN
ENGLISH LEVER
ESCAPEMENT

COMPENSATED BI–METALLIC
BALANCE

COMPENSATED BALANCE
FOR A CHRONOMETER

ARNOLD'S DOUBLE-S COMPENSATED BALANCE

The most important part of any watch is the *balance* in combination with the *balance spring*, for on this depends its accuracy. Steel balances with three arms were usual in the 18th and 19th centuries; for some better class watches gold was used as it is a denser metal and not affected by corrosion or magnetism. The vibrations of a balance depend largely on the *mass* of the body and its *diameter*, regulated by the balance spring. The *arc* of the balance is that part of the vibration during which it is locking and unlocking the escapement and receiving impulse, any further vibration in either direction being called the *supplementary arc*. The *complete* arc of vibration of a lever watch should average $1\frac{1}{2}$ turns, which is the distance traversed by a given point on the edge of the balance through 270° *and back again*, while a verge balance in good condition will vibrate through an angle of about 135°, that is a $\frac{3}{4}$ turn or *half* that of a detached balance.

Balances were temperature compensated to increase the effective diameter in cold and contract it in heat. This was done by making the balance rim from a *bi-metallic strip* of brass outside and steel inside, with a *cut* (A) on opposite sides near the arm. As brass expands more readily in heat than steel, the rim bends slightly *inwards* to compensate, and conversely in cold. Gold *timing screws* fitted in the rim could be moved and adjusted during the timing of the watch, and the *quarter screws* at the ends of the balance arm and in the centre of the rims could also be adjusted. Chronometer balances were the first to use this principle. The one illustrated has large weights (B) which could be moved closer to or further away from the cut to compensate, while Arnold's *double 'S'* balance was another way. The two springs (B, B) and (C, C) are of bi-metallic construction, riveted together and controlling the inward and outward movement of the adjustable weights (A, A) in temperature changes.

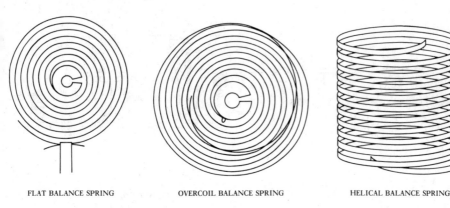

FLAT BALANCE SPRING   OVERCOIL BALANCE SPRING   HELICAL BALANCE SPRING

The *balance spring* is the thin spiral of flat tempered steel or other metal attached to the balance of a watch to render its vibrations as far as possible isochronous (p. 102). Most balance springs are made of blued steel, though gold was occasionally used and palladium, which is non-magnetic, was introduced in 1877. Various alloys have been perfected which are both non-magnetic and not affected by changes of temperature, the most important being *elinvar* which is a type of nickel alloy, its name derived from '*élasticité invariable*'. Balance springs lose their elasticity in higher temperatures, thus changing their control on the balance. Many precision makers introduced compensation devices to overcome this problem in balance springs as well as in the balances. The simplest form of balance spring is the flat one, the inner end pinned to the balance collet and the outer to a stud on the top plate. Early verge balance springs were of only 3 or 4 turns, while modern ones may have 8, 10, 12 or more.

In the *overcoil* balance spring, often called a *Breguet spring* after its inventor (p. 180), the outer terminal curve is bent up and over the main coils of the spring to a point midway between the collet and the outer turn. The main advantage here was that the 'breathing' of the spring, as it expanded and contracted during the balance oscillations, was more evenly divided between the inner and outer coils. Another form is the *helical spring*, in which the coils are of the same diameter but spirally arranged in a vertical manner. With inward curving terminals John Arnold found that this type of spring possessed important isochronal properties and its use became standard in chronometers and deck watches. The length of the spring, however, made it inconvenient for ordinary watches, apart from expense, as it considerably increased their thickness. Other forms of balance spring were devised, mostly of an experimental kind for precision work, the flat or overcoil springs being most commonly used in ordinary watches.

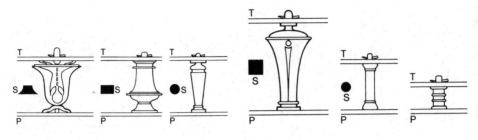

WATCH PILLARS

a. Tulip pillar
b. Square section baluster
c. Round section baluster

d. Inverted baluster
e. Cylindrical
f. Cylindrical with rings

The decorative *pillars* of watch frames are important both in helping to date a watch and also because of the superb quality of many of their designs, particularly in early examples. Watch pillars were presumably the work of a specialist, as with all other watch parts, and six are shown here illustrating some of the principal types. In each drawing (T) refers to the *top plate* which is *pinned* to the pillars, and (P) refers to the *pillar plate* to which the pillars are *riveted*. The *tulip pillar* of the late 17th century reminds us of the tulip as a decorative feature on engraved dials (p. 88), while the two *baluster pillars* of square and circular section (S) are clearly derived from architectural work and are to be found on late 17th and early 18th century watches. The mouldings on these pillars are of superb precision and proportion and can be closely related to similar forms on both buildings and furniture of the period.

The baluster with a slit down the centre is often referred to as an 'Egyptian' pillar, but it should perhaps be called an *inverted baluster* as with the similar profile of 18th century wine glass stems. The turned *cylindrical pillars* indicate something of the effect of the increased production of watches in the late 18th and 19th centuries, for they could be produced on the lathe far more quickly than cast and engraved pillars of earlier design. The first of these cylindrical pillars is not unlike the pillars of a long case clock frame without the central *knop* (p. 20), while the last pillar from a watch of the mid-19th century is simply turned with *annular rings* and shows the short, squat pillar form used with the thinner watches of the time. All the pillars shown here have the top plate *pinned* to them, but late 19th and 20th century watches, like the clocks, have plain pillars drilled and tapped at their ends to hold them with *screws* to the plates.

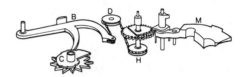

REPEATING WORK
For an 18th century watch

Repeating work, invented in the 17th century (p. 105) was popular in good quality watches throughout the 18th and 19th centuries, and many fine *minute* repeaters have been made in Switzerland in the present century. There were many forms of mechanism for repeating, early ones being on a *bell* and 19th century ones mostly on *gongs* housed round the outer edge of the movement, between the movement and the case. *Quarter* repeating is sounded by two sharp blows on the bell for each quarter, while two gongs of different pitch are used in later work. *Dumb repeating* was introduced about 1750 by Julien Le Roy (p. 174), in which a dull sound is made by striking on a *block* inside the case. Repeating watches must have been extremely useful after dark. A system for the repeating work of an 18th century watch is illustrated here, its various parts being mounted between the dial and the pillar plate of the watch; the illustration is from the horological section of Diderot's encyclopaedia (p. 168).

As the pendant is pressed the *push piece* (A) depresses a *depthing lever* (B) against the *snail* (C) mounted on a *star wheel* (p. 32) which regulates the striking for the hours. A chain is pulled round a *pulley* (D), winding the *repeating spring* (H). A small arm on the spring arbor engages a pin on the *quarter striking piece* (G) and pushes its right end up to one of the 'steps' of the *quarter striking snail* (E). Providing that the *all-or-nothing piece* (F) has been pushed sufficiently firmly to allow the quarter striking arm to be released, all is now ready. As the spring unwinds two hammers (M), of which only one is shown in the sectional view, alternately strike the quarters by means of the teeth at each end of (G) engaging with pawls on the hammer arbors, *after* the hours have been struck by the right hand hammer as the spring (H) unwinds to a distance determined by the amount it is possible to depress (B) to the snail (C).

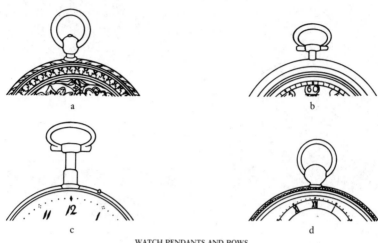

WATCH PENDANTS AND BOWS

a. Mid 17th century   b. Early 18th century
c. Late 18th century   d. Early 19th century

An important feature illustrating the development of the watch case is the shape of the *pendant and bow* or loop which is used to secure the watch, either by a chain or a cord. Cords or ribbons appear to have been the most usual form of attachment in the 17th and 18th centuries, while later the chatelaine was used by the most fashionable owners (pp. 74, 124). The chain, often complete with a dangling ornamental *fob* called an 'Albert', was a 19th century fashion. Early pendants had simple circular loops or bows, but by the late 17th century the *stirrup bow* had developed, its ends being curved and pivoted to swivel on a pin through the pendant proper. The circular bow, however, remained in fashion and about 1700 it is often very thin and small in comparison with the round and thick proportion of the case. The pendant of course is attached directly to the case containing the movement, an aperture being left at the top of the outer case to enclose it.

Rococo ornament (p. 108) made its effect felt on watch bows of the mid-18th century in the form of scrolls on each side of the bow. Bows of this type had to be *cast* instead of being shaped from circular section wire, while in the late 18th century the bow developed a distinctly oval form in keeping with Neo-Classical styles (p. 118). 18th century watches often employed the pendant as a means of activating the repeating work (p. 47) and in these cases the pendant stem appears longer than in a non-repeating watch. The 19th century saw a return to the circular bow which remained popular until pocket watches went out of fashion, though it was generally much larger than its early predecessors. Though this simple evolution of the pendant and bow gives a rough indication of date it must not be relied upon too closely, for the various styles overlapped considerably and bows particularly were subject to breakage and subsequent repair in another style.

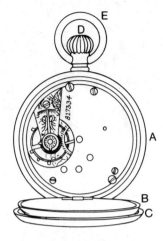

KEYLESS WATCH MOVEMENT AND CASE
Late 19th century

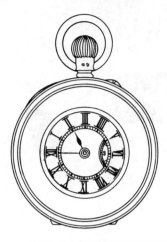

HALF HUNTER OR DEMI-HUNTER WATCH CASE
Late 19th century

In most watches until the second half of the 19th century the movement was *hinged* to its case, access being gained by opening the *bezel* at the front which held the glass or crystal. Until the first half of the 18th century it was common for the bezel to be split in the middle of its hinge so that when the hinge was pinned the glass would be firmly held in its groove. Later, with more precise casework, the glass was of 'snap-in' fit. By the second half of the 19th century the hinge was gradually displaced by screws, though the old, hinged, *bolt and joint* method died hard with English makers and survived into the present century. Movements which are screwed into their cases are generally of the *keyless* type; the screws used are known as *case screws*. Some case screws are made with their heads half cut away to allow the movement to be taken out without removing the screws entirely; these are known as *dog screws*.

The band forming the edge of the watch case is called the *middle* (A) while B is the *dome* and C is the *back cover*. E is the bow (p. 48) but this watch is *keyless* and has *stem winding* which passes through the *pendant pipe* below the *winding button* (D). Keyless winding was attempted by *Pierre Auguste Caron* (1732–99) in 1752, who made a watch for Madame de Pompadour which was wound by turning the bezel, and in 1820 *Thomas Prest* took out a patent for keyless winding from the pendant. Keyless winding early became standard in American watches (p. 165) but some English makers retained key winding until after 1900. The second drawing shows the *half hunter*, or *demi-hunter* in which the watch glass is protected by a cover through which part of the dial could be seen, a *full hunter* having a hinged cover over the glass which springs open when the winding button is pressed. In some watch cases of about 1900 the back cover and bezel were screwed on.

Sterling standard

Town marks

Date letters

HALL MARKS ON SILVER AND GOLD

Gold and silver are the traditional metals from which watch cases have been made; gold plating or 'gold filling', as it is called, gives an appearance of gold but without the permanence of the solid metal. *Rolled gold* is produced either by laminating a thin gold sheet on a plate of base metal, or by electro-gilding. A metal for cheaper watches in the 18th century was a zinc/copper alloy resembling gold and known as *Pinchbeck* after its inventor *Christopher Pinchbeck* (1670–1732), a fine maker of musical and astronomical clocks. During the 19th century many watches, particularly Continental ones, were cased in nickel alloys and some were silver plated. All cases of gold and silver in England must conform to the laws relating to these metals and must be *assayed* and *hall-marked* before they are retailed, whether of English or foreign manufacture. Many escaped being tested and marked by the Act of 1738, which exempted various articles of jewellery from assay, but most are marked and can be dated easily.

The craft of making gold and silver watch cases properly comes under the subject of goldsmithing and silversmithing, quite separate from that of horology; in the making of watches it was a completely different trade. Gold and silver articles are tested for purity at an *assay office* where a *town mark* is stamped, the three examples shown here being the *leopard's head* (uncrowned) used for London after 1821, *three wheat sheaves and sword* used at Chester between 1779 and the closure of the assay office there in 1962, and the *anchor* used for Birmingham since the opening of the office there in 1773. The *sterling standard* mark of a *lion passant* indicates the purity of the metal and the rows of dates and letters show how assay offices used codes of letters of different designs for their yearly cycles of dating, the ones shown here being from the London series. The *initials* of the case-maker are included on watch cases also, for each gold and silversmith registered his punch.

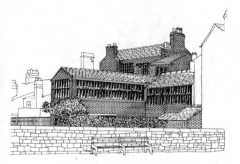

WATCH MAKING WORKSHOP
Prescot, Lancashire, 19th century

WATCH CASE MAKING WORKSHOP
Clerkenwell, London, 19th century

Few of the old workshops remain, where clocks and watches were made by handcraft methods. As they were mostly humble, utilitarian buildings this is not surprising. Of the two workshops shown here, the *watch case making* shop of the firm of A. T. Oliver in Spencer Street, Clerkenwell, has already disappeared and the buildings of the *wheel cutting* firm of Saggerson Brothers in Prescot, Lancashire, form a group of the few remaining workshops in that area, long unused, whose future is far from certain. Yet it was in small buildings such as these that the splendid movements and cases of watches were made over the years, where men lived out their lives, often in a precarious way owing to the vagaries of trade, making specialised parts, and whose names go largely unremembered. The buildings shown, like the few remaining in Coventry too, have long lines of windows above the working benches and were situated close to or above the dwellings of the workmen and apprentices.

Hundreds of firms like Oliver and Saggerson have come and gone not only in Prescot and Clerkenwell, but in Liverpool, Coventry and Birmingham too, where as centres of the trade they were most numerous. The firm of Saggerson Brothers started in Prescot in 1836 when John Saggerson (d. 1871), a watch wheel cutter, made agreement with William Rowson for the use of the land on which to build his workshop and house, while his son Robert was described as a watch movement manufacturer some years later. The firm of A. T. Oliver, watch case maker of Clerkenwell, survived in business until 1970 having started about eighty years earlier in nearby Northampton Square. R. J. Oliver, A. T. Oliver's son, was forced to terminate his case-making trade in Spencer Street by enforced demolition; although his firm did not use this particular workshop until 1940 the building was erected for the firms of Joseph Hurst and Edward Culver, watch case maker, chainmaker and jewellers about 1857.

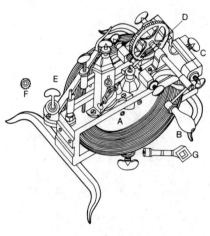

WATCH WHEEL CUTTING ENGINE
English, 18th century

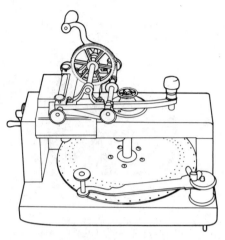

CLOCK WHEEL CUTTING ENGINE
American, 18th century

Cutting the teeth of wheels before the second half of the 17th century was apparently done by *hand filing*. Although the accuracy and skill of this method was a critical factor in good work, it is clear that methods of *dividing* had been developed long before the use of a dividing or *wheel cutting engine*. It is not known when the first wheel cutting engines were made. Conservative estimates suggest a date about the middle of the 17th century, for in 1675 John Smith in his '*Horological Dialogues*' advised 'First be satisfied if possibly, (sic) whether the teeth of the wheels be cut down by an ingine or not, for there is no man can cut them down by hand so true and equal as an ingine doth.' This would suggest that the wheel cutting engine had been in use for some years. The toolmakers of Lancashire made fine engines in the 18th and 19th centuries, and equally fine ones were made in France.

The wheel cutting engine depends on an *index plate* (A) on which concentric circles have been accurately divided into different numbers of divisions. The wheel blank (D) to be cut is mounted on the index plate arbor and as each separate cut is made the index plate is turned to the next notch according to the number of teeth required. Location is by the *index arm* (E), which has a point to engage with the index plate holes; the *cutter* (F) is driven by turning the handle (B). *Depthing* of the cutter is adjusted by the screw (C) which can then be locked tight with a key (G). Although the wheel cutting engine retailed by Wyke and Green above (p. 108) is *hand driven*, much larger and later iron-framed engines were driven by cords and pulleys from a treadle, which with high gearing caused the cutter to rotate at high speed. *Single* watch train wheels were usually cut in tools such as these above; the American wooden-framed engine was used for clock wheels.

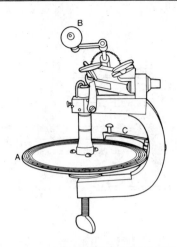

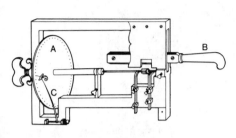

PINION ENGINE
French, 18th century

CROWN OR ESCAPE WHEEL CUTTING ENGINE
English, 18th century

Large pinions for clocks could be cut on a *pinion engine*. This machine employs the same principle as the wheel cutting engine, an *index plate* (A) with 'count' holes in its edge being arranged vertically in an iron frame on which the arbor and pinion to be cut are mounted. The *index arm* (C) is fitted to the bottom of the frame and counts off the holes required on the index plate. The pinion being cut in the diagram has 9 leaves, therefore the index plate would be turned for 6 divisions of the 54 on its edge for the *initial* dividing. The other holes would be used for widening the pinion leaf spaces equally on each side of the first cut, as required. Cutting is by a narrow file mounted in the handle (B) and the plates of the frame ensure that the work is kept true as it progresses. The bracket supports on each side of the pinion avoid possible distortion of the pinion arbor.

Tools such as the pinion engine and the *escape wheel engine* were fixed firmly in a vice for use. The crown or escape wheel engine by Wyke and Green of Liverpool is described in their catalogue as a *balance wheel engine*, meaning for cutting the wheel which activates the pallets of the verge on a watch balance staff. In the catalogue the drawing is labelled *John Wyke, Prescott*, which suggests that the engraving was made prior to 1758 when Wyke left Prescot for Liverpool, where he continued his business and supplied tools to the trade, including James Green of Fenchurch Street, London. The tool works on the same principles as the wheel cutting engine, with its *index plate* (A), *index arm* (C) and handle for turning the cutter (B). In this tool, however, the cutter descends on to the upturned edge of the crown wheel and is shaped to produce teeth of 'saw-tooth' form for the verge escapement (p. 40). The depth of the cutting was controlled by an adjustable stop.

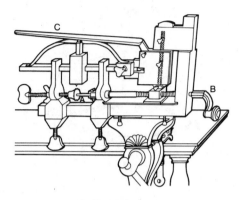

FUSEE CUTTING ENGINE
French, 18th century

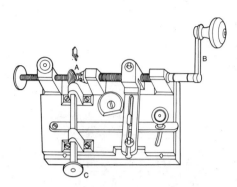

FUSEE CUTTING ENGINE
English, 18th/19th century

The method of making *the fusee* was to use a *fusee engine*, i.e. a type of lathe in which the spiral turns of the fusee cone were accurately cut both in profile and pitch. Two such engines of the 18th century are shown, the first being a French design illustrated by Thiout in 1741 and the second English, as advertised by Peter Stubs of Warrington, Lancashire and retailed about 1800. The conical shape of the fusee was first cast in moulds and turned true in an ordinary lathe. It was then mounted on a fusee engine in the position (A) and rotation of the handle (B) not only turned the fusee but it also caused the carriage of the cutter to move sideways, these two actions together determining the *pitch* at which the fusee groove would be cut. Although the lateral movement of the cutter carriage could be predetermined on each of these tools the final *profile* must have been gauged by the skill and eye of the workman using it.

In both engines pressure on the cutter is hand applied using the handles (C) into which the hard steel cutter itself is fitted. The French one is of greater delicacy in that the handle of the cutter is tensioned by a steel spring bow which would release the tip of the cutter when pressure was relaxed. Some engines of the English type are fitted with an adjustable profile plate to guide the depth of cutting and so regulate the profile, sometimes these plates being fitted to tools which were not originally provided with them. Peter Stubs described the tool as a 'Common Fusee Engine' and in his catalogue engravings of three other models are illustrated, all working on the same general principle. A price list from the Stubs firm dated 1807 shows that the engine illustrated was available for watch fusee makers at 4 guineas, while a wheel cutting engine, exactly the same as the Wyke and Green one on p. 52, described as a 'Watch Engine' could be bought at £13 10s.

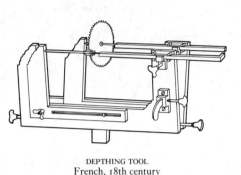

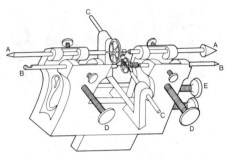

DEPTHING TOOL
French, 18th century

TRIPLE DEPTHING TOOL
English, 18th/19th century

For true running of wheels and pinions the *depth* of engagement had to be correct when the wheels were in the clock or watch frame (pp. 21, 22). In early days, before the advent of careful machine drawings, this process was somewhat empirical and wheels and pinions were tried in a *depthing tool*, the distance apart of the pivots of the arbors then being measured for transferring directly on to the clock or watch plate or template. The French depthing tool is less complicated than the second one, from the catalogue of Peter Stubs. The wheel and pinion being tried can be seen clearly, their arbors pivoted to an adjustable frame which has a tang below for fixing in the vice. The frame is adjusted in width until the wheel and pinion engage smoothly, then the frame is 'locked' by the set screw on the right and the measurements are taken. The Stubs tool is more complicated in that this is a *triple* depthing tool, described as 'Triple Brass Turns for trying wheels'.

The 'set-up' on the Stubs tool is for trying the engagement of the crown wheel with the pallets on the balance staff of a verge escapement for watches. Between the *runners* (A, A) a balance with its staff and pallets is mounted, and between the runners (B, B) the contrate wheel is placed which engages the pinion of the escape or crown wheel. This is mounted between the runners (C, C) so that the relationship of the escape wheel and the pallets can be tested. Once set up, adjustment of the screws (D, D) at the side and (E) at the end will cause the frames carrying each of the three parts to be correctly related to each other. The measurements can then be transferred to the watch plates and potence in the watch. The runners (A) and (B) at the right-hand end are so shaped that the *conical nose* of A can be placed in a pivot hole already determined, while the *pointed* end of B can be used as a scriber.

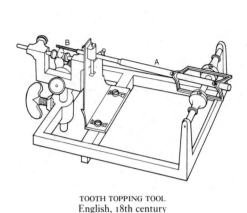

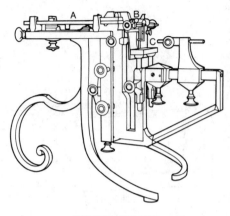

TOOTH TOPPING TOOL
English, 18th century

TOOTH TOPPING TOOL
French, dated 1766

When a newly-divided wheel left the wheel cutting engine its teeth were square ended and had to be shaped. A special tool known as a *tooth topping tool* or *rounding up tool* was used, in which a file (B) for cutting the tips of the teeth was held true by being carried on a sliding bar or handle (A) which it was possible to move only in a line directly at right-angles to the plane of the wheel being cut. In the English example the wheel being 'topped' can be seen clearly on the left, but the French tool has no wheel mounted in it, though one of the runners to take the arbor of a wheel to be topped appears on the right (C). In both these tools the power is applied by hand and accuracy is assured by the frame and rollers which guide the file carrier. The files had hollow curving concave faces to give the correct shape to inside edges of two teeth at a time.

The French tooth topping tool is of particularly elegant workmanship; perhaps one might feel that it is strange to see such a graceful finish on what is essentially a utilitarian object, intended for the workshop and not the 'salon'. The inscription '*B. Samuel Gautier à Caen No. 3 au Roi 1766*' in all probability suggests that this was specially made by an 'horologer du Roi' (p. 168) for an aristocratic client who wanted the very best for his studio workshop. In some 18th century catalogues of tools some are shown very elegantly finished with flourishes described as 'furbelows'. Such details may be seen on the end of the *turns* on p. 58 from an English source, and in the trade card of Wyke and Green on p. 108 we see that this 18th century firm advertised 'Likewise Gentlemen's Chests of Tools &c.' which suggests that specially finished tools were made for dilletante craftsmen, as well as plain and entirely functional items for the ordinary watch and clockmaking tradesman.

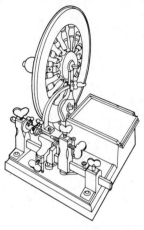

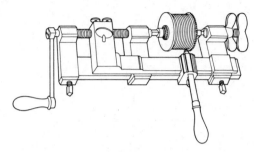

CLOCKMAKER'S THROW, OR LATHE
English, 18th century

BARREL ENGINE
English, 18th century

Just as the early tooth topping tools were replaced by automatic power-driven tools, so the hand turned *lathe* seen here was later supplanted by the powered lathe. Turning of arbors, pivots, wheel blanks, collets, screws, pillars and many other parts was performed in the 18th and 19th century *hand craft tradition* either on a lathe of this sort, providing motion in one direction only, or by the *turns* which were powered by the *bow*, which alternately rotated the work backwards and forwards (p. 58). This nicely made lathe, sometimes described as a clockmaker's *throw*, was advertised as a 'Gentleman's Leath with wood complete' in 1801 which meant that the tool had its own independent base-board and chest at the back for accessories. Much lathe work was done using a separate *bench wheel*, mounted directly on to the bench top, to drive turns clamped in a vice on the bench edge. Bench wheels were usually made of brass or iron but the hand wheel of this lathe is made of wood.

A specialised type of lathe or engine is shown which is clamped in a vice and used to make the sixteen turns or spiral groove for 8-day long case clock winding barrels (p. 29). This tool works on much the same lines as the fusee engine (p. 54) in that the work is made to rotate by turning the handle on the left, at the same time causing the carriage holding the cutter to travel in a lateral direction. The carriage is driven sideways by a screw thread on the left hand runner on which one end of the carriage is mounted. Turning on this engine would be done in one direction only, towards the operator, using the left hand to turn the handle and the right to give pressure to the cutter. In order to make the groove deep enough at the end of the first 'run' the handle is reversed and the cutter travels back to its starting point, and this could be repeated as many times as was necessary.

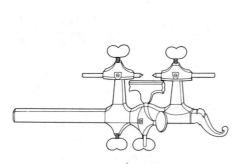

WATCHMAKER'S TURNS
English, 18th/19th century

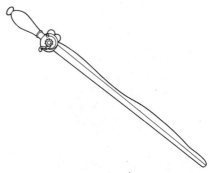

WATCHMAKER'S BOW
English, 18th/19th century

Turns were made in a wide variety of sizes for clock or watch work and were adaptable to many different operations, such as turning arbors and cutting and polishing pivots, for which several different types of steel runners were available. In the barrel engine and fusee engine (pp. 54, 57) the steel cutter is held firmly by a carriage, but the *engraving tools* which are used with turns are supported on a T-shaped *rest* which is situated between the runners and is adjustable in height and depth. The left-hand runner stock may be moved on the sliding bar to accommodate work of differing sizes and the tool is clamped in a vice below the right-hand stock, where it is faced with brass to give better grip. Work to be turned is held between the runners and a small pulley or *ferrule* is either clamped on to the work with screws or is provided with a tapered arbor on to which the work can be held friction tight.

Power for the turns could be provided by a bench wheel (p. 57) or with the *bow*. This particular bow, made of flexible steel, has a ratchet winder at the handle end to give the correct tension to the line. This line could be of gut, horsehair or even human hair according to the size and nature of the work. To operate it the bow is held in the left hand and one turn of the line is passed round the ferrule or pulley on the turns. Tension is adjusted on the bow itself then backwards and forwards motion of the bow rotates the work backwards and forwards. Cutting or polishing is done on alternate strokes while the rotation is *towards* the workman. Most bows are made of simple strips of cane or whalebone and many old craftsmen would use no other method for turning. The 'feel' of the bow interacting with the work and the *graver* gave precise control such as was impossible with either bench wheel or treadle.

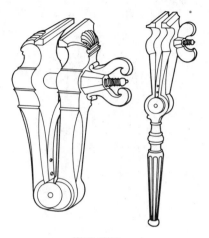

HAND VICES
French, 18th century

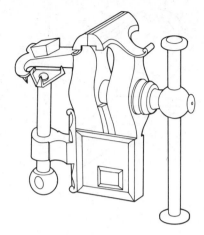

BENCH VICE
English, 18th century

There are two basic types of *vice* in clock or watch work, the *bench vice* which is clamped or screwed to the front edge of the bench top and the *hand vice* which allows work to be held firmly in one hand but which can be turned to various positions at will. Two hand vices are shown here, both of French design but almost identical to English vices of the same date except for the ornamental *scallop shell* motifs on the jaws of the larger one, the graceful *chamfering* of the arms and the elaborately scrolled *wing nut*. Both these vices have a *spring* inserted between the lower arms of the jaws so that they open automatically as the vice is undone. Some hand vices have brass inserts in the jaws to prevent marking any brass parts held and some hand vices were designed to hold special parts of clocks and watches, such as the open jawed *balance vice* for gripping the balance collet without touching the pallets.

Although modern engineers' vices are usually screwed directly on to the bench, clock and watchmakers' vices were *clamped* on so that they could be moved about easily. The bench vice was often used for holding some specialised tool such as the fusee engine, barrel engine, turns or swing tool. The vice shown here was intended to be opened to a comparatively short distance as the jaws are *hinged*; in *sliding vices* the jaws remain parallel to each other and can thus accommodate large items. Sometimes a clock or watchmakers' vice was made to *swivel* on its base so that work could be turned round to a new position and locked without having to remove it from the jaws. Vices which might be used for heavy hammering were made with a leg down to the floor and known as *pole vices*. Tools such as vices are impossible to date with any degree of accuracy, for once the best functional form had been established they changed little in style over the years.

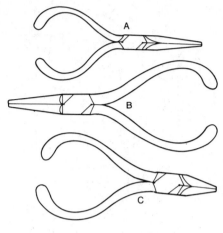

WATCH AND CLOCKMAKERS' PLIERS
English, 18th/19th century

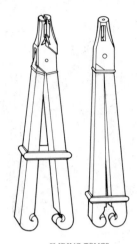

SLIDING TONGS
French, 18th century

In the Wyke and Green catalogue of about 1760–65 (p. 108) twenty different designs of *pliers* and *nippers* are advertised for the clock and watchmaker, including such types as 'half round half flatt', 'cutting nippers cross chops and slant chops', 'pendulum plyers', 'spring makers round nose', 'hawk bill' and an elegant design combining tweezers and pliers. The three shown here from another catalogue slightly later are described as 'pendulum plyers' (A), 'round nose' (B), and 'watch plyers' (C). Like some hand vices, pliers could be obtained with brass cheeks in the jaws for holding delicate parts safely, and making good pliers was a specialist craft requiring great skill. Pliers are useless unless the working faces fit accurately together and, unlike scissors, the joint of good pliers is 'boxed', i.e. the arm of one half *passes through* the other to give firm support to the handles and jaws when the joint pin is riveted home. To get one half through the other required opening and closing of the outer part of the joint.

In use pliers must always be gripped firmly and a tool was evolved which is something between pliers and a hand vice. This was the *sliding tongs* illustrated here from an 18th century French source, though they appear in almost exactly the same shape in English catalogues of the time. The work is gripped as when using ordinary pliers but once held, the *sliding bar* could be moved down the handles to keep the jaws closed and the work in place. The advantage is that the tongs can then be loosely held without the work falling out and being flat sided, as they invariably were, they could be held in a bench vice in the upright position. In designs for English sliding tongs a notch was provided on the inside of one arm just above the sliding bar. A peg could be slipped into this notch once the sliding bar was down to prevent it from accidentally being released while the tool was in use.

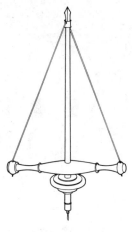

ARCHIMIDEAN DRILL STOCK
English, 18th/19th century

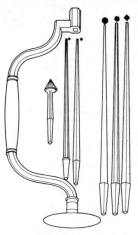

BROACHES AND BRACE
English, 18th/19th century

Drilling of pivot and other holes in clock and watch plates can be done in various ways. For some parts it is possible to drill them in a *mandrel lathe*, where the work rotates and the drill remains stationary. Drills held in a separate stock with a ferrule and powered by a bow can be used either with one end against a *breast plate*, held against the chest of the workman, or using a pivoted block in one hand. Vices were often used to take the rear end of a bow-driven drill stock and some have small holes in the end of the jaws for this purpose. For reciprocating drilling the *Archimedean drill stock* was sometimes used. The drill stock is held with a pivoted block at the upper end and a counterweight on the shaft gives inertia to its motion. The cords of the drill wrap themselves round the stock, first in one direction then the other as the handle is moved up and down.

After drilling, pivot holes have to be *broached* or *reamed* to the exact size required. A *broach* is usually five-sided, the sharp edges between the flat surfaces cutting the side of the hole as the tool is turned. As the broach is tapered it is used first on one side of the pivot hole, then on the other. This action produces a hole which is slightly tapering from each end and at its narrowest at the centre. This means that the pivot is only in frictional contact with the hole at its centre and the space at each side gives adequate access for oil. The broaches shown here are for use on large clocks and the *brace* is used for turning them, ensuring smooth cutting action. The round broach is a *burnishing broach* used to burnish the inside of the holes after they have been broached to size. Broaches vary from large ones over 1 ft. long and $\frac{1}{2}$ in. thick at the wide end, to tiny ones like fine needles.

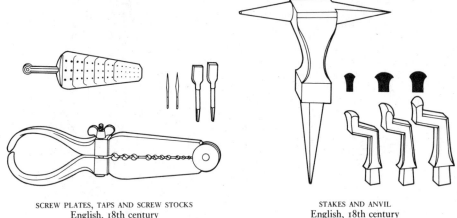

SCREW PLATES, TAPS AND SCREW STOCKS
English, 18th century

STAKES AND ANVIL
English, 18th century

Before the days of standard sizes of screw threads, individual clockmakers made their own screws and even at times made their own tools to make their own screws. The illustrations show a *screw plate* and *screw stocks*, the former for small screws and the latter for larger ones. The action of the old screw plates is somewhat different from that of the dies used today in that the screw plate tends to *impress* rather than *cut* the thread of the screw. The *taps* were made of a size to fit the holes in the screw plates and once a tap was inserted into a new hole to make a thread it could be turned with a hand vice or other suitable tool. Tapping blind holes was impossible with this type of tap and this is one reason why clock and watch makers for long continued to pin their movements together, screws for this purpose not appearing before our modern era of machine tools.

Absolutely vital to the clockmaker, watch-maker and casemaker, was a good selection of *stakes* and small *anvils*. For any type of controlled hammering of small parts, and particularly for riveting, the anvil would be mounted in a solid, well-supported part of the bench, and if of large size might well be mounted in a heavy wooden block on the floor. The round or curved headed stake, mostly used for delicate work such as shaping part of a thin metal watch case or taking a dent out of the back of it, would not need to be so solidly mounted, indeed some slight resilience might be an advantage. Stakes, therefore, are usually square at the foot to be held in a vice when used. Watch case makers have a very wide variety of stake tools of various curvatures and sizes, as do silversmiths generally, and it is extremely important that the heads of stakes should be kept in a smooth, clean and polished condition.

1a (*above left*). Enamelled watch, verge escapement; signed Thp. Masseron à Paris, *c.* 1650. *City of Liverpool Museums.* 1b (*above right*). Cruciform watch, verge escapement; signed Josias Cuper, Blois, *c.* 1620. *City of Liverpool Museums.* 2 (*below*). Table clock with striking and alarm, verge escapement; signed Johannes Somer, south German, *c.* 1650. *City Art Gallery, Manchester.* 3 (*right*). Movement of clock in illustration 2.

PLATE II

4 (*left*). Bracket clock, quarter striking on two bells, pull repeat, verge escapement; signed Richard Fennel, Kensington, *c.* 1690. *City Art Gallery, Manchester.* 5 (*below left*). Back plate of clock in illustration 4. 6 (*below*). Long case clock, external locking-plate striking, anchor escapement, marquetry case with cresting missing; signed Joseph Knibb, Londini fecit., *c.* 1690. *Museum and Art Gallery, Salford.*

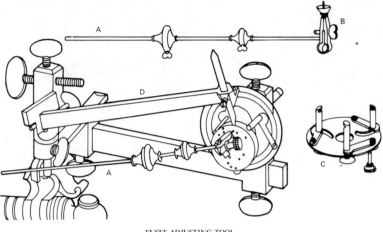

FUSEE ADJUSTING TOOL
English, 18th century

For high precision adjustments to a watch fusee a set of turns is mounted in a vice at right-angles to the normal position and at the right-hand end a watch movement is clamped to the stock by a *movement holder*, shown at C. A long arm (D) is pivoted through an adapted tool rest and its upper end is fitted with a steel cutter arranged to ride in the groove of the fusee. On the square of the fusee a clamp at the end of a long *adjusting rod* is fitted (upper diagram), the clamp (B) holding a fusee and the adjusting rod (A) having a large and small weight sliding upon it. When the mainspring of the watch and the fusee are linked by their chain the *torque* of the spring can be measured and compared at different parts of the winding by the way in which the adjusting arm (A) balances the force as delivered through the fusee.

In setting up the tool the large weight on the adjusting rod would be used to balance the turning power of the fusee, and manipulation of the smaller weight would detect any subtle inequalities, rather like the small weight on the arm of a weighing machine. If adjustment of the groove was found to be necessary the cutter mounted on the pivoted arm (D) could be used to cut the groove slightly deeper where necessary without dismantling the fusee and spring. Naturally all this would be done without the wheel train or other parts of the watch in place, and such treatment would be reserved for fusees and springs which were required for really accurate work. The important point is that the individual fusee by this method could be matched to the individual qualities of a given mainspring in an age when standard behaviour of hand-wrought springs could not be relied upon. It is also an interesting example of 18th century workshop ingenuity.

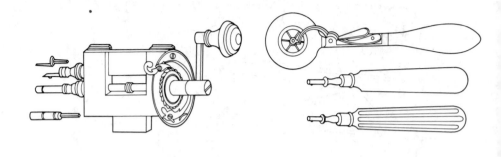

SPRING WINDER
English, 18th/19th century

BLUEING TOOL AND HAND WINDERS
English, 18th/19th century

The mainsprings of clocks and watches had to be tightly wound to introduce them into their respective spring barrels before assembly. Although this can be done by hand except with strong springs, it is not good for the springs as inevitable distortion and strain takes place which might affect the action of the spring later. *Spring winders*, made of brass and steel, were therefore used, the spring to be wound being hooked at its inner and outer ends on to the respective hooked projections on the left-hand side of the winder. As the handle was turned the spring was wound and it could not unwind because of the ratchet and click on the winding handle. Once the spring had been wound to a smaller diameter than the inside of the barrel, the barrel was slipped over it and the hooks of the winder withdrawn. Like several of the other hand tools shown the spring winder has a tang below allowing it to be held in a vice.

Small springs for watches could be wound into their barrels by a simple tool with a handle, because there is comparatively little power in the springs. Two of these hand winders are shown with a hook on the end to attach to the spring. Clock and watch springs are almost always blued, that is they have a thin film of blue oxidation, used to check the *tempering* of the steel. Tempering is the process used to soften hardened steel to the state most suited to its purpose. The polished, hardened steel goes through a range of colours from pale straw to a deep blackish blue as heat is increased, watch springs being tempered to a bright blue colour at about 580°F. This must be done evenly throughout the spring, so a *blueing tool* is used, its broad flat pan distributing the heat evenly to the spring which is held firmly to it by a spring-loaded clamp from which it can be dropped as soon as the correct temperature is reached.

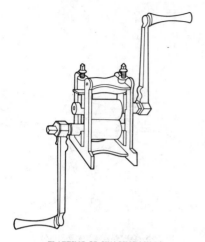

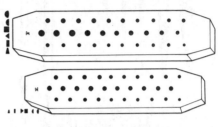

FLATTING OR SWAGING MILLS
English, 18th/19th century

DRAW PLATES
English, 18th/19th century

The *rollers* or *flatting mill* shown here is really a simple type of mangle with which strips of metal such as steel, silver, gold, brass, or other alloys could be reduced in thickness by evenly narrowing the gap between the rollers at each successive 'pass'. A hand operated mill of this kind was generally more at home in a case maker's workshop than in that of a watch or clockmaker, and usually interchangeable rollers were available, some having engraved mouldings cut round their surfaces. With rollers of this kind thin strips of silver, for example, could be passed through them to impress the required moulding on a piece to be used for a watch case *middle* or the *bezel*. The projecting ends of the iron frame were clamped with stout iron hooks to a heavy wooden stand as a mill of this kind needed stability. Another name for this machine is a *swaging mill*.

The *draw plate* is also important to the casemaker. When a wire of a certain section is required, a piece of wire of larger diameter is sharpened at one end and pulled through the largest hole of the plate giving the section required. The holes diminish in size along the plate and taper from front to back to squeeze the wire as it is drawn through. Once the wire passes easily through the first hole it is pulled through the next smallest until the right size is reached. With square, circular, semi-circular, triangular and other section drawplates available, all manner of mouldings could be made, the work being done on a strongly built *draw bench* in which the end of the wire is gripped by a pair of pliers which are pulled by a leather strap wound round the narrow barrel of a large capstan wheel. After several drawings the wire must be heated to *anneal* it otherwise it will become very brittle and will snap when being drawn through.

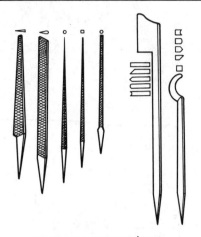

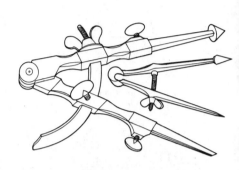

WATCH AND CLOCKMAKERS' FILES
English, 18th/19th century

WING COMPASSES AND DIVIDERS
English, 18th/19th century

The steel *file* is perhaps the most important tool of all in the clock or watchmaker's workshop. A file is a strip of good quality steel, swaged or hammered to shape and cut to provide it with teeth, the cuts either being *single cut*, i.e. rows of parallel cuts alone, or *cross cut*, with two sets of parallel cuts crossing each other. The cut is made with a steel chisel which brings up a ridge or edge, the following cut being made by bringing the chisel to the ridge already cut and cutting the next one. Originally all files were made *by hand*, the hand cutters working at tremendous speed since they were paid for the quantity produced. After the cutting is done the files have to be hardened, by heating to a dull red and then quenching in a saline solution. One of the oldest firms where file making was first put on an industrial footing is that of Peter Stubs of Warrington.

A wide range of different sections and cuts of files were made, such as 'half round', 'lozenge', 'square', 'round' and so on, particular files being made for specialised purposes, e.g. the *crossing file* for cutting out the 'crossings' of wheels. *Rifflers* were a specialised type of file with shaped ends on which the file teeth were cut to be used on parts difficult of access for ordinary files. Such tools are difficult to obtain today. The two other tools shown on this page, *compasses* and *dividers*, were made in many sizes and both were invaluable to the maker of watches and clocks. Both have one foot of conical shape to give exact location in a previously drilled hole, and both could be used for *scribing out* a clock plate (p. 22), or for making comparative measurements. Compasses are adjusted by hand and locked in position on the curved quadrant plate, while dividers are hinged by means of a strong steel spring integral with the arms and are screw adjusted.

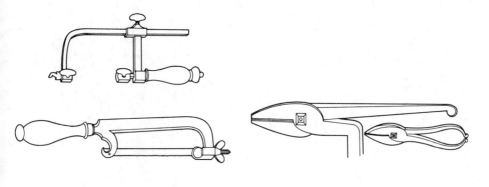

WATCH AND CLOCKMAKERS' SAWS
English, 18th/19th century

METAL-CUTTING SHEARS
English, 18th/19th century

One tool factor's list which has survived from over a hundred years ago itemises more than three hundred different tools available to the trade, though where the trade itself was so specialised different craftsmen would only need the tools for his own type of work, and not the whole range. At the same time many tools were made by the craftsmen themselves to suit their own specialist needs in the days when it was impossible to get hold of a particular item required. The last tools shown are those required for cutting metals, *saws* and *shears*. Saws were made in many sizes and styles, the *piercing saw frame* being used with very fine blades to cut out apertures in movements and the fine decorative frets which are met in both clocks and watches. The thicker saw, described as a 'saw with nut'—the nut being used to tension the blade—is the ancestor of the well-known hack saw of today.

The two types of shears were used for cutting comparatively thin sheets of metal and, like the draw-plates (p. 65), were used by the casemaker as well as the clock or watchmaker. In the case of the larger shears one handle is cranked at right-angles to insert into a hole in the bench. By this method the workman could operate the other handle with one hand and guide the metal being cut with the other. Cutting tools of this kind were made by the trades-men of Sheffield, an important retailer early in the 19th century being *Joseph Smith*. His catalogue entitled '*Explanation or Key to the various Manufactories of Sheffield*', published in 1816, illustrates a wide range of tools made there, many of which were of particular use to the clock-maker. This same Joseph Smith was responsible for the production of Peter Stubs' first catalogue of 1801 and it was through dealers such as Smith that Stubs got his steel for making his files.

3
Mechanical Clocks before c. 1550

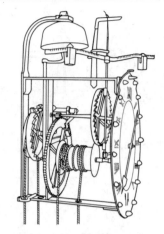

GOTHIC IRON WALL CLOCK WITH ALARM
German, c.1400

Informed opinion gives a tentative date for the introduction of the mechanical clock in Europe at about 1270 A.D., a suggestion which presupposes the knowledge of toothed wheels and pinions for driving machinery very much earlier. The transmission of power and motion through toothed wheels was known in the western world by the ancient Greeks, and in China as early as the 4th century B.C. Much of our knowledge of early science has been preserved in European monastic libraries, and it was within the monastic system itself that the first clocks, as we know them, were undoubtedly made. The mediaeval horologium when found in early writings is a difficult word to interpret, for it might mean a sundial, a water clock or hand-struck time bells, but by the 1340s we know that it could be used for a mechanical clock with weighted power source and regulated escapement. By 1550 the clock was taking its place in domestic as well as religious life and its basic principles were firmly established.

In mediaeval monasteries, of whatever religious order, fixed times were allocated for devotions, known as the *canonical hours*. These occurred as many as three times in the night—the Nocturns; Matins at dawn; at 6.0 a.m., 9.0 a.m., noon and 3.0 p.m., with Vespers about 6.0 p.m. and Compline as daylight departed. Particularly for the night hours an alarm was essential, and such a clock of about 1400 is shown. Powered by a weight and regulated by the *verge and foliot*, it has gearing for a *sixteen hour dial*, with *touch pieces* on the edge for checking the time in the darkness. With sixteen hours on the shortest day of the year, and eight hours on the longest, the clock was adjusted to sound the bell at hourly intervals throughout the night. With the *great wheel* engaging directly with the *escape wheel pinion*, in a single iron strap frame, this is the most primitive form of verge and foliot clock devised and the earliest known ancestor of the range of clockwork devices made in following centuries.

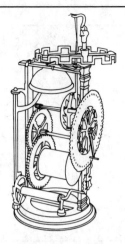

MONASTIC ALARM CLOCK, BRASS AND IRON
Italian, early 15th century

GOTHIC IRON DOMESTIC CLOCK
German, late 15th century

The iron *alarum* of about 1400 on the previous page used the verge and foliot type of escapement, and although this system continued for more than two hundred years, a *circular balance* instead of a foliot was sometimes employed. Initial regulation was supplied by fitting weights to the balance arms, with subsequent adjustment by altering the driving weight. A peg fitted into one of the holes on the edge of the *twenty-four hour revolving dial* would 'trip' the elongated arm of the star-shaped *detent* below and release the alarm work which itself was worked by a type of crown wheel acting on two pallets on the alarm hammer staff. In the Italian clock above, the front supporting column is moulded with a classical *Ionic capital*, while the *trefoil cusping* of the pierced openwork dial is reminiscent of Gothic rose-window tracery. The classical style was never entirely absent in the art of Italy in the mediaeval period, nor did Italian Gothic develop as fully as the Gothic of northern Europe.

Although a touch of Gothic design is seen in the Italian alarum, the style of the German clock is entirely Gothic, and it was doubtless made for domestic rather than for religious use. The corner pillars, which are the principal members of the open iron frame, are shaped like *Gothic buttresses*, with three stages of 'offsets' and tapering pinnacle terminals. The pointed arched support of the bell is decorated with attached *crockets* which simulate those of wood and stone in 15th century architecture. Mechanically the clock has two trains, the *going train* at the front and the *striking train* behind, an arrangement which persisted until the later years of the 17th century, and later still in many country districts. This is the precursor of the *lantern clock* (pp. 88, 89) and has an early example of the *locking plate* or *count plate* system of striking. A circular balance is fitted below the bell and its single hand marks the hours against Gothic style numerals or *chapters*.

GOTHIC PILLAR CLOCK
From a French miniature, 15th century

GOTHIC PILLAR CLOCK
From a French miniature, mid 15th century

Much of our knowledge of mediaeval clocks is derived from illustrations in manuscripts, missals and other books of devotions. One of the most important discovered is the *Brussels Miniature* (p. 72) which is particularly valuable in its depiction of an early *fusee*; other miniatures show us the form of Gothic clocks even though the artists do not always appear to have understood the way in which the clocks they were drawing worked! Both the illustrations here are from French manuscripts and each clock is weight-driven with going and striking trains. The absence of a dial in the first illustration is unlikely to be the result of artistic licence as many early clocks were without dials, recording the time simply by striking the bell. Both clocks are supported on a single Gothic column, a functional form which must have been made though none, apparently, are extant today. It is difficult, however, to make a final judgement in this case for mediaeval ideas of scale in their paintings were not the same as ours.

The second miniature is more accurate horologically, and the artist had observed and understood the motion of the wheel work. The *great wheel* of the going train is geared through a pinion to the *motion work* behind the dial, and the striking train seen in part in the upper half, is clearly making use of a *birdcage pinion* as it drives the *fly* which in this clock is a most extraordinary feature like windmill sails, appearing above the dial. A hammer above is pivoted to strike the bell and perhaps the figure of Temperance, emerging from the clouds, is in the act of attending to *capstan winding?* The four Evangelists, depicted as an Angel, Eagle, Lion and Bull appear in the upper and lower corners of the dial while the quatrefoil plan of the base of the column is a shape often seen in encaustic tile designs of the late mediaeval period, or as the foot of a silver chalice.

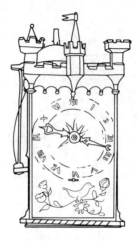

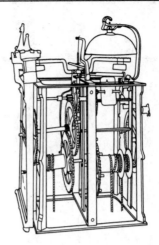

GOTHIC CHAMBER CLOCK
Probably German, late 15th century

MOVEMENT OF GERMAN CHAMBER CLOCK

While the form of the Gothic clock (p. 69) is suggestive of ecclesiastical architecture, the clock above reminds us of military forms of building. At the top of the dial the crenellated turrets and the overhanging machicolations are derived from later mediaeval defence works in castles and fortified houses. Unlike the Gothic clocks (pp. 68, 69) the dial is painted on an iron plate occupying the *entire front* of the clock, the hours, or chapters, being accentuated by painted radiating arms from the dial centre, alternately wavy and straight. Though much worn on the original the painted bird and flowers remind us of decorative margins in mediaeval manuscripts, and the use of rectangular dials of this kind heralds an era when movements were largely hidden, not to be uncovered again until the advent of the *skeleton clock* in the late 18th and 19th centuries (p. 134). This type of painted decoration might also be thought of as the precursor of the painted wooden clocks of southern Germany, made in the 18th century (p. 187).

In the movement of the clock we see the same arrangement of going and striking as in the German clock (p. 69). The *winding barrels* are narrow and although requiring a heavier weight than with a wider barrel the clock will run longer at each winding, since one revolution of the great wheel requires less 'drop' for the weight. The escapement is of *verge and foliot* type and the *studs* on the striking great wheel, which operate the *tail* of the bell hammer, are clearly seen. The *strap iron frame* is a miniature version of the frame of the Salisbury Cathedral clock on p. 72, and the corner posts have Gothic offsets above and below. The frame is of riveted construction, the three central plates being held at the top by *wedges* as in later lantern clocks, easy to remove when dismantling the movement. The open structure of these early clocks freely admitted dust and dirt, but the coarseness of their construction and the inaccuracy of their timekeeping made this of little consequence.

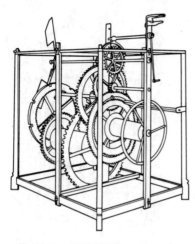

TURRET CLOCK
From Salisbury Cathedral, 1380–85

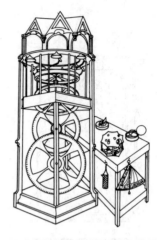

DETAIL FROM THE BRUSSELS MINIATURE
Between 1455–88

The great *tower clock*, or *turret clock*, at Salisbury Cathedral is said to be the oldest working clock in England and is a larger version of the domestic Gothic iron clocks. It was constructed in the early 1380s and housed in the bell tower, near the north porch of the church; there was no dial on the clock at this period. The movement was placed in the central tower when the bell tower was demolished in 1790 and remained there in daily use until 1884. In 1931 it was brought out and cleaned, and in 1956 the escapement, which had earlier been converted to a pendulum type, was re-converted to its original verge and foliot design. It is now displayed in the cathedral aisle in going order, the replacement parts painted dark green to distinguish them from the original movement. Like the domestic clock on p. 71 the turret clock of Salisbury has its corner pillars set at an angle of 135° to the frame and has similar Gothic mouldings. The drawing shows the clock with an anchor escapement after its first conversion.

Of all the mediaeval manuscripts giving horological information there are two, perhaps, which are of the greatest importance and both of approximately the same date. One is the *Almanus Manuscript* written by Brother Paulus Almanus after 1475 and the other is known as the *Brussels Miniature* of between 1455 and 1488. In the detail shown we see a type of monastic alarum in a Gothic iron frame, presumably intended to be powered by a weight and causing the bells to be sounded by pivoted hammers, actuated by a large horizontal revolving wheel. The hammers are pivoted to the fixed iron frame. On the table on the right we see a *quadrant* and three *sundials—horizontal*, *equatorial* and *pillar* (pp. 15, 16, 17) while a clearly drawn spring-driven table clock movement shows that by this time the *fusee* was well-known and possibly in regular use. The movement is shown lying dial downwards with its balance and balance cock removed; perhaps the artist observed it on a workshop bench awaiting repair.

TAMBOUR–CASED GILDED BRASS TABLE CLOCK
German, c.1540

TAMBOUR–CASED GILDED BRASS CLOCK AND ALARM
German, c.1560

The spring-driven fusee movement so clearly seen in the Brussels Miniature (p. 72) is important. It is the earliest representation we have of this feature, designed to equalise the *torque* of the mainspring (p. 31), though it is quite likely that the device had been known for many years before the miniature was produced. If, as is sometimes stated, the coiled mainspring as a source of power was introduced about the third quarter of the 15th century, it is not impossible that the spring in a barrel and the conical fusee to *equalise* the varying torque of the spring were *developed together*, at least for use in clocks, though the *stackfreed*, being much easier to make and smaller in construction, was mainly used for watches or very small clocks (p. 31). It is quite unknown which came first, the fusee or the stackfreed, but the latter could well have been devised as a more simple and cheaper way of replacing the principle of the fusee.

The development of the spring-driven portable clock must have been of tremendous importance in the late 15th and early 16th centuries. The *tambour cased* clocks shown here were made about 1540 or slightly later, powered by springs in barrels connected to fusees by *gut lines*, with *frames* of steel and controlled by the *verge and balance*. The single hand on the horizontal dial can be 'read' by the fingers when it is dark and its position related to the *touch pieces* round the edge, while the clock on the right has a spring-powered alarum clipped on the top, released by the hour hand as it contacts a projecting lever at the time desired. The gilded brass cases of these clocks are of early Renaissance style, with engraved scrolls, leaves and classical heads in circular roundels, reminding us of those in terra-cotta which flank Anne Boleyn's Gateway at Hampton Court Palace (1531–6), where the great astronomical clock, installed by Henry VIII about 1540, has recently been restored.

4
Early Renaissance Clocks and Watches
c. 1550 to 1650

HAND HOLDING A WATCH
Detail from an Italian painting, c.1560

It was probably in Italy, towards the end of the 15th century, that the watch, as distinct from the domestic clock, began to appear though none of this date are known to exist. A watch is only a very small portable clock, and in its earliest appearance it closely resembles the drum-shaped clocks we have seen (p. 73). Knowledge of the introduction of watches is largely based on pictorial representations and the drawing here is based on one of the earliest portraits known in which the sitter is holding a watch. From the fact that the watch is being held out as though for inspection, we can see that it was regarded by its owner as an important possession; to have owned it at all would indicate a status in life of some note, for watches as well as clocks were the property of the rich. The opulence of those who could afford watches in the 16th century is reflected in the elaborate decorative treatment which these timepieces received.

Like the drum-shaped *tambour* and early Gothic clocks, the watch shown here has *touch pieces* on the dial for use at night and has a cord through the *pendant* to fasten it to the owner's clothing. Sometimes the watch was of globular form, often being known as a *musk-ball* or *musk-apple watch*, perhaps of the type said to have been made by the famous *Peter Henlein* (c.1479–1542) of Nuremberg, who though credited with making a watch as early as 1510 was probably not the first maker of watches at all. The drawing shows a watch with a *double* or *24 hour dial* and a pierced metal cover to protect it in the pocket. Its portable *alarum* (p. 73) stands on the table by the brim of its owner's hat with its velvet-lined carrying case immediately behind. The watch and alarum at this stage were separate, but it was not long before the alarum mechanism became incorporated with the movement of the watch itself.

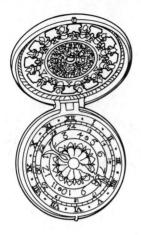

DRUM-SHAPED ALARM WATCH
German, c.1575

The detailed views of the watch above show the type from the portrait on the opposite page. Dating from about 1575 this watch has an alarum, of which the *setting dial* is in the centre of the main dial. To set it to the time required the disc is turned until the hour selected coincides with the hand. It is surprising how long this form of alarm-set persisted, and it is often met in American mass-produced clocks of the 19th century. The dial with normal 12 hour divisions in Roman numerals also has a complete set from 13 to 24 in Arabic characters on an inner ring, a style of dividing known as *Italian*. Only quarter-hour divisions are marked on the dial for with but a single hand and far from accurate timekeeping, this was all that was required at the time. The relief decoration on the sides of the case and the cover was produced by *casting*, finished by *engraving* and *chasing* and later *gilded*.

Whereas the movements of tambour-cased clocks were *slid* into the cases and held in place with *pins* or *swivel latches*, the movements of most watches were *hinged* to the case, a system which survived until the early 20th century. Movement frames in early clocks were often *skeletonised* on the top plate, and while both were of steel the watches were of *full plate* construction. Brass had not yet begun to replace steel for the wheel work and movements, when compared with later ones, were reasonably plain. A touch of decoration appears in the splendid foot of the *stackfreed spring* and the early *balance cock* is made as a simple S-shaped piece of soft brass which could be bent for adjusting the depth of the *verge escapement*. No balance springs appear on any of these early watches unless added at a later date, and *regulation* is achieved by the *hog's bristle* to control the balance oscillation, acting against the balance arm.

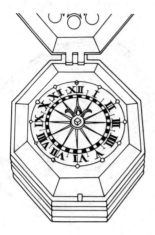 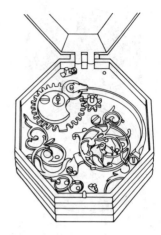

OCTAGONAL WATCH WITH STACKFREED
German, *c.*1580

A fine example of about 1580 is this anonymous German octagonal brass-cased watch. It is believed to be German partly because of the use of the *stackfreed*, an essentially German characteristic at the time. Beautifully simple, its short and stubby hand is *pinned* to the *centre arbor*, reading against a dial with touch pieces and quarter-hour divisions. The octagonal and oval-shaped watch began to evolve from the circular drum cases of the middle of the century, and the stage was set for the elaborate '*form*' watches after about 1600. This watch is an interesting transitional piece for though the case and interior treatment suggest a date towards the end of the century, the fitting of the movement follows the earlier pattern, sliding into its case and held by swivel latches instead of being hinged as one might expect. The plain back and pierced dial cover plates are fitted on stout brass hinges and are held against a small protruding catch when closed.

What the movement of this watch lacked in accuracy it certainly gained in elaboration. The *balance cock* is of an early form which was fashionable for a short time only, the cock itself being circular and entirely protecting the balance. Both the cock and its foot are widely pierced in flowing scrolls and leaves; this is characteristic of early watches, the pierced designs on later cocks being more concentrated. A notable feature is the large stackfreed and spring with its *roller* terminal. The watch is *key-wound* in a clockwise direction on the steel pinion to the right of the stackfreed, and is shown about three-quarters up. With full winding the pinion would lock on the stackfreed edge where a tooth has been left uncut to prevent over-winding. In its initial movement the mainspring of the watch would expend its early power by pushing the roller up the first slope of the *cam*, but in its later revolution it would be aided by the roller on the long downhill slope of the cam (p. 31).

STAR-SHAPED WATCH
English, c.1620

OVAL-SHAPED WATCH
French, c.1590

By the turn of the 16th century the art and science of making watches was spreading through Europe; in such centres as Nuremberg, Geneva, Blois and London craftsmen were settling and establishing their trade. From similarities of cases and movements from these centres alone it is clear that the craft was international in structure; it was, after all, not until 1631 that the *Clockmakers' Company* was founded to protect the English makers from foreign competition, when the resident workers were becoming conscious of their own identity. European watches of the early 17th century are frequently called *form* watches, from the diversity of shapes of their cases, and it is in this period that the watch emerges as an article of jewellery, a facet of the industry which, from this point onwards has always been important. External appearance has always been an important factor in retailing watches of whatever date, combined with the reputation of the manufacturer for mechanical reliability. (Plate 11.)

The form watch evolved as oval, octagonal, stellar, cruciform and other shapes, some of which are remarkable as imaginative shapes of birds or skulls. By the 17th century brass had begun to be used for all parts of the movement except the steel arbors and pinions, clicks and springs, the mainspring and a few screws. Elaboration of cases was matched by much decoration on the easily accessible movements and the ornately designed and pierced balance cock was here to stay, in various evolving forms, until the end of the 19th century. Although most watch cases had hinged metal covers a few were made from *cut crystal* (p. 84) and such was the international character of these elaborate though inaccurate devices that it is improbable that all the parts were made in such widely varying places suggested by the signatures and cities engraved on the plates. To what extent this was due to emigration of craftsmen or the trading of specialised watch parts in this early period we shall perhaps never know.

TABLE CLOCK
Augsburg, c.1635

TABLE CLOCK
Hamburg, 1638

Elaborate watches in the early 17th century were matched by equally elaborate clocks from Germany, Italy, Switzerland and France. Many of the clocks of this period are now in public museums and those still on the market command high prices. The quality of the casework of the best of these clocks puts them in the highest order of decorative metalwork and in some ways the applied sculpture and ornament is more important than the clockwork contained within, for the cases were the work of artist-craftsmen and the clocks were but indifferent timekeepers. Elaboration was not only confined to cases, however, for the clockwork was often elaborate too, and many are equipped with information such as *lunar phases*, *month*, *date*, *day of the week* and *alarm*, with *striking work* as well. In their gilded splendour these clocks display the richness and opulence to be seen in the gold and silver ewers and bowls, goblets, steeple ' cups and salts which adorned the tables and cupboards of early Renaissance Europe.

Both the table clocks here are essentially *octagonal watches* with elaborate movements, mounted on magnificent stands. Composed mainly of silver and gilded brass, with Renaissance detailing, the form relates in some ways to the *Gothic monstrance*, some clocks actually being made in monstrance form, mounted at the top of a pillar. *Casting, piercing, repoussé, chasing* and *engraving* were the metalworking techniques of goldsmiths, not the products of the clockmaking trade (p. 50). The clock on the left has calendar information on its moulded base, with a revolving moon at the top; the one on the right presents these details on separate small sub-dials which we see in some watches later in this chapter (pp. 83, 84). Perhaps one should relate the general form and design of these clocks to the Gothic pillar clocks from mediaeval miniature paintings (p. 70). The gearing of these spring-driven clocks was such that they rarely had a running period of more than 14 hours, and had to be wound twice each day.

PLATE III

7 (*left*). Silver pair-cased watch, 'sun and moon' dial, verge escapement; signed Richard Vernon, Liverpool, *c.* 1700. *City of Liverpool Museums.* 8 (*below left*). Dial of the Exeter Lovelace clock. *City of Liverpool Museums.* 9 (*below*). Long case clock, musical work and quarter striking, anchor escapement, ebonised case with coloured prints applied to the door; signed John Ellicott, London, *c.* 1750. *Lady Lever Art Gallery, Port Sunlight.*

PLATE IV

10 (*top*). Enamelled pair-cased watch, quarter repeating, lever escapement (probably a later conversion); made for the Spanish market and signed Higgs y Evans, Londres, *c.* 1775–80. *City Art Gallery, Manchester.* 11 (*above*). Gilded pair-cased striking watch, strike/silent catch on right, verge escapement; signed Dan. De St. Leu, Watch Maker to her Majesty, London, *c.* 1790. *City Art Gallery, Manchester* 12 Two watches for the Turkish market: a (*far left*). Silver and tortoiseshell pair-cased quarter repeater with dial removed to show repeat work, cylinder escapement; signed Balthazar Granier & Cie. French, *c.* 1780. b (*left*). Triple-cased silver and tortoiseshell watch, verge escapement; signed George Prior London. Hallmarked 1780–81. *Museum and Art Gallery, Salford.*

CRUCIFIX CLOCK
German, c.1600

TABERNACLE CLOCK
Italian, c.1580 with later conversion

The introduction of the *coiled mainspring* (p. 73) made possible the production of watches and also gave rise to the development of clock forms which were very different from their weight-driven predecessors, mounted in cases of splendid craftsmanship and decorative ingenuity. Some were *square*, with a dome for the bell (p. 81), or *cylindrical*, derived from drum-cased clocks, while *pillar*, *tabernacle* and *hexagonal* clocks evolved of the highest quality of case and movement (see Coole and Neumann, *The Orpheus Clocks*) (Plate I, 2, 3). Whether German, Italian or French the designers and sculptors of the casework understood the classical principles of design and were familiar with the work of the foremost artists of the day, and it is to the studios of such artist-craftsmen as *Wenzel Jamnitzer* (1508–85) of Nuremberg that we must look for the production of these fine pieces. It is said that Jamnitzer could cast in relief in his metalwork the shapes of animals and plants, just as the French potter *Bernard Palissy* (c.1510–90) did in his extravagant earthenware dishes.

There is no better evidence for the flowering of the early Renaissance than these small but significant collaborations of art and science. At no other period do we find this same 'marriage' except perhaps in the late 17th and 18th century styles of France (Ch. 9), where clock cases were works of art in their own right irrespective of the quality of the movements inside them. The *crucifix clock* above is but a religious form of the pillar clock type (p. 78) with its revolving dial and movement in the base, while the *tabernacle clock*, of architectural inspiration, is a good example of an altered clock, for it was 'improved' at a later date by conversion of the movement to a more accurate pendulum controlled escapement and fitted with a new dial and hands quite out of sympathy with the original design. The *cyma reversa* moulding of the base, common to both these clocks, was a favourite base moulding of Renaissance architects and in both it is ornamented with applied engraving.

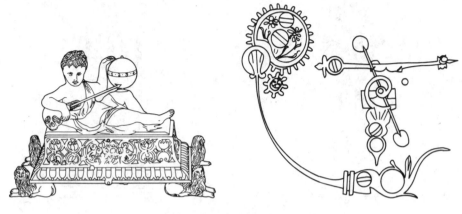

CASE AND PART OF MOVEMENT OF TABLE CLOCK
Augsburg, c.1590

This Augsburg rectangular clock is a good example of the elaborate casework of an early Renaissance sculptor. Reclining on his plinth, a cherub supports a revolving globe, indicating the hours with a pointer. With his elbow resting on a skull, that emblem of death already seen twice on clocks of this period, we are reminded of the passage of time (pp. 78, 79). Tomb-like, the case rests on four lion feet; the movement is contained in the base, held in place with *swivel latches* turning into slots. The bottom of the case is also latched and carries the bell, which is sounded by a hammer on the underneath side of the movement. The tradition of using sculptured figures on clocks was continued into the 18th century by the French and many French clocks have revolving dials (Plate V, 13 and p. 176). Piercing of the sides of the base below the cherub's elbow allows the sound of the bell to be heard and the whole group of the case and figure is engraved, chased and gilded.

As the movement of the clock is easily accessible, it is decorated with engraving and other ornament (Plate I, 2, 3). The second illustration shows the *foliot* which regulates the escapement, for the foliot did not give way entirely to the balance in these early years of clockmaking (p. 69), though by 1600 it would have been very uncommon. This type of foliot is often known as a *dumb-bell foliot* and it is poised beneath an S-shaped *cock* (p. 75). The foliot is controlled in its oscillations by a *hog's bristle regulator* which can be moved nearer to the centre or further away on the pivoted arm seen above the cock. The *stackfreed* (pp. 31, 76) with its powerful steel spring is located on the left, the top of the *cam* being engraved with flowers, while the splayed-out end of the spring contains the roller which is resting in the hollow of the cam, indicating that the mainspring has completely run down. The foot of the stackfreed spring is finely scrolled.

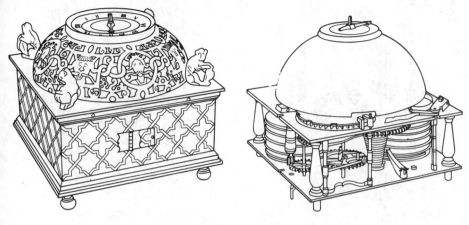

CASE AND MOVEMENT OF TABLE CLOCK
Abbeville, c.1620

Instead of fitting the bell beneath the clock as in the last example (p. 80), in this French clock of about 1620, signed by *Nicholas Plantard* of *Abbeville*, it is ingeniously mounted above the movement as in contemporary weight-driven clocks, but being for table use the dial is placed above the bell. The case is of pierced, engraved and gilded brass, the outer dome being of *strapwork* design reminiscent of plasterwork ceilings of the Elizabethan and Jacobean periods. The sides are engraved with interlocking geometrical forms which remind us of Persian tiles, a Near Eastern influence which spread through southern Europe in the wake of the Moslem Empire. Another clock of very similar form in the Victoria and Albert Museum is signed by *David Ramsay*, who came to London from France about 1610, and among his other claims to fame became the first Master of the Clockmakers' Company in 1632. One difference between the two clocks is that Ramsay's has classical *caryatids* at the corners, while the corners of Plantard's clock are plain.

The movement of the clock with its turned *baluster pillars* is inserted from the base. The conical *fusee* is driven from the spring barrel on the right through a twisted *gut line* round its spiral groove of sixteen turns. Part of the barrel for the striking train is on the left, and just below the bell the edge of the *count* or *locking plate* appears (p. 32), its locking *detent* projecting upwards through the pillar plate. As the locking detent falls into a notch in the locking plate the arm half way down its arbor engages with the locking wheel of the train, and the clock cannot strike again until unlocked at the following hour. The bell is cut away at its edge to make room for the arm of the bell hammer, while the *fusee stop-work* appears between the fusee and the spring barrel to prevent overwinding and breaking the gut line. The stopwork is pivoted to the *top plate* which is at the bottom of the clock, pinned underneath the pillars.

ASTRONOMICAL CLOCK OF PAINTED IRON
Austrian, dated 1545

Comparatively simple calendar work has already been noted in clocks of the early 17th century (p. 78), but many years earlier elaborate astronomical clocks were constructed, the 'grandfather' of them all being the astronomical clock of *Giovanni Dondi* (1318–89) professor of astronomy in Florence and Padua. Descriptions of the clock which he completed in 1364 have survived, though the clock itself has vanished, but a reproduction has been made by Thwaites and Reed of Clerkenwell for the Science Museum in London, and others are in the Smithsonian Institution in Washington and at the Time Museum in Rockford, Illinois. *Astronomy* and *astrology* were very much interdependent in the mediaeval period, a reminder of the inheritance of learning from the Moslem world. The famous astronomical clock made for Wells (1392), and the first and second Strasburg clocks (1352–4 and 1574), the latter by the *Habrecht* family, are notable examples, while the one at Hampton Court (1540) has already been mentioned (p. 73).

The astronomical/astrological clock above is dated 1545 and is a small iron chamber clock, driven by springs with *verge and foliot* escapement. Motion to its many dials is through *cords* passing round pulleys, an unusually rare solution to transmission and gearing in clocks. On its several dials are depicted the daily hours, the phases of the moon, the position of the sun and moon in the Zodiac, the day of the week and the ruling planetary hours. The influence of the planets, the planetary positions and other complex calculations must have been of utmost concern in 16th and 17th century life and therefore many elaborate dials were made, difficult if not impossible to understand today. Although it is easy to dismiss such astrological preoccupations as the superstitions of an earlier age, let us not forget the continued popularity of the 'horoscope' columns of our magazines and newspapers, and the serious way in which they are sometimes regarded.

WATCH WITH CALENDAR AND ASTRONOMICAL WORK
French, c.1620

WATCH WITH CALENDAR AND PHASES OF THE MOON
German, second half of the 17th century

Although complex astronomical clocks were made it was not possible to combine all their details in the compact movements of watches. Nevertheless many watches of the early 17th century provided such details as the phases of the moon, day of the week, month and date as well as the hours. The watches above are both of this kind, French and German in origin, the second being considerably later than the first and provided with a *glass* or *crystal cover* to protect the hand and dial instead of a flat metal plate (p. 76). The French watch shows on its upper dial the date of the month, the month of the year with its appropriate number of days and the position of the sun in the Zodiac. In the left-hand aperture the day of the week is shown with its astrological sign and on the right the age and phases of the moon. The other watch provides more simple information, but this also gives the date on its upper dial.

A significant development to be noted in these watches is the addition of a separate *silvered* dial or *chapter ring*, pinned to the flat brass dial plate. In some of these the ring was made of silver, but in most it was a fine silver film applied to the brass base, most of them now being worn down to the base metal. The silvering was chemically applied and the engraved numerals were filled with black wax, melted into the engraved lines to increase their legibility. The chapter rings of clock dials of this period were of similar design, with silvered finish, and examples may be seen on pp. 85, 86 and 88. In the early 17th century it was normal to have the dials divided for hours and half hours, and occasionally into quarters. The apparently complicated information on the calendar dials was provided by motion work driving flat discs between the dial and the movement, on the same basic principle as is used in calendar wristlet watches today.

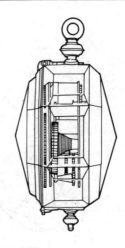

OCTAGONAL WATCH WITH ROCK CRYSTAL CASE
English, c.1630

A beautiful oval watch, encased in a piece of *solid rock crystal*, is the example above signed by *Simon Bartram* of London, an early supporter of the Clockmakers' Company and its Master in 1650. The watch is now in the Metropolitan Museum of New York. The dial follows the same basic style as those we have seen on p. 83 but in its transparent cover the movement may be examined without opening it at all. The *crystal* of the case is a very hard, transparent type of *natural quartz* and many early watch glasses were of this material, when it was presumably difficult to obtain the right type and shape of glass for the purpose. The *facet-cutting* of original crystal covers for watch dials gives its name to a type of modern watch glass with angular edges, known as raised, i.e. convex, or flat *crystal*. In the glassmaking trade the term crystal is used for a very clear type of lead-glass which is particularly suitable for cutting.

Simon Bartram's watch follows the same international style of form, decoration and movement as we have seen in the watches from Germany and France. How much of this style can be traced to the influence of Italy is hard to define, but the beautifully engraved *lettering* of the signature can be associated with the *humanistic cursive script* which originated in Italy in the 15th century and was carried throughout Europe by the engraved pattern books of the writing masters (see illustration of lettering on p. 87). Lettering is perhaps the most difficult of decorative forms to copy, for any style of writing has a character peculiar to its own age. A specialised engraver would have cut the signature of Bartram on this watch, just as other specialist engravers were employed to cut dials and the decoration on cases and movements. The study of lettering and the design of numerals on dials is important in trying to determine an approximate date of any particular piece.

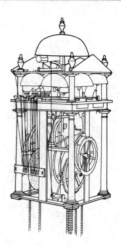

CASE AND MOVEMENT OF CHIMING CLOCK
Nicholas Vallin, London, dated 1598

Although the watches and clocks in this chapter have been concerned with *spring-driven* movements, the *weight-driven* clock continued to be made both for domestic use and for the *turret clocks* of churches. All weight-driven clocks have a double advantage in timekeeping over portable spring clocks, for their frames remain motionless, firmly fixed on a bracket or to the wall, and the power of the weight is *constant* throughout its run. In the weight-driven clock by *Nicholas Vallin*, dated 1598, we meet again a square, four-posted frame clock directly evolved from the Gothic tradition (p. 69), but no longer in the Gothic taste. The four corner pillars of Vallin's clock are of *Roman Doric* design and the *architrave* and triangular *pediment* on the front and back show direct influence of the Roman Classical style. The clock was made in London not many years before the architect *Inigo Jones* (1573–1652) was to introduce the pure Italian 'Palladian' style of architecture to the London scene with his Banqueting House in Whitehall, built between 1619 and 1622.

Stylistically the casework is new and in the fashionable classical manner, but horologically the clock is very little different from those of a hundred years before. The *going train* is controlled by a *verge and balance* which is not seen because it is hidden behind the architrave, and in the rear half of the clock is the *striking train*, controlled by a *locking plate* on the back. One feature, however, is of particular note and unique in this clock. It is equipped with *musical work* playing on thirteen bells, the hammers being operated from a *pinned barrel* like a musical box. It is the earliest known English *carillon* clock. The motion work and double hands for hours and minutes are thought to be a later addition, particularly since the dial has no divisions for minutes. This clock by Vallin is in the Ilbert Collection at the British Museum; Nicholas Vallin himself was a Protestant refugee from the Netherlands, born about 1565 and dying in a London plague in 1603.

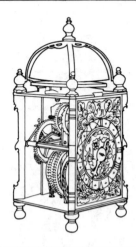

LANTERN CLOCK, TRANSITIONAL STYLE
English, early 17th century

LANTERN CLOCK
English, c.1625

The transitional style of English Renaissance art was to continue from the early 16th century to the second quarter of the 17th. A beautiful example of this stylistic transition is the English weight-driven clock on the left, with its classical *urn finials, ball feet, flat engraved dial plate* and its mediaeval style angle-set *buttresses* and *buttress offsets* (pp. 69, 70, 71, 72). The square form of the clock is similar to that of Nicholas Vallin, though of more simple design, with a bell on the top; this is the type which is popularly known as a *lantern clock*, from its basic lantern-shaped frame (p. 89). The lantern frame was not peculiar to England and it has its parallels in Germany, France, other European countries and Japan (pp. 191, 192). The four posted frame was to survive even into the 20th century, in particular in the wooden clocks of the *Black Forest* (p. 187) and in the *Morez* or *Morbier* type of clocks made in France until about the'time of the First World War (p. 183).

The clock on the right is of typically English form, with classically moulded feet, pierced *frets* to hide the balance, bell supported at the top and hinged brass *side plates*. The *chapter ring* is pinned to the flat brass dial plate and is 'silvered with black wax numerals. In the centre of the dial the *alarm-setting disc* (p. 75) has projections round it to give grip while it was being turned. The arrangement of the movement follows the now familiar pattern, while the presence of the feet, not really required since the clock is *hung* and steadied by *projecting spikes* at the back, would suggest that its prototype was a clock which had stood on a bracket like the Vallin clock on p. 85. In a sense the feet have become more like *pendants*, though they were to remain as long as the lantern clock survived. Most lantern clocks which are found today have been converted to pendulum controlled anchor escapements, and many are now being converted back to a verge and balance (pp. 88, 89).

CASE AND MOVEMENT OF A 'PURITAN' WATCH AND
DETAIL OF THE SIGNATURE
English, c.1645

This watch was made just before the middle of the 17th century by *David Bouquet* (?–1665), a Frenchman practising his trade in London. It heralds the beginning of that restraint in design which was in large part to separate the English decorative arts from the heavily ornamented Continental tradition. Puritan the watch certainly is, with restrained decoration and plain silver case. The dial has a gilded *calendar ring* which revolves with reference to a fixed pointer above the hour XII. A small hole in the date numeral 10 allows the ring to be set to the correct date by inserting a pointed tool, at the end of every month with less than thirty-one days. The inner edge of the chapter ring is divided into quarters and the 'tail' of the hand not only gives a satisfying appearance but it is also useful in helping to turn the hand when setting the watch to time. The movement is powered by a *spring and fusee* and controlled by a *verge* and small steel *balance*.

At the hinged end of the movement the newly introduced *worm set-up* for the mainspring is fitted, of blued steel between scrolled brackets. All early spring-driven clocks and watches depended partly for their timing on the 'pull' or *torque* of the mainspring, transmitted through the wheelwork to the escapement. This torque was made even, as far as possible, either by the *stackfreed* or by the *fusee*, but when setting up a spring some extra power must be put into it first (pp. 31, 38). This *initial* power was adjusted from the *spring barrel arbor* in most cases by a *ratchet wheel and click*, but the alternative method, more convenient for the owner, was the *endless worm screw* with a squared end to take a small key. Throughout the 17th century and into the first half of the 18th the worm set-up continued as a useful though more expensive device, but with the advent of better wheelwork and improved escapements its use declined and the ratchet wheel and click remained as the standard practice.

5
Classical English Horology
c.1650 to 1740

DIAL OF LANTERN CLOCK
English, *c*.1670

It is impossible to compress into a few pages the significance of the immense steps forward which were taken in horology during the ninety years covered by this chapter. This 'golden age' of the later Stuart and early Hanoverian dynasties in England embraced the careers of Sir Christopher Wren and his contemporaries Webb and Hawksmoor, Sir John Vanbrugh, Robert Hooke, Robert Boyle, Isaac Newton and many others of their stature in the world of architecture, mathematics, astronomy and philosophical science. It also saw the birth of the Royal Society and one must not forget the encouragement to the arts and sciences, including those of horology, by the royal patrons Charles II, James II and William III. It was in 1675 that the Royal Observatory was founded by Royal Warrant, the first Astronomer Royal being the Rev. John Flamsteed, appointed expressly with the purpose of improving the methods of navigation at sea and helping to solve the problem of determining longitude, of paramount importance to a seafaring nation.

Before embarking on the clocks and watches of that period of the 17th century in which the great and famous clockmakers were working—Tompion, the Knibbs, Quare, East, Windmills, Clement, Gould, Graham and many others—or analysing the new devices which were to have such profound importance in the history of the clock and watch, we must recognise that the more humble domestic clock in 1650 was still the *lantern* form (p. 86), single handed with verge and balance escapement. The clock above is a typical example, made 'Neare ye New Exchang' and signed *Thomas Fenn* presumably soon after the Great Fire of London in 1666 when the Royal Exchange was rebuilt, or near the New Exchange of 1608 in the Strand. Dutch influence is very strong in the lively tulip engraving in the centre of the dial and the design of the blued steel hour hand, with its pierced and scrolled head, links the robust forms of decoration of earlier periods (p. 76) with the developing styles of hour hands yet to come (pp. 93 and 97).

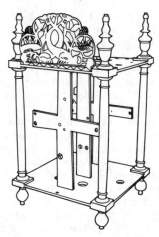

FRAME OF LANTERN CLOCK ON P. 88

LANTERN CLOCK
English, c.1650

The drawing above shows the *Thomas Fenn* lantern clock (p. 88) stripped of its dial, side plates and most of its parts. The 'lantern' frame is now quite clear, with solid brass plates at top and bottom and finely proportioned classical columns, turned urn finials and rounded feet. The columns are of subtly swelling form, an architectural feature known as *entasis* and used extensively in early 17th century buildings. The three vertical plates in the centre, to carry the movement, are slotted in the base and held with wedges at the top, as in the Gothic predecessors, and the pierced brass *fret* is of wide scrolled formalised leaf and flower design, closely resembling the decorative style seen in early watch balance cocks (p. 87). Interweaving dolphins on each of the frets were popular decorative features in English art of the time, and were long to remain so in a country dependant for its prosperity and security on the sea.

Lantern clocks were powered by weights on woven ropes which passed through the holes in the base of the clock. The ropes were held firm on the *great wheel pulleys* by spikes in the pulley groove, though later lantern clocks were sometimes driven through chains. The *going train* had three wheels and pinions, the *great wheel*, *second wheel* and crown-toothed *escape wheel*, its teeth interacting with the *pallets* of the *verge*. The striking train at the rear comprised the *great wheel* with its striking pins, the *locking wheel*, the *third wheel* and *fly*; the *count plate* was on the back, moved forward by the striking great wheel pinion, and the *locking detents* and *bell hammer* were supported in the *pivot holes* at the ends of the cross-shaped plates. All the wheels were of brass, with steel pinions, arbors, detents and hammer. A later form is the *winged* lantern clock, shaped to accommodate the swing of an anchor-shaped *pendulum*, a device which was to revolutionise the precision of timekeeping.

The principle of *isochronous* motion of the simple *pendulum* was noticed by *Galileo Galilei* (1564–1642) and a way of controlling clockwork with it was devised by him in 1641; this may or may not ever have been made. *Leonardo da Vinci* (1452–1520) may well have made experiments to do the same thing very much earlier, to judge by the evidence of one of his drawings made about 1500, and *Christiaan Huygens* (1629–95) successfully applied the principle in 1656. *Salomon Coster* (?–1659), a clockmaker at The Hague, made some of these clocks on Huygens' principle and showed the method to *John Fromanteel*. Fromanteel was a man of Flemish/French descent who worked with Coster for a few months between 1657 and 1658. After returning to London Fromanteel started to make pendulum clocks which were retailed under the name of his father, *Ahasuerus Fromanteel*; these, as far as we know, were the first English pendulum clocks to be made.

The first pendulum clocks were controlled by a 'bob' pendulum and so much improved was their accuracy over the verge and balance that, at one step, it was reasonable to make clocks go longer than for a single day and to have an 8-day or even longer run and to include minute as well as hour hands. The bob pendulum was connected to a horizontal verge (Ch. 2) and the two trains for going and striking were now, for the first time, arranged side by side between solid brass plates. The tall, slender, ebonised *long case*, to protect the hanging weights of the Fromanteel clock left, is characteristic of the severe architectural case style of the time. The second clock signed *George Harris*, of similar proportions, incorporates yet another innovation; this clock, with *slide-up hood*, is controlled by a pendulum 61 in. long with a period of $1\frac{1}{4}$ seconds each swing. This clock utilised a new form of escapement called the *anchor* (p. 25).

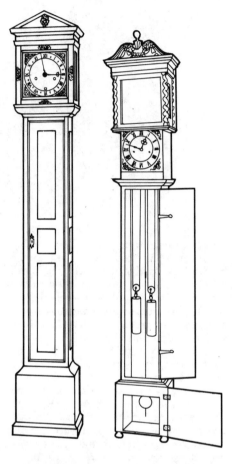

LONG CASE CLOCK
Ahasuerus Fromanteel, London, c.1660

LONG CASE CLOCK WITH SLIDE-UP HOOD
George Harris, London, c.1675

HOODED WALL CLOCK
Christopher Gould, London, c.1685

HOODED WALL CLOCK
Edward East, London, c.1665

There were more changes in the fundamental design of clocks from about 1660 to 1675 than had happened in several hundred years before. This was primarily due to the introduction of the pendulum, either in its short 6- or 7-in. 'bob' form, or in conjunction with the anchor escapement with a 39-in. 'Royal' pendulum beating seconds, or even occasionally a 5-ft. pendulum of $1\frac{1}{4}$ seconds swing. The purpose of the long case, at least for the period between about 1660 and 1670, was to support the clock and protect the weights only; the severe, splendidly proportioned classical design was the contribution of the furniture maker to the domestic interior. At the same time *hooded wall clocks* were being made, some with rope-driven 30-hour lantern type movements (on the old style), some with 30-hour rope-driven movements with trains side by side between brass plates like the one by *Christopher Gould* (on the new style), and some with 8-day movements, with *compounded weights* on gut lines, like the *Edward East.*

The period from about 1660 to 1690 was one of experiment, transition, adaptation and innovation. The classical, slender, ebonised case was the result of bringing the new, accurate, desirable clock into the well-furnished room, while the loud striking lantern had its proper place in the outer hall. The hooded clock by East shows the continuity of the classical tradition found in the lantern clock and in the earlier one by Vallin (p. 85) with classical urn finials and pendant feet (pp. 88, 89). The dial of the clock is also engraved, with 'matted' centre and raised separate chapter ring, though new features such as *bolt and shutter* winding and date aperture appear. While the East clock is at the beginning of the period 1660 to 1690, Gould's comes at the end, introducing a new case style of veneered *marquetry*, of Dutch influence, popular in the late 1600s. The variations are many in the clocks of these years, both in mechanics and cabinetwork; the technical changes and innovations are explained in Ch. 2.

Now the designers of furniture were having to provide a style of case for which there had been no precedent. The long case gives sturdy support, protection for weights and pendulum and a relatively dust-free enclosure. The case styles and proportions follow contemporary classical design, while Baroque features such as *twisted columns*, used architecturally in England as early as 1637 at St. Mary the Virgin, Oxford, are often to be found, as are the *cresting* and *strapwork piercing*, created in the same tradition. Both cases shown have the typical 17th century convex mouldings beneath the hood, and the *bun feet* on the Knibb clock were usual in much other furniture of the time. There may have been similar feet on the Tompion case, as the base appears to have been altered by the addition of a wide, ill-proportioned plinth, and the cresting of the hood has certainly gone.

Particularly important is the *marquetry* on the Knibb clock and *parquetry* on the Tompion. Both are forms of decorative veneering, the veneers being cut in thin panels and glued to the doors and fronts of the bases. Whereas marquetry is the term used for naturalistic, mostly floral designs, with leaves and sometimes birds, parquetry follows more geometric patterns. The background, in these examples, is of '*oyster-shell*' veneering in olive wood or laburnum and the edges of the trunk doors are fitted with *cock beading*—a half round, cross-veneered strip of moulding which overlaps the edge, hiding the gap between door and trunk. By no means universal, the Tompion case has an oval *lenticle* or window aperture through which the bob of the pendulum could be seen to swing. The dials of both clocks have early, *winged cherub spandrels* at the corners, and both these clocks, by such famous makers and in such sumptuous cases, would command very high prices in the salerooms today. (Plate II, 6.)

LONG CASE CLOCK
John Knibb, Oxford, c.1680

LONG CASE CLOCK
Thomas Tompion, London, c.1685

LONG CASE CLOCK IN EBONISED PEARWOOD
Tompion and Banger, London, c.1705

Although the Tompion clock on p. 92 has a parquetry design, it is said that Thomas Tompion himself favoured the dignified simplicity of the undecorated, ebonised case. This assumption would correlate well with the high standards of craftsmanship and taste which characterise the works of this master. Rather later than the previous clock by Tompion, this example of his in ebonised pearwood retains the cock-beading on the tall, narrow trunk door, but the moulding below the hood is now concave, a style which persisted throughout the long tradition of the English long cased clock. Three gilded spires or finials now crown the hood instead of the earlier crested forms, and the top of the hood is domed, to increase the height and give balance to the design. By the end of the 17th century extreme height was often achieved in English long case clocks, and the earlier fashion of slide-up hoods (p. 90) gave way to hoods which slid forwards, with glazed doors hinged to open and three-quarter columns integral with the door.

The elegant architectural motifs of columns with *entasis* (p. 89), brass moulded bases and capitals, combined with the simple lines of the trunk and the richness of the dial and pierced frets above, add up to perhaps the most splendid and dignified design of long case clock ever produced. The spandrels of the dial still contain a cherub's head, but with scrolled and formalised leafwork more closely filling the corners between the chapter ring and edge than earlier examples. The date aperture appears below the nameplate in this clock by *Thomas Tompion* and *Edward Banger*. Banger collaborated with Tompion from about 1701 until 1708, a few years before Tompion's death in 1713, an association which ended in a quarrel. Thomas Tompion is considered one of the greatest, if not the greatest English clockmaker; we should perhaps regard him as a man not only of immaculate taste and exacting standards, but also a successful businessman whose fortune and good standing earned him a resting place in Westminster Abbey.

LONG CASE CLOCK
Edward Faulkner, London, c.1705

DOOR OF LONG CASE CLOCK WITH MARQUETRY
DECORATION

The taste for marquetry and parquetry designs for clock cases was a fashion widely adopted by the best case makers, particularly in London though at times in the provinces as well. By the 1690s until the early 1700s this style, however, became overdone, the lavishness of the decoration detracting from the elegance of the overall proportions. The clock left signed by *Edward Faulkner* is of this kind, for though the case is of fine proportion, except for the cut-down hood in the bottom stage of the dome, the surface embellishments prove distracting. Wealthy clients of the time of William and Mary and Queen Anne were fond of this style, which was much used in their other furniture. In its final form, known as *seaweed marquetry*, the veneered designs are incredibly detailed and the era of what had been a dignified, pleasing technique degenerated into one of technical virtuosity before finally going quite out of fashion.

In the clock door of about 1690, flowers and leaves are combined with architectural scrolls and the figures of classical fawns and a bird, hidden in the foliage; the design is arranged, more or less symmetrically, down the whole length of the door. The tonal qualities and some of the fine detailing was done by scorching lines with a hot tool (an early type of poker work) while staining and colouring to produce hues not available in the natural woods are sometimes found. This kind of decoration is sometimes mistakenly called 'inlay' work. The patterns are made by sawing out a 'sandwich' of thin veneers of different woods, sorting out the pieces and fitting them together in a kind of jig-saw puzzle. The whole is glued to the basic carcase of the case, which was usually of oak. Light coloured woods such as sycamore were used for these veneers giving an overall colour of warm gold and brown.

In the early years of the 18th century a new decorative technique known as *lacquering* came into vogue. Furniture from the Far East, decorated with resinous colours forming a warm, lustrous surface applied in many layers and with great skill, had been arriving in Europe from the middle of the 17th century. It was the contact with the Far East, particularly Japan, which came with the formation of the East India Company in 1600 which brought this style to England, and we thus have the beginning of an oriental influence which continued well into the 18th century in articles of furniture, porcelain, earthenware and even hand-painted wallpapers which were sometimes actually Chinese. As original oriental lacquer was difficult and expensive to acquire, English designers produced imitation lacquer, of which the popular name was 'japanning'.

Lacquered long case clocks continued the fashion for surface decoration until about 1740. Oriental figures, birds, plants, houses, furniture and animals were prepared in gesso, in low relief, on a flat ground of black, or in some cases dark blue, dark green, deep red and even yellow. Colours and gilding in the finer details enriched the design and produced a blend of oriental treatment on an English classical case. Lacquered cases have not stood the test of time as well as marquetry veneers and many are now worn and cracked as the carcase beneath has expanded and contracted, loosening and damaging the lacquer on the surface. This clock illustrates another important change in case design—the introduction of the semi-circular *break-arch dial*. This mannerism was used by the clockmakers to contain a strike/silent dial or a name-plate roundel and later for the popular phases of the moon. The shape of the break-arch is echoed in the arch-shaped top of the door of the trunk.

LONG CASE CLOCK, LACQUERED DECORATION
London, c.1730

DOOR OF LONG CASE CLOCK WITH LACQUERED DECORATION

BRACKET CLOCK
Robert Seignior, London, c.1670

BRACKET CLOCK
John Fromanteel, London, c.1685

With the advent of the pendulum a portable clock of *English style* immediately evolved in a form never previously seen. The spring and fusee, combined with a pendulum controlled verge, produced clockwork approaching the accuracy of the weight-driven long case. The 'lying down' posture of early portable clocks (p. 81) was changed for all subsequent spring-driven clocks to the upright position, the two separate trains being side by side between solid brass plates. This was a natural evolution as the verge could now be mounted horizontally at the top, with the pendulum hanging down outside the back plate. Upright movements of early date such as the tabernacle clock were often converted from balance to pendulum for better timekeeping (p. 79). The portable English version of the second half of the 17th century is known as a *bracket clock*, presumably because many had brackets to support them, and the name persisted when brackets were never intended. (Plate II, 4 and 5.)

The clock shown here, made about 1670, is a form of mantel clock. It has plain, almost severe, classical lines which remind us of the hooded clock by East (p. 91) or even the early Vallin (p. 85). This clock, fitted with a *central dial alarum*, *date aperture* below XII and *winged cherub spandrels* is cased in ebony and tortoiseshell, the latter perhaps being an influence from France, where this material was extensively used by *André Charles Boulle* (1642–1732). The clock on the right by John Fromanteel (p. 90) of about 1685 is truly portable, for it has a carrying handle above its domed, gilded brass basket top, and bun feet, like the long case clock by Knibb (p. 92). The finial urns at the corners persist and the clock has quarter striking, employing three trains between vertical brass plates, the pillar plate being in one piece but the top or front plate divided into three separate parts for dismantling any one of the three trains of wheels without disturbing the others.

BRACKET CLOCK AND MOVEMENT
Joseph Knibb, London, *c*.1670–75

Any study of clocks, either as furniture or as machines, always shows continuous development and rarely sudden changes. Even the revolutionary introduction of the pendulum, which altered the timekeeping properties and overall form of both weight-driven and spring-driven clocks, did not prevent earlier fashions from influencing their design. The fine bracket clock here shows this well, for the back of the movement plate is finely engraved, as had been the custom with both clock and watch movements much earlier. The clock is from the workshop of that famous maker *Joseph Knibb* and dates from 1670 to 1675; the engraved *back plate* is designed with formalised arrangements of naturalistic tulips and leaves, with a rose round the pivot of the going train fusee. This should be compared with the engraving on the dial of the lantern clock on p. 88, and the pierced and scrolled ornament on the 'apron' of the pendulum cock bears remarkable similarity to the style of the watch cock on p. 87. (Plate II, 5.)

Mechanically the clock is a straightforward, two train, spring and fusee movement, with *count plate* progressive striking, and the bell on its stand is of the flat-topped 'pork pie' style which was easier to accommodate in the confined wooden case than the larger, domed versions used earlier. The *dial plate* is brass, with cast and gilded *winged-cherub spandrels*, and the *chapter ring* is of silvered, pinned-on type with hour divisions on its inner edge and minute numbering *inside* the narrow minute ring divisions. Of great importance are the *blued steel hands*, the pierced and scrolled hour hand continuing the fine evolution which began with the pierced single hand of the lantern style (p. 88). The case, of veneered olive wood, has bun feet like the John Knibb long case (p. 92) and a narrow pierced panel above the dial, backed with fabric, to allow the striking to be heard. The cranked *carrying handle* is of earlier form than that on p. 96, and it 'marries' well with the plain lines of the case.

BRACKET CLOCK
Daniel Quare and Stephen Horseman, London,
c.1720

NIGHT CLOCK
Joseph Knibb, London, c.1670

Just as the break-arch dial appeared in long case clocks by about 1725, so it also appeared in the bracket (or perhaps more properly 'mantel') clocks. The result was a case of much increased height, to accommodate the arch which in this clock by *Daniel Quare* and *Stephen Horseman* of London (p. 105) was utilised for calendar work. The tops of cases, formerly of basket form either in wood or pierced and gilded cast brass, correspondingly increased in height, and were known, when in the form shown here, as *inverted bell*. The upper moulding is concave, with a convex moulding below; in later clocks after about 1770 what is known as the *true bell* became fashionable, with convex moulding above and concave below (p. 113). Appearing in the dial of the Quare and Horseman clock is a *pendulum aperture* —a narrow slit above the centre. This *false pendulum*, fitted to the true pendulum arbor, swings to and fro and so it is easily seen whether or not the clock is going.

Very unusual, is the *night clock* by *Joseph Knibb* of about 1670 in the National Museum of Antiquities of Scotland. To tell the time at night the old method of touch pieces was no longer valid and many clocks were equipped with repeating work which struck the bells, on demand, by a cord pulled through the side of the case (p. 105). This method in quarter striking clocks could tell the time to the nearest seven and a half minutes but more accurate readings could be made on the Knibb night clock above. An oil lamp inside, requiring a chimney, shone through the quarter slits I, II, III and the tiny holes at five minute intervals indicated the position of a revolving disc beneath. Within this disc the pointer is a small pierced disc showing each hour in turn. As one hour departed at the right-hand side the following hour appeared on the left. This required an elaborate and ingenious mechanism driven by an ordinary clock; its special nature may be recognised by the elaborately painted dial.

ASTRONOMICAL, AUTOMATA, MUSICAL CLOCK
Henry Bridges, Waltham Cross, Herts. 1734

ASTRONOMICAL, AUTOMATA, MUSICAL CLOCK
Jacob Lovelace, Exeter, unfinished 1755 and
completed later

The two clocks above were huge and very special productions, with astronomical motion work and dials, automata figures enacting diverting scenes, wind-powered organs and many other elaborate 'amusements'. Both stood about 10 ft. high and both were designed in the Baroque 'grand manner', the one by *Henry Bridges* (c.1697–1754) on the left being made near London, and the other at least begun by *Jacob Lovelace* (1656–1716) of Exeter and probably completed by his son *Jacob* who was born in 1695 and died in 1755. In the state we see them here neither has survived—the movement and dials of Bridges' clock are in the British Museum, but only fragments remain of the one by Lovelace which was irreparably damaged in Liverpool Museum in the Second World War. Though clearly no longer collectors' pieces, and never ordinary domestic clocks, they show a type of triumphal 'tour de force' of the early 18th century, combining Baroque aspirations with a mediaeval desire for mathematical astronomical complexity (p. 82).

When Vanbrugh was building his immense country houses of Blenheim or Castle Howard, Bridges and Lovelace were working on their horological masterpieces with the same sense of scale! The flanking caryatids, reclining figures and broken-arch pediment of Lovelace, or the ascending 'orders' of architecture, with triumphal figures, classical columns and pilasters of Bridges, illustrate a common architectural heritage. The painted scenes on both—though more provincial on the Lovelace (Plate III, 8)—perhaps remind us of Thornhill's painted ceilings at Greenwich or inside the dome of St. Paul's. Space forbids an adequate description of the working of these clocks or their interesting history, but the Henry Bridges is described by Lloyd and Tait (see Bibliography) and the Lovelace is the subject of research by the author in *Antiquarian Horology*, Volume 5, Number 3, 1966. The Bridges clock is shown from a dated drawing of 1734 while the Lovelace illustration is from a lithograph of the clock as it appeared in 1833.

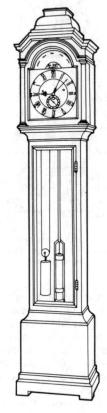

REGULATOR CLOCK
George Graham, London, c.1740

MARINE CHRONOMETER
John Harrison, London, 1759

Between 1660 and 1760, English horological inventors and craftsmen made many of the finest clocks and watches of their time and the trade developed in such a way that England became the centre of the clockmaking world. There were many political and economic reasons for this and the desire to extend knowledge and investigate the regions of pure science, as seen in the work of the Royal Society, coupled with the official stimulus to solve the problem of finding longitude at sea, brought forth clocks of superb precision which are outside the domain of the domestic timepiece (p. 88). Two of this type are illustrated, a fine *regulator* of about 1740 by *George Graham* (1673–1751), and the fourth *marine chronometer* by *John Harrison* (1693–1776). Harrison's chronometer was the climax of a lifetime of patient endeavour, beginning before he was twenty years of age in 1713.

The Graham regulator, with its break-arch dial and glazed trunk door, is a month-going timepiece only. Its accuracy depended on two important inventions for which Graham is famous—the *dead beat escapement* introduced in 1715 (p. 26) and the *mercurial pendulum* of 1721 which compensates the pendulum for changes of temperature (p. 28). Other refinements of the clock include a separate hand to indicate the equation of time (p. 19) and calendar work in the arch. The Harrison chronometer, in external appearance very like a mid-18th century pocket watch, but very much larger at over 5 in. diameter, is of such superb precision that in trials at sea in 1761, for five months to Barbados and back, the watch gained only 54 seconds. This fantastic performance was eventually to bring Harrison his deserved award of £20,000 from the Board of Longitude, after many trials and difficulties in obtaining it. (See Quill and Gould, Bibliography.)

DIAL, OUTER CASE AND MOVEMENT OF A PAIR–CASED
WATCH
English, c.1670

To return to the design of watches, the example above is of about 1670 and although some twenty-five years later than that on p. 87 it is similar in many ways, such as the single hour hand and quarter hour dial divisions, the hinged movement, worm set-up for the mainspring, an engraved signature and an oval-footed pierced and scrolled balance cock. The form of the watch, however, has changed to circular, a functional design which has persisted in watches to the present day, though 'form' watches have reappeared recently. The puritan watch on p. 87 has an outer case (not illustrated) which fastens with a latch, and the one shown here also has its outer case, hinged on the left and fastened with a spring catch on the right, opened by pressing a raised button to be seen nearly level with the figure III. This extra case gives its name to the watch, for we now call them 'pair-cased', a style which lasted until well into the 19th century.

The outer case clearly evolved as the need was found to give the watch more protection, and perhaps more important because it gave opportunity to decorate the exterior in a way not appropriate to the case which held the movement. In this example the outer case is embellished with silver *pinwork*—small, round-headed pins riveted through the leather cover to the metal and decoratively arranged in a design of formalised tulips, roses and leaves, reminding one of contemporary designs used on slipware pottery dishes of the type made by Thomas Toft, a famous Staffordshire potter working in the 1660s and 1670s. Two characteristics of the early pair-cased watches which we see here are the small round *pendant* which is fitted to the inner case, and the large square hinge which projects from the side of the outer one. In the watch movements of this period even the pillars separating the plates are of Dutch inspired tulip shape, reminding us of the engraving seen in the clocks on pp. 88 and 97.

DIAL, OUTER CASE AND MOVEMENT OF A PAIR-CASED
WATCH
English, *c*.1680

Just as the introduction of the pendulum made tremendous improvements in time-keeping in clocks (p. 90), so the addition of a thin, coiled spring to control the balance oscillations of a verge escapement improved timekeeping in watches. This device is attributed to *Christiaan Huygens*, who had already in 1656 applied the principle of the pendulum to clocks, and also to *Dr Robert Hooke* who claimed, with *William Clement*, the invention of the *anchor escapement*. It is generally agreed that the principle was established by about 1675. The *balance spring* is pinned at its outer end to the watch top plate and at its inner end to the verge staff, beneath the balance wheel. As the balance vibrates one way the spring expands and on the alternate swing contracts. By adjusting the length, thickness, strength and materials from which this spring is made with the mass of the balance and torque of the mainspring, this natural period of vibration keeps the balance oscillations to a steady and pre-arranged rate.

The early balance springs, unlike those of today, were of only two complete turns from outer to inner end and regulation of length was comparatively crude. At first watches fitted with the balance spring continued to have only one hand, for its ultimate advantages had not been realised. The watch above is similar to that on p. 101, except for two important changes—the *balance cock* is now quite circular, though still of scrolled and pierced design with pierced *cock foot*, and to the left of the cock is a little dial, similar to the one on the mainspring set-up on p. 101, but used here to regulate the acting length of the balance spring through a *rack and pinion* fitting. The outer case is decorated in tortoiseshell inlaid with silver, and the watch is by a London maker, *Joseph Windmills*. The drawing of the movement clearly shows the conical *fusee* and the typical *tulip pillars* which are often seen at this period, as well as the architecturally designed *baluster* form (p. 46).

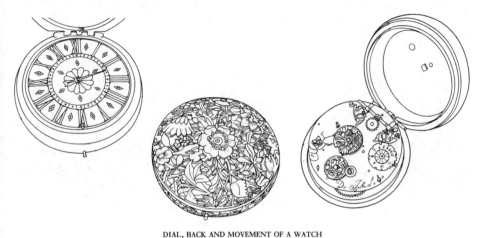

DIAL, BACK AND MOVEMENT OF A WATCH
Richard Marsh, Ipswich, c.1660

Another example of a single-handed watch, signed *Richard Marsh* of Ipswich, contains striking work on a bell. A bell inside a watch had been used from the later years of the 16th century, sometimes as an alarum and also as shown here, for striking the hours. These watches are known as *clock watches* and were intended for use at night as an alternative to touch pieces, now that the dial is protected by glass or crystal. The striking train is housed between the same plates as the going part, and a *count plate* can be seen on the movement, in miniature form like that on the clock by Joseph Knibb (p. 97). The locking detent enters the slots in the progressive count plate from the edge of the movement and in the position shown is in process of striking four. The separately wound spring for the strike is on the left of the balance cock and the bell is inside the case, held in place by a central, square-headed screw.

As the movement is folded into the case the hammer swings out from between the movement plates to strike the bell. The catch which holds the movement firmly in place is of early form and can be seen below VI on the dial—a small projection hooked by the finger nail to release the spring catch. To enable the bell to be heard clearly the body of the silver case is elaborately pierced, the pattern being of a central rose with inter-twining stems, flowers and leaves spreading from it. The silver dial, with central, quarter hour divisions and lozenges at two-hourly and half-hourly intervals is of *etched* design, the background being removed with acid to reduce the level below the numerals and form a dull, matted surface. In fine dials of gold and silver this style of treatment persisted until the early part of the 18th century, but with different grouping of the hour and minute numerals (p. 104).

DECORATIVE DIALS FROM LONDON WATCHES
a. 'Wandering hour' dial, c.1690
b. Multiple dial, c.1710
c. Sun and moon dial, c.1695

As balance sprung watches came into vogue a fascinating crop of unusual dials appeared. The style was short-lived, from about 1690 to 1710, the result of the characteristic desire for pomp and splendour, like the marquetry clock cases with which they are contemporary. All three watches shown above have London signatures, with movements similar to that on p. 102. The first watch has a *wandering hour* dial, in principle like the night clock on p. 98, the hour number moving against a semi-circular minute scale from 0 to 60 which, when it disappears on the right is replaced by the next number appearing on the left. The time by this watch is almost 4.15. The watch with multiple dials has a normal minute hand recording on the outer edge, but the hours are shown in the aperture below, with dials for calendar on the right, adjustment on the left and an oscillating disc in the dial above showing the watch in motion, like the false pendulum of the clock on p. 98.

The moving disc on the dial described left is fitted to one arm of the balance wheel, involving a reorganisation of the movement inside. These watches were termed *pendulum watches*. Sometimes watch dials were made with an aperture to show a series of small portraits or other pictures which could be changed by pressing the pendant; another characteristic feature of this period is the gilded and decorated outer edge of the silvered dial. The last ingenious dial is called the *sun and moon*. The minute hand is conventional but the hour indicator appears as a sun, moving against the semi-circular scale of VI to XII then on to VI again; when the sun has completed its course past the hours and is 'setting' a moon and stars appears at VI and take over the task. The action is simple in that both sun and moon are painted on the same revolving disc which takes the place of the hour hand, but is set beneath the dial. (Plate III, 7.)

DIAL AND BACK OF REPEATER WATCH
Daniel Quare and Stephen Horseman, London,
*c.*1720

The early 18th century saw the emergence of the watch in the basic form it was to maintain, with subtle variations and changes of style, for almost a hundred years. In this example the *pendant* is no longer a loose-fitting ring but is of *stirrup* or *horseshoe* shape, swivelling on a horizontal pin. This pendant is especially long for by depressing it with the thumb the hour and quarters are sounded on a bell inside. This *repeating watch* performs the same action as repeat work in clocks, (p. 98) and the competition to be the first to achieve this on a miniature scale is the story of the contest for royal approval between *Daniel Quare* (1649–1724) and the *Rev. Edward Barlow* (1639–1719). Barlow, who had changed his name from *Booth*, was an outstanding theoretical horologist who came from Lancashire; he invented *rack striking* work in clocks and, with *William Houghton* also of Lancashire, is thought to have been responsible for an escapement like the *cylinder*, which they patented in 1695.

The repeater by Quare and the one by Barlow, made to his design by Thomas Tompion, were demonstrated to the King and Privy Council in 1688. The king preferred Quare's because its action was simpler. It would seem, however, that the invention which Barlow had made in the 1670s was well-known to London makers by this time. The watch shown is by *Daniel Quare* and *Stephen Horseman* who were in partnership from 1718 until Quare's death in 1724. There is evidence to show that London makers such as these were making use of Lancashire-made *ébauches* (rough movements) at this early date, a matter to be referred to later (p. 143). The dial on this quarter-repeater watch is of *white enamel*, with blued steel *beetle and poker* hands, the dial being probably a later replacement, for the style and date of the watch would suggest an original of etched and engraved gold. Early metal dials were not always easily legible and were sometimes replaced when the white enamel type came into favour.

A SELECTION OF ENGLISH WATCH COCKS
a. c.1650
b. c.1680
c. c.1710
d. c.1750

The balance cock, that small brass bracket which supports the upper pivot of the verge and balance staff, was universally decorated from its earliest appearance in the 16th century to the beginning of the 20th century, though in comparatively modern times the decoration has become a mere ghost of its former glory (p. 143). Always included while movements were easily accessible to the owner, the decoration and general shape can help us to date a watch. Curiously enough there is little evidence to be found about the makers of these balance cocks, with their intricate pierced designs. With the introduction of the balance spring about 1675, balance wheels became larger and the balance cock became larger to match, entirely covering the balance wheel and with a wider, larger foot. It is known that a large number of cocks were made in Switzerland or southern Germany, and used by makers in England and elsewhere, though many must have been of English make.

The illustrations show development in design of the balance cock from the mid-17th century until about 1750. (a) shows the early, elongated oval form, with wide formalised scrolls and open piercing; (b) shows the form after the introduction of the balance spring, of wide circular shape, symmetrical scrollwork and wide foot following the line of the plate; (c) shows the early 18th century type with straight inner edge of the openwork foot and (d) has the wide flowing scrollwork, deeply engraved and sculptural in quality, of the English Rococo style. The foot of the last example (d) is more narrow than ever before in the 18th century, roughly triangular and no longer pierced but only surface engraved, and the grotesque head of a man or lion is now a definite feature of the base of the cock. These balance cocks are so attractive that in the last century particularly many fine watches were despoiled of their cocks, to make necklaces, bracelets and other jewellery articles.

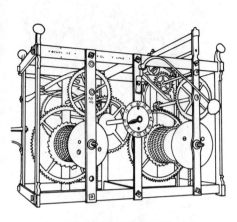

IRON-FRAMED TURRET CLOCK
William Clement, London, 1671

TIMBER-FRAMED TURRET CLOCK
Barton-in-Fabis, Notts. late 17th century with
alterations dated 1735

The last church tower or *turret* clock we saw was that of Salisbury (p. 72). Turret clocks continued to be made with far less change in design than the domestic clocks and watches as turret clocks are rarely seen except for their dials. Of the two above the first was made in 1671 and is now in the Science Museum, London. It is signed by *William Clement* and employs the anchor escapement (p. 25), which was Clement's great contribution to clockwork history. The pendulum, escapement and some other parts of the clock as we see it today are, however, 19th century replacements. Unlike the *pegged* jointed frame of the Salisbury clock, this one is of iron straps screwed together, though the curved corner finials and offsets of the posts remind us of mediaeval predecessors. With striking train of iron wheels on the left and going train on the right, we now see the *setting dial* and long armed and weighted *maintaining power*, for use when the clock was being wound.

Timber being cheap and readily available, it was often used for turret clocks and the *timber-framed* example is from Barton-in-Fabis in Nottinghamshire. A date of 1735 on one of the timbers might indicate the period of construction, or more likely the date of its conversion to anchor and pendulum. The three trains are arranged vertically, the going train in the centre, hour striking train above and quarter striking train below. The count plate for striking can be seen on the right at the top, internally driven, and the anchor and 'scape wheel on the left replace an earlier verge. All the wheelwork is of iron except for the brass escape wheel and it is unlikely that this clock ever had a dial; it would have indicated the time by striking the bells, one for the hours and two for the quarters. This accounts for the double great wheels of the quarter striking train with their pins for operating the tails of the bell hammer levers.

6
English
Rococo and
Neo-Classicism
c. 1740 to 1800

TRADE CARD OF JOHN WYKE
AND THOMAS GREEN, LIVERPOOL,
c.1765–70

From about 1740 until the end of the 18th century many important changes in the design of clocks and watches may be seen. While the London trade continued to flourish it did not have quite as important a place in the clockmaking world as it had held in the period discussed in Ch. 5 and more clocks and watches with provincial English names are to be found. In the north of England, for example, such names as Liverpool, Warrington, Wigan, Manchester, Oldham, Huddersfield, Halifax and Derby begin to appear on splendid clocks of proportion and style quite different from their southern cousins and exhibiting a quality all their own. We find that northern watch-makers too, already steady suppliers of movements to the London trade, were increasing their business both at home and overseas. It is appropriate, therefore, that we should begin this chapter with the stylish trade card of one of the most important Liverpool tool factors and clock-making firms, John Wyke and Thomas Green.

The trade card reproduced here dates from about 1765 to 1770, for the engraver, *Thomas Billinge*, was engraving for the pottery trade about this time, and the style is pure Rococo. This Rococo manner, derived both in name and form from the French 'rocaille' had a brief but important effect on English decorative art from the 1740s to the mid-1760s and is characterised by asymmetrical scrollwork of delicate and frivolous style, unlike the ponderous manner of the earlier Baroque. In this example the various tools which Wyke retailed are seen dangling in ordered disarray—wheel engines, turns, stakes, shears, arbors, saws, drills, callipers, sliding tongs and many others for which the Lancashire trade had long been famous. By the end of Wyke's life in 1787 another style had become established which affected clocks and watches as profoundly as it changed the direction of English art, the *Neo-Classical* manner of *Robert Adam* (1728–92) and his followers, a style to be seen in the catalogue cover of a Birmingham tool firm about 1785 (p. 118).

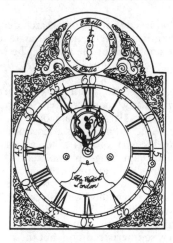

LONG CASE CLOCK DIAL
John Westcott, London, c.1750

LONG CASE CLOCK DIAL
Benjamin Barlow, Oldham, c.1775

Clock dials of the period show the same Rococo decoration as that in the trade-card opposite. Not only the spandrels changed, the proportions and other details of the dials were different too. Both dials here follow the break-arch tradition which had begun in the 1720s, but both London and north of England makers had abandoned the central, quarter-hour divisions and not only were dials larger but the chapter ring was wider in proportion, with taller figures. In the 1750s the closely scrolled corner spandrels of the London clock can be compared with the widely scrolling, Rococo manner of the Oldham clock of about 1775. While the calendar aperture appears in the London clock just above VI, the northern example displays the date with a separate hand, the dates being marked on the inner edge of the chapter ring.

The hands on clock dials can be used to help to date a clock. Care, however, is needed for many clock hands are replacements and this is certainly the case in the *John Westcott* dial shown here. The minute hand is later in style than the more delicate hour hand and is heavier; the wavy scrolling is not characteristic of its partner. Most important it does not fit, for the end of the hand projects beyond the line of the minute circle, whereas it should terminate on it. Minute hands are particularly prone to breakage through careless handling when setting the time. Two final points should be noticed in these dials—the minute numerals are now getting larger and are *outside* the minute ring. They had begun to appear inside by about 1700 and moved outside, though very small, by about 1705 (compare pp. 93, 97). The later northern clock by *Benjamin Barlow* has *dots* for minutes instead of a divided circle scale, as frequently happened in later *painted* dials (p. 120).

LONG CASE CLOCK
Nathaniel Brown, Manchester, c.1780

30-HOUR LONG CASE CLOCK
William Porthouse, Penrith, 1755-60

The outer edge of the break-arch dial was frequently used in the north to engrave the name and place of the maker. The Manchester clock signed *Nathaniel Brown*, recorded as working between 1773 and 1800, dates from about 1775 to 1780; it shows many northern characteristics, though the alarm is not common. The *swan's-neck pediment* was almost universal in good clocks of this kind, as was the scrolled engraving in the centre dial, sometimes on a ground of 'matted' brass and sometimes silvered with vertical 'graining', then filled with black wax. The 'arrow-heads' at half-hour spaces and the calendar aperture show a link with the earlier, southern tradition, but the mahogany case is heavier and wider. The *columns* of the hood are now free-standing, no longer part of the glazed hood door, and '*quarter columns*' on the corners of the trunk are a feature introduced just after the middle of the century.

Late 18th century break-arch dials, at least in the north of England, are almost always used to show the phases of the moon. The new moon appears on the left, advancing for $29\frac{1}{2}$ days across the opening to disappear on the right. Though the edge is engraved and silvered, the face itself is normally painted with landscape or seascape scenes behind. There are, of course, two moons on the disc and it is advanced by a *ratchet mechanism*, engaging one tooth at a time, every twelve hours, of the total of 118 teeth on its outer, hidden edge. The *lever and ratchet* is operated by a pin on the *hour wheel pipe*, though occasionally a moon dial might be advanced by a *worm-screw* system. The *Brown* clock and those on p. 109 are all 8-day with *compounded weights* on gut lines, but the *William Porthouse* of Penrith shows a northern oak case of about 1755-60, with a fine brass dial, but with a 30-hour movement wound by the Huygens' endless chain (p. 29).

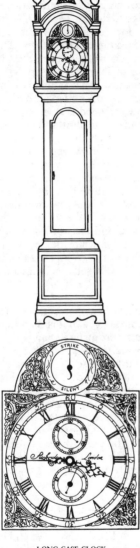

LONG CASE CLOCK
Charles Puckridge, London, *c.*1775

While the northern makers were developing their own style, fine quality London clocks were still made, reminiscent of the early 1700s. In this example of about 1775 the arch in the hood is still reflected in the arch-shaped door, and the *hollowed pediment* is quite unlike the *swan's neck*, giving emphasis to the height and continuing in fashion until almost the end of the century. Like the northern clocks, however, the case is of mahogany veneer, a vogue which had begun to replace the lacquered style by the 1740s (p. 95). Importation of mahogany from the West Indies and North America was encouraged by parliamentary action in 1721 and until the end of the 18th century it was popular for good quality clock cases. Oak with cross-banded veneering of mahogany on the edges was fashionable for medium-priced work; quarter columns, when they were used, were normally of mahogany. The London clock does not show the Rococo influence like its northern contemporaries, retaining classical proportions. (Plate III, 9.)

The dial of the *Puckridge* clock is conservative, for the arch has *strike/silent* work instead of a moon. A later feature, however, is the silvered dial centre and the fact that the seconds circle is *engraved* on the dial, and *not* pinned on. A new idea, not mentioned before, is the *calendar dial* instead of date aperture, which came into fashion in the 1770s, and the *lettering* of the signature should be noted, for this is pure 'copper plate' and in its sharpness and elegant precision is quite unlike the lettering of the previous century (pp. 87, 88, 97, 101). The calendar work is operated by a separate wheel, geared to the *hour wheel*, on which a pin engages with one of the 31 teeth of a wheel fixed to the back of the dial, carrying the calendar hand. Every 24 hours, therefore, the calendar hand is pushed to the next date, though for short months it must be adjusted by hand.

LONG CASE CLOCK
John Wyke, Liverpool, c.1770–75

DESIGN FOR A CLOCK CASE
Gillows of Lancaster, 1788

The English *Gothic Revival* had begun by the mid-18th century and the Gothick taste became part of the English Rococo, found a good deal in *Thomas Chippendale's* designs for furniture of the 1760s. A splendid example of its influence in clocks is the one shown here from the Liverpool workshop of *John Wyke* (1720–87), though the mahogany case would have come from elsewhere. On the underside of the moulding below the hood is an arcade of cusped arches and on the plinths below the corner columns, which are *full* not quarter columns, is a tracery fret of Gothic design. Mixed with these elements are classical columns, *bracket feet, quoins* on the corners of the base, *swan's neck pediment* with *dentil band*, 'Chinese' *frets* round the door of the hood and in the corners of the panel at the base, and elegant *wooden finials* to crown a design which is the apotheosis of the northern style, from the establishment of one of Liverpool's most famous entrepreneurs. (Plate VI, 17.)

Cases and clock movements were the combined efforts of two distinct trades. As clock dials were made to standard sizes (12, 13, 14 in. etc.) it was, *and still is*, easy to fit a movement to a case. Unfortunately much less is known about case-makers than clockmakers, but in the records of the firm of *Gillows of Lancaster* many details of clock case designs are recorded. The drawing left is from a Gillow pattern of 1788, recording the exact dimensions, types of wood and other details, and this firm may have been responsible for the case of the clock by Wyke. There were other cabinet makers in the north of England who could have made the case, but Gillows, founded at the end of the 17th century, sending furniture to London by 1740 and opening a branch there in 1770, is well-known for high quality products. The name of the firm still survives in the establishments of Waring and Gillow Ltd.

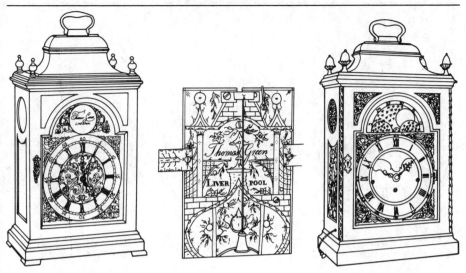

BRACKET CLOCK AND DETAIL OF BACK PLATE
Thomas Green, Liverpool, c.1785

BRACKET CLOCK
James Smith, London, c.1775–80

It is not known exactly when the partnership of *John Wyke* and *Thomas Green* started, but they were probably in business together from the late 1760s and Green continued the business after Wyke's death in 1787, until about 1805. They *retailed* a wide range of clock and watch-making tools, as well as clocks, the tools being produced by numerous small firms in the surrounding area of south-west Lancashire. The bracket clock by Thomas Green has an engraved *back plate* in the old tradition (p. 97), but in a later style which combines a touch of '*Chinoiserie*', a hint of *Gothic* and sprays of leaves and flowers in *Neo-Classical* taste. The movement is fastened to the case with right-angled brackets on either side, a later and cheaper method than the earlier fastenings, where the movement and dial were held by circular swivel catches on the back of the dial, fitting into slots on the inner side of the front of the case.

The pendulum cock of this clock has been spoiled by later conversion from a verge to an anchor escapement. The front remains unchanged except for the filling of what were pierced frets with solid panels, on either side of the arch of the dial, as the original fabric-backed, thin pierced wooden frets were easily damaged by careless handling. The top is of the *true bell* form (p. 98) and the centre of the dial is finely engraved with intertwining scrolls in the northern tradition (p. 110). The London bracket clock signed by *James Smith* is similar, though of more sumptuous quality, with moon's phases in the arch and *quarter-repeat striking*, operated by the cord seen hanging from the left-hand side (p. 98). A particularly 'London' feature is the segment of the inner dial, below XI, XII and I. In this open part of the dial the name-plate of the 'maker' was fitted, a sure sign that the dials were made for the trade at large, and could be fitted with any retailer's name-plate.

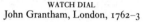

WATCH DIAL	REPOUSSÉ OUTER CASE OF	ENAMELLED CASE OF WATCH
John Grantham, London, 1762–3	GRANTHAM WATCH	William Turner, London, 1768–9

By the middle of the 18th century watch dials were plain white *enamel*. Against the white enamel, blued steel *'beetle and poker'* hands stood out clearly, and Roman numerals for the hours with comparatively large Arabic numbering at 5-minute intervals, was the general rule as with clock dials of the time. Plain English watch dials sometimes have *Dutch-style arcaded minute rings* as in the example here, datable from the hall-mark to 1762–3. White enamel is a fusible, vitreous, silica-based compound, rendered opaque white by the addition of tin oxide, a layer of which is *fired* on to a thin disc of copper, on which it melts and to which it adheres. Several layers separately fired and polished were often required to produce a good finish and the numbers were finally painted by hand in a black enamel, fixed by firing for the last time. Such dials remain pristine permanently because of their glass-like quality and usually suffer from damage by cracking only through careless handling.

The outer cases of pair-cased watches could often be of the utmost splendour in terms of Rococo decoration. The two outer cases illustrated here, both with Rococo conjoined 'C' scrolls round their outer edges, represent two distinct methods of case elaboration—on the left finely wrought *relief decoration* and on the right *coloured enamelling*. The relief decoration represents Perseus rescuing Andromeda from the sea monster; it is a superlative gold case, *part cast*, *part engraved* and *part chased*, while the enamel case of 1768–9, some six years later, is of a type where bright, clean, coloured enamels, hand applied, are fired on to a plain white enamel ground—a cheaper technique than working in metal, yet decorative and attractive. This design depicts Penelope and her suitors; in the original the surface is scratched and worn which was something of a weakness in both these types of casework and which was sometimes guarded against by the provision of a third, protective carrying case. (Plate IV, 10, 11.)

WATCH MOVEMENT AND DUST COVER
William Turner, London, 1768–9

CLOCK DESIGNED FOR THE TURKISH MARKET
c.1770

This watch movement and dust cover belong to the enamelled case opposite. The balance cock is a splendid example of the Rococo style, of deeply cut and pierced asymmetrical scrolls and wedge-shaped foot (p. 106). In the centre of the cock is a *diamond endstone* or *cap-stone*, to form the end bearing surface for the upper end of the balance staff. The pivot holes, both in the balance cock and *potence* at the lower end, are fitted with jewelled bearings, to reduce wear and friction and to help retain the oil. Although the art of piercing *rubies*, *sapphires*, *garnets* and *crystal* for watch pivots was first devised by a Frenchman in London as early as 1704, the *jewelling* of watches in the main train holes was only undertaken on pieces of the highest quality until about 1800. The diamond endstone here is faceted, to catch the light, and we see this feature in many watches from the 1740s though it was used by Graham from about 1725.

Another innovation and refinement with which George Graham is credited is the *dust cover*. These nicely fitting, gilded brass covers to protect the movement appear quite early in the 18th century, when greater precision and refinement developed in watch construction. They were formed by first pressing a flat piece of brass in a screw press, then turning in a lathe of sophisticated design for the eccentric parts of the work. Sometimes engraved with the name of the watch-maker, they are held in place by a sliding steel curb locating on two notched pillars on the watch top plate. Dust covers continued in use until the early part of the present century. Illustrated here is a clock designed for the Turkish market, similar to normal English examples but having the dial set out with Turkish numerals. These were made for export to Turkey from the later 17th century until the early 19th, latterly in quite large numbers; 'Turkish Market' watches were often made fitted with triple cases. (Plate IV, 10, 11, 12.)

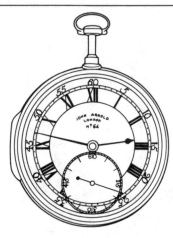

CHRONOMETER
Richard Pendleton, Robert Pennington and others,
London, 1797

POCKET CHRONOMETER
John Arnold, 1789

The watches illustrated of the 1760s (pp. 114, 115) are good quality London-made products, utilising the *fusee* and the *verge escapement*. Other types of escapement, however, were being tried out from the early part of the 18th century onwards, most notable being the *cylinder*, introduced by George Graham in 1726 (Ch. 2 and p. 122). *George Graham* (1673–1751), *John Harrison* (1693–1776), *John Ellicott* (1706–72), *Josiah Emery* (1725–97), *Thomas Mudge* (1715–94), *John Arnold* (1736–99), *Thomas Earnshaw* (1749–1829) and *Paul Philip Barraud* (1752–1820) and their French counterparts *Peter Debaufre, Julien le Roy* (1686–1759), his son *Pierre* (1717–85) and *Ferdinand* (1729–1807) and *Louis Berthoud* (1754–1813), contributed many inspired ideas and refinements which were to improve the watch and establish standards which are commonplace in good watches today. There is space to cite only one example, the use of the *spring detent escapement* for *chronometer* work, one version being by John Arnold and another by Thomas Earnshaw.

Intense rivalry existed between Arnold and Earnshaw over the invention of the spring detent device; Arnold obtained his patent first but Earnshaw, being poor and leaving his patent in the hands of others, always claimed—perhaps rightly—that the idea was his. The 1789 pocket chronometer above by John Arnold, employs a balance, which is temperature compensated by two 'S' shaped curbs of laminated brass and steel, and a detent escapement (pp. 41, 44). Also shown is a chronometer of 1797, by *Richard Pendleton, Robert Pennington* and other craftsmen under the proprietorship of Thomas Mudge *junior*, who was anxious to establish the reputation of his father. Thomas Mudge *senior* is to be remembered particularly as the inventor of the *detached lever escapement* about 1770 (pp. 43, 141). During his partnership with *William Dutton*, from 1759 to 1790, Mudge produced many superb watches, some with cylinder escapement; his famous chronometer and its two copies, the 'blue' and the 'green', were too complicated for commercial reproduction.

Regulators, being firmly fixed and weight-driven, were not involved with the complications inherent in ships' chronometers. Left is a London made regulator of about 1800, or slightly later, and of particular note is the design of the dial which is quite different from that of a domestic long case clock. The minutes are indicated by a single central hand marking the outer scale, with subsidiary dials for seconds above and hours below. This arrangement not only adds clarity in reading the dials accurately, but also avoids any possible effect on the timekeeping by having the *hour wheel pipe* supported by the *bridge pipe*, or by the *pipe of the minute wheel* and *central arbor*, as in conventional domestic clocks. Striking trains are not included in regulator clocks because the stresses in the movement frame and vibrations when striking would undoubtedly affect the accuracy of the clock, as well as the complication of 'unlocking' the striking action.

A regulator is a scientific instrument, of particular use in watch and clockmaking establishments. In the Clerkenwell watch-making district of London, many years ago, boys were sent to Greenwich to 'get the time' from the Observatory. In 1833 a visual *time ball signal* was instituted at Greenwich, whereby a ball about 5 ft. in diameter was released to fall down its mast at precisely 1.0 p.m., warning being given by hoisting it half way up the mast at 12.55 and close up at 12.58. In Liverpool, where ships' masters and manufacturers of clocks required precise time, the firing of a cannon at exactly 1.0 p.m. has only recently been discontinued. Although a regulator is not a domestic clock the one shown here in a mahogany case follows the same basic lines of the English long case clock, but it is devoid of all decoration apart from the simplest of mouldings to enhance its proportions and make it suitable for the shop of a good clockmaker.

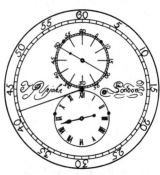

REGULATOR CLOCK
T. J. Upjohn, London, *c*.1800

TITLE PAGE
OF A TOOL CATALOGUE
Ford, Whitmore & Brunton,
Birmingham, c.1785

Some of the main features of the Neo-Classical style which affected the decorative arts in the last quarter of the 18th century are seen in the title page of a catalogue of tools by *Ford, Whitmore & Brunton* of Birmingham, published about 1785. Particularly characteristic is the *oval cartouche*, used extensively in the furniture designs of *Robert Adam* (1728–92) and amongst designs by *George Hepplewhite* in the'*Cabinet-Maker & Upholsterer's Guide*', published two years after his death in 1788. The restless 'C' and 'S' scrolls of the Rococo style had been used in furniture designs by *Thomas Chippendale* in his '*A Gentleman and Cabinet-Maker's Director*' in 1754 and, just as Chippendale's use of this style in furniture affected clocks, so the Neo-Classical style had its influence. On the catalogue cover design are the symmetrical and carefully disposed *ribbon-bow* at the top, with *husking* behind, balanced mistletoe sprigs at the base and *reeding* and *fluting* on the 'frame', all typical elements of this cool and refined style.

The firm of Ford, Whitmore & Brunton seems to have started in Birmingham with *Richard Ford*, 'Engine & Ovil Lathe Maker' in 1767 and continued until 1798 when it became *William Whitmore & Sons*. Retailers of a wide range of horological tools and other equipment, they must have relied on the Lancashire makers for their goods, for the catalogue is similar to, if not in part copied from the one by *Wyke and Green* (p. 108), which was also copied by Warrington file-maker and tool retailer *Peter Stubs* (1756–1806). The relevance of these three catalogues, the first ever published in England, apart from the light they throw on the tools and techniques of the period is that, in horology as in most other trades, they show the effects of the Industrial Revolution. With increased specialisation in manufacturing processes, better retailing and communications and increasing availability of tools and materials, large numbers of English and foreign clock and watchmakers were emerging to supply the needs of an expanding market.

A group of outstanding northern English makers were emerging in the second half of the 18th century (pp. 108, 109, 110, 112), including for example *Thomas Lister* (1745–1814) of Halifax (p. 127), *William Barker* (?·married 1745–d. 1786) of Wigan (pp. 120, 126) and *Joseph Finney* (*c.* 1708–1772) of Liverpool (p. 127). The clock left is an 8-day long case by Listèr, of about 1785, with typical northern hood, columns and pediment, though the columns on the hood and on the trunk are of *coupled shafts*, in the Gothic taste. Most important is the fact that the door and base contain veneered designs in the *Neo-Classical* manner. The symmetrical designs with *urns, ribbon bows, swags and festoons* and *acanthus scrolls* are of Adam style, often to be seen in his painted or plaster-moulded interiors, such as Syon House in Middlesex, Kedleston in Derbyshire and many others. This style was also much used by *Josiah Wedgwood* (1730–95) in his jasperware ornaments. (Plate VI, 17.)

The dial of the Lister clock is of straightforward northern pattern, with engraved centre dial, break-arch top and with calendar and moon. The calendar is of the latest and cheapest type, being pushed forward at each complete revolution of the hour wheel in half-day or 12 hour intervals. This type of aperture was used extensively in the *painted iron dials* of the early 19th century (p. 129). The moon, appearing in an inverted segmental aperture, is also a later and cheaper replacement for the moon in the arch (p. 110). Like the date, this kind of moon is moved forward each 12 hours by the *same pin* as the one which works the date. The *roundel* in the arch has a figure of Father Time engraved upon it and such reminders of mortality were popular in the north of England, along with such mottoes as 'Time is Valuable' and 'The Man is yet Unborn that Duely Weighs an Hour'.

LONG CASE CLOCK
Thomas Lister, Halifax, *c.*1780–5

 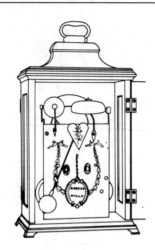

BRACKET CLOCK
William Barker, Wigan, c.1785–90

William Barker of Wigan, whose date of birth we do not know, petitioned for the Freedom of Wigan to ply his trade of gunsmith and clockmaker, which was granted in 1751, married a Wigan lady about 1745 and died there in 1786 or '87. Barker's great horological masterpiece will be considered later (p. 126), but here we have a bracket clock, signed by Barker on the backplate and dial, curiously enough with *Wigan* on the back but *Warrington* on the front. Why this should have been done we do not know, but research may show that either Barker had a retailing shop in Warrington, not far from Wigan, or that perhaps the clock was retailed by a member of his family in the town of Warrington, after his death in the 1780s. With typical moon work in the arch and calendar inside the chapter ring, this *quarter striking* and *repeat striking* clock has a *painted dial*, of a type often seen in the long case clocks of the period.

In appearance the clock is similar to the Thomas Green on p. 113, but it is ebonised, decorated on the front with *inlaid* Neo-Classical designs—*ribbon bow* at the top, *symmetrical scrolls* and *husking* down the sides (pp. 118, 119). This theme is taken up on the engraved back-plate, with a pair of *ribbon bows*, festoons of *husking* and a large *oval cartouche* containing the signature. On each side of the central line are two oval *paterae*, very common in Adam-style architecture and furniture where it was often used in coloured veneers with shell motif centres. Particularly of note is the *heart-shaped pendulum cock*; the symmetrical heart design is very much a late 18th century feature and occurs again in clock hands (p. 121) and watch hands (p. 122). The clock has three bells, one for the hours and two for the quarters and in the view above the pendulum, with its *lenticular bob*, is seen hooked to one side, to prevent possible damage to the verge escapement while the clock was being moved.

BRACKET CLOCK
William Bull, Stratford, Essex, *c*.1795

TAVERN CLOCK IN LACQUERED CASE
c.1750

The *low arch style* of hood seen in the regulator on p. 117 developed in other types of clock towards the end of the 18th century. Exactly this shape is seen in the bracket clock above, which although retaining a carrying handle like that on p. 113 has features which date it to the last years of the century. In particular we notice the *circular dial*, devoid of any ornament and, like the watches, of enamelled manufacture to provide a clear white surface against which the scrolled and pierced hands stand out well. The *enamelling* of clock dials of this 7-in. size or larger was technically a difficult matter compared with watch dials and many of the later dials are simply *painted* white, though often described as enamelled. The *bracket feet* are an earlier form which survives on these and on long case clocks too (p. 119), but the large brass *bezel* and *domed glass* front are new features which display a change in the fashions of the day.

Bracket clocks are for private use, but the clock on the right, of earlier date, is a *public* clock for use in taverns or sometimes churches. The black lacquered case and arched trunk door are evidence of the period of the clock (p. 95) though the *heart-shaped terminals* of the hands might suggest either a later date for the clock or later additions, which is far more likely. The extension of the arms of the hands beyond the centre is to provide *counterweights* for hands of large size. These unglazed, 8-day tavern clocks, averaging about 3 ft. in diameter, are frequently mis-named 'Act of Parliament Clocks', being placed in public taverns for the benefit of customers when a tax on watches and clocks was instituted by Act of Parliament in 1797, though repealed the following year. Clocks of this type, however, are known to have been made throughout the 18th century and as public clocks they are the direct ancestor of what are now known as *dial clocks* (p. 144).

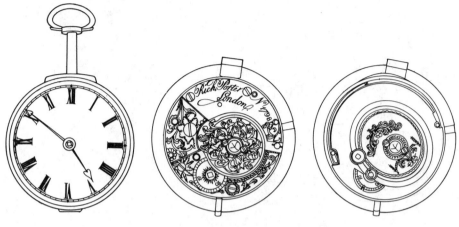

DIAL, MOVEMENT AND DUST COVER OF A WATCH
Richard Porter, London, *c*.1780

Even in the details of the decorated dust cover of a watch the Neo-Classical forms are used, the *oval* raising to accommodate the cock, the symmetrical *ribbon bow* and *swags* and *festoons*. Such decorative details are extremely useful in determining the date of a clock or watch, though we must take into account the movement too and not be confused by the revival of earlier designs in the 19th and early 20th centuries (Ch. 7, 10). The watch shown here, signed by the unrecorded *Richard Porter* of London, dates from about 1780, and contains the *cylinder escapement*, first devised by George Graham in 1726 (pp. 40, 116). The cylinder escapement was sometimes known as the *horizontal escapement* in that the escape wheel is in the same plane as the other wheels and interacts directly with a cut-away cylinder on the balance wheel staff. When the escape wheel 'locks' it does so without *recoil* and in this sense is *dead-beat*, like the dead-beat anchor in clocks, also introduced by Graham.

The balance cock of the watch is still very much in the Rococo tradition of asymmetrical, formalised leaf scrolls, with surface engraved decoration on the foot and on the *regulator plate*, the latter carrying the silvered disc *regulator* which is used to move the balance spring *curb pins* by a rack and pinion system hidden underneath. The plate containing the signature, of good 'copper plate' script, is known as the *barrel bridge* or *bar*, as it holds the upper end of the *spring barrel arbor*. This is a useful construction in full-plate watches, since in the case of mainspring breakage it allows the barrel to be withdrawn with minimal disturbance to the rest of the movement. The dial is of white enamel, with black enamelled chapters and heart-shaped gold hands. The *stirrup pendant* (p. 105) appears long in the stem, but this is because the watch is shown without its outside 'pair' case, which at this date would be of plain design, perhaps with some engraving of Neo-Classical inspiration.

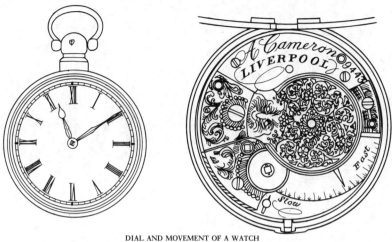

DIAL AND MOVEMENT OF A WATCH
A. Cameron, Liverpool, c.1800–10

According to G. H. Baillie's *Watchmakers and Clockmakers of the World* A. Cameron of Liverpool died in 1800. The watch above, by this maker, appears to have been made about this time but the death of a watchmaker does not mean that the firm which carried his name would not continue to use that name, perhaps for many years. Superficially the same layout as the Porter watch on p. 122, this has a *verge escapement* and a very important change appears in the regulator. The silvered disc, with its squared centre for a key, is now blued steel without any index figures; although it operates exactly as formerly through a rack and pinion to adjust the balance spring curbs, an *index pointer* attached to the rack moves on a *divided scale* engraved on the top plate, when setting the watch 'fast' or 'slow'. This index hand with rack and pinion is a transitional form, for in the early 19th century the rack and pinion was dispensed with altogether, the index being moved manually (p. 141).

The balance cock piercing is now very fine, cut in tight little scrolls, but with its foot unpierced. Now that the regulator details are changing, the engraved portion of the regulation plate is much smaller, and capital letters are used for the word 'Liverpool' to contrast with the script lettering of the name. This watch shows how the design of movements was gradually changing in the early 19th century, particularly in the form of the balance cock. The foot of the cock now achieved its final segmental shape and apart from the bell-shaped cock with its serpentine edged foot used with *rack lever* escapements (p. 141), the whole cock gradually took on a triangular form decorated with surface engraving only (Plate VIII, 25 a and p. 143). The reason for this was that the balance cock was no longer required to protect the balance completely and, with better fitting cases and more difficult access to the movement, such decoration was no longer necessary. In modern watches decoration of the movement has disappeared altogether.

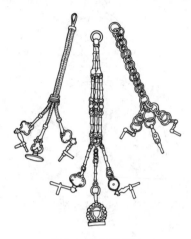

A WATCH PAPER FROM HUDDERSFIELD

FOBS AND WATCH KEYS
18th century

No illustrations of watches of the 18th century would be complete without some assessment of their accompanying 'furniture'. In the backs of pair-cased watches it is common to find a *watch-paper*, a thin printed circular slip which was placed inside to 'cushion' the inner case and to act as an advertisement for the retailer or repairer. Records of repairs and cleaning written on these papers are much to be preferred to the defacing scratch marks one often meets in old watches. The watch-paper here, with shield-shaped cartouche and some Gothic lettering, carries the useful information round its edge: 'To make the Watch go Slower, turn the Regulator the same way you wind up— Faster the Contrary' and also the rider: 'Engraving neatly executed'. Watches were wound, of course, by small keys of which we see a selection attached to a 'fob' and worn with the watch on a gentleman's waistcoat or front trouser pocket. Many keys were of superb quality, many being 'cranked' like a car starting handle.

Towards the end of the century *Abraham Louis Breguet* (1747–1823) (p. 181) introduced the *tipsy key* which contained a ratchet mechanism, preventing the watch from being wound backwards when its owner was in a 'tipsy' condition, though this invention is claimed by *Samuel Harlow* (1751–1815) of Ashbourne, Derbyshire, who received patent No. 1708 for it in 1789. The keys shown here are accompanied by seals, used when sealing letters. Another useful article for carrying a watch and other appendages was the *chatelaine*, of first importance to women who had no convenient pockets in their clothing yet who wished to carry an assortment of articles such as keys or scissors. As superintendant or hostess of her household, called in French the 'châtelaine', a woman would carry it hooked to her girdle. A wide range of these small, personal chatelaines was made for 18th century ladies and gentlemen, often elaborately decorated with imitation stones, Wedgwood medallions, cut-steel work and coloured enamels.

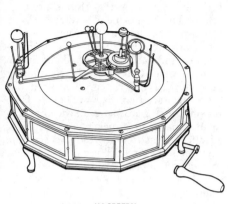

AN ORRERY
English, mid 18th century

CLOCK WITH GLOBE
John Whitehurst, Derby, c.1780

Closely associated with clockwork is the *orrery*, an 18th century device sometimes powered or sometimes turned by hand, which indicates the motions of the planets round the sun, the moon round the earth and in some examples, the satellites of Jupiter and Saturn. The first known example was made about 1710 by *Tompion* and *Graham*, another in 1716 being made by *John Rowley* of London, which was owned by Charles, Fourth Earl of Orrery, who gave it his name; another name is the *planetarium*. They were used for lectures and demonstrations in an age when popularisation of science was very much in vogue. From 1784 *W. & S. Jones* of London were making simple ones for teaching children, at 3–6 guineas each. In the example here the 'sun' in the centre is a polished brass ball, but oil lamps were also provided to give light and thus display eclipses of the moon and the progression of day and night.

In a painting called the 'Orrery', by *Joseph Wright* (1734–97) of Derby, a group of people watch a demonstration by the light of an orrery lamp. One of the principal figures is *John Whitehurst* (1713–88), a member of the *Lunar Society* which also included Josiah Wedgwood, James Watt, Joseph Priestley, Erasmus Darwin and Matthew Boulton. Whitehurst of Derby was a skilled mechanic who made turret clocks, domestic clocks and other mechanical devices, maintaining a lifelong interest in mechanics and science. The astronomical clock shown here displays a 24-hour rotating globe of the earth, mounted above the movement with its 24-hour dial. The gilded brass case and mounts were made by *Matthew Boulton* (1728–1809), who made decorative metalwork at his Soho Foundry, Birmingham. Some of Boulton's clock cases are mounted with blue-John stone from Derbyshire and he also provided Wedgwood with cut-steel and ormolu mounts for his jasperware jewellery. (Plates V, 13, VII, 22).

The interest in science and astronomy in the second half of the 18th century is reflected in the making of several clocks by some of the famous northern makers mentioned on p. 119. This was a continuation of a tradition which started very much earlier (p. 99) but which, by the closing years of the century, was scientifically far more accurate than had previously been possible, taking advantage of the improvements made in timekeeping methods, advances in astronomy and the accurate division of the circle. The clocks shown on this and the opposite page could hardly be called domestic clocks, though they are housed in cases of the northern domestic tradition (p. 112, 119), and one is fitted with musical work. The clock on this page is the masterpiece of *William Barker* of Wigan (p. 120) which must be dated to about 1780. The rounded form of its upper dial is its most characteristic feature and it shows what is known as a 'Halifax' moon.

The upper dial of the Barker clock, like the Finney clock opposite, shows the time of rising and setting of the sun by means of rising and falling shutters, left and right, behind which the daily sun appears and disappears every 24 hours. A slender hand, revolving annually, indicates the daily calendar *Old Style* on the inner chapter ring edge, and the *New Style* on the outer. The New Style came into use in 1752 when the Old Style or *Julian Calendar* had become eleven days wrong since its beginning in 325 A.D. Various ecclesiastical details are given on the outer ring which can be altered annually to allow for variations of the date of Easter, a *solar time* pointer is located above XII and below the moon (pp. 19, 100), and the moon itself is spherical, half black and half silver; it revolves every $29\frac{1}{2}$ days and has a central scale to show the moon's age and the time of high tide in Liverpool, London, Bristol and Hull.

LONG CASE CLOCK WITH CALENDAR AND
ASTRONOMICAL WORK
William Barker, Wigan, *c.*1780

PLATE V

13 (*above left*). Mantel clock with revolving dial, of gilded bronze, white jasper and marble, Wedgwood cameo plaques; designed in the French manner and signed Vulliamy, London, *c*. 1795. *Lady Lever Art Gallery, Port Sunlight.* 14 (*above*). Lyre mantel clock, porcelain case, ormolu mounts, paste brilliants round the pendulum, calendar work showing date and month; signed Roblins & Fils Frères à Paris. Style Louis XVI, *c*. 1785. *Lady Lever Art Gallery, Port Sunlight.* 15 (*left*). Mantel clock in patinated bronze with ormolu mounts, attributed to Antoine Ravrio, a famous Parisian case-maker. Empire style, *c*. 1805. *The Bowes Museum, Co. Durham.* 16 (*below*). *a*. Heart-shaped watch with paste brilliants, verge escapement; signed André Hessen, Paris, *c*. 1785. *b*. Watch in the form of a beetle, dark blue enamel, seed pearls and ormolu, verge escapement; unsigned, Swiss, *c*. 1830. *City of Liverpool Museums.*

PLATE VI

17 (*above left*). Long case clock in mahogany, Gothic and Neo-Classical detailing, centre seconds, dead beat escapement; signed William Kirk, Stockport, *c.* 1770. *Lady Lever Art Gallery, Port Sunlight.* 18 (*above*). Regulator in mahogany case with brass inlay, jewelled dead beat escapement, Harrison's maintaining power, gridiron pendulum; dial signed Ollivants, Manchester; movement signed G. Jamison, *c.* 1815. *Private collection.* 19 (*left*). Skeleton clock, quarter striking on eight bells and gong with pull repeat, lever escapement with compensated balance and helical spring; signed James Condliff, Liverpool, 1862. *City of Liverpool Museums.*

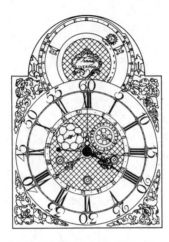

DIAL OF LONG CASE MUSICAL CLOCK
Joseph Finney, Liverpool, c.1775

DIAL OF LONG CASE CLOCK
Thomas Lister, Halifax, c.1775

These clocks are both housed in cases of the northern English tradition. The *Lister* clock has a dial which gives astronomical and calendar information, while that by *Finney* has musical work also, playing on eight bells with two hammers for each bell. The clock by *Joseph Finney* (1708–72) of Liverpool has a *mercurial barometer* in the door of the trunk and an upper dial for showing the length of daylight throughout the year. The moon's age and tides appear on an inner dial on the right, with the names of the tunes it plays at 9.0, 12.0 and 4.0 o'clock being recorded on the left. It has a central *sweep second hand* and the monthly dates are shown in northern fashion on the inner edge of the chapter ring, making use of a fourth, separate hand. One refinement which cannot be shown is the rhomboid pendulum (p. 28), a diamond-shaped frame for the pendulum rod made of brass and steel strips to compensate for temperature changes.

The shutters for the rising and setting of the sun in both Barker and Finney clocks are moved by wheel work revolving once in a year, a low-geared drive achieved through the use of worm-toothed wheels. The so-called 'Halifax' moon on Barker's clock is thus named because others by *Thomas Lister* of *Halifax* are known with this attractive and rational arrangement. The clock by Lister has an annually rotating dial in the arch to show calendar information, month, day, saints' days, equation of time and signs of the Zodiac. The small dials in the corners are for choice of striking or not and for regulation. The flat engraving of the centre dial and spandrels shows a desire for the later style of plain engraved and silvered surface and includes a good deal of Neo-Classical inspiration. These northern clocks show a development of English craftsmanship which has been for too long neglected in the shadow of the 'golden age' of the southern school of the 17th and early 18th centuries.

7

English Eclecticism in the Nineteenth Century c.1800 to 1900

LONG CASE CLOCK
T. Lees, Bury, Lancashire, c.1800-10

Though confusing in its complexity of styles, the 19th century is perhaps one of the most interesting periods for the study of clocks and watches, when looked at from over 100 years later. It saw the evolution of new techniques in manufacture, particularly in America, and vastly increased production to meet the needs of a rapidly expanding market in both cheap clocks for the working people and expensive ones for their masters; it saw the introduction of electrical power to horology and a continuing tradition of fine hand-craftsmanship which was finally to suffer its death throes at the end of the century. The changes and developments which took place in English social and technological history during the long reign of Queen Victoria, from 1837 to 1901, are reflected in the world of clocks and watches and in this same world we also see something of the self-assurance which characterised the era and yet which, paradoxically, caused it to look for inspiration to artistic standards of the classical and mediaeval worlds.

Many books on furniture, clocks or the decorative arts generally conclude with the period of the *Regency*, a term rather roughly used to cover from about 1800 to 1830, although the Regency proper lasted only between 1811 and 1820. The long case clock shown here, of about 1800 to 1810, is seen to continue in basic form its 18th century predecessors, veneered in mahogany, but there are notable differences. The columns of the hood are ornamentally turned instead of following classical precedent, the 'corner columns' of the trunk are but flat and reeded pilaster strips, the dial is of iron with painted chapters and spandrels and the whole case is wider in proportion than it had been previously, a tendency which led to some extremely fat and ungainly shapes by the 1830s and 1840s. The Gothic revival motif on the top of the trunk door should be noted (p. 112), but this clock represents the 'beginning of the end' of the English long case tradition, though it lingered on for many years.

LONG CASE CLOCK
From Otley, Yorkshire, *c*.1810

PAINTED DIAL
From a Yorkshire long case clock, *c*.1815

The long case clock shown here, of Yorkshire origin, is similar in form to the one on the opposite page. The veneered case, with *stringing* of thin strips of light coloured wood, is basically a cheap and superficial design, with chamfered corners, short or squat trunk door, medley of motifs of classical origin and flimsy construction. Such cases were simply glued together and present on their fronts a decorative 'facade', concealing an ordinary movement of a type manufactured by specialist firms well into the 19th century. In 1813 *Samuel Harlow* (1751–1815) published *The Clockmaker's Guide* and shortly after left to his son Robert a flourishing business, which specialised in making movements for 'clockmakers', all the parts being pre-fabricated and requiring little more than assembly. Clocks of this kind are now the most commonly found of the long case type, for they were made in enormous numbers.

The dials of northern, 19th century clocks are invariably painted. Whereas brass dials are fitted directly on to the movement with dial pillars riveted to the dial plate, *painted iron* dials have a *false plate* behind, to which the dial itself is connected. These false plates were fitted by the dial makers, then appropriately placed pillars could be fixed to the false plate rather than to the dial itself, which would have been impossible once the dial had been painted. More often than not the false plates give the name and place of the maker, produced in Roman capital lettering when the plate was cast. Birmingham appears to have been an important centre for the production of these dials and C. Osborne of Clerkenwell has compiled a list of about forty dial makers from that town. On ordering his dials from a dial making firm the provincial clockmaker would specify the name and place to be painted on it; or commission a local sign-writer.

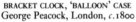

BRACKET CLOCK, 'BALLOON' CASE
George Peacock, London, c.1800

BRACKET CLOCK WITH LOW ARCH TOP
George Jamison, Portsea, c.1800

BRACKET CLOCK WITH ARCHED TOP
John Barwise, London, c.1810

While the long case clock had begun its decline, the making of fine quality *bracket* or *mantel* clocks continued, particularly in London. No longer portable, they were intended for the mantelpieces of the wealthy merchants and industrialists who were joining the ranks of, if not replacing, the aristocracy. Six clocks of the period are shown. Gone, except in one example, is the top carrying handle, since they were intended to stay in one place, though in some we do find carrying 'rings' on each side. In all but one specimen the dials are round, painted or enamelled (pp. 114, 121) and the hands, though varied, are of simpler profile than their 18th century precursors, either of symmetrical, open-pierced form, straight with ornamental terminals, or wavy. The movements are mostly controlled by an *anchor escapement*, with pendulums longer than those used with a verge. The verge will perform quite reasonably on slightly different levels and even while being carried, but the anchor, once set 'in beat', is better left in a permanent position.

The curved 'balloon' clock is datable to about 1800 in a form which owes something to French styles, but with English restraint (p. 172). The example is veneered with satinwood and mahogany and has a Neo-Classical oval with shell-motif filling. The second clock, by *George Jamison*, who had been associated with *Paul Philip Barraud* (p. 116) and who made fine quality chronometers and regulators (Plate VI, 18), follows the low arch top tradition (pp. 117, 121) and also dates from about 1800. The third clock, also arched, with quarter columns at the corners, is from the firm of *John Barwise* who was later in the century to become Chairman of the British Watch Company, London, founded in 1843 and which, like the English Watch Company of Birmingham (c.1872) and the Lancashire Watch Company (1889), was an attempt to introduce new methods of manufacture into an essentially conservative tradition (p. 143). All three clocks on this page relate closely to, and are a development from, the late 18th century style of casework and ornament.

BRACKET CLOCK WITH BRASS INLAY
Septimus Miles, London, c.1815

BRACKET CLOCK IN GOTHIC CASE
R. Widenham, London, c.1835

BRACKET CLOCK IN CLASSICAL CASE
Coleman and Chapman,
Liverpool, c.1820–5

From about the 1830s onwards England was to witness the growth of a *Gothic Revival* which profoundly influenced all design in London and the growing provincial cities. One may cite the work of *A. W. N. Pugin* (1812–52) who provided the Gothic detail to Sir Charles Barry's plan for the Houses of Parliament, or *Sir George Gilbert Scott* (1811–78) with, for example, his façade of St. Pancras Station, London, in which he used his rejected designs for the Foreign Office Building (1856), and the Albert Memorial (1863) to say nothing of his countless Gothic churches throughout the land (p. 145). *John Ruskin* (1819–1900) published his 'Seven Lamps of Architecture' in 1849 and preached his advocacy of the Gothic style, and with other critics, designers and architects stamped 19th century England with the Gothic image. It is not surprising, therefore, that clocks should be designed in the Gothic manner too, both in English workshops and in 19th century America (pp. 135, 137, 157, 158 and Plate VI, 18).

Two clocks here in the Gothic style are of about 1815 and 1835. In the first we see the *brass strip inlay* in a mahogany veneer, a form of ornament popular in the Regency period, and the second has a *flattened pointed arched dial*, with *finials*, 'lancet' *side frets* and 'coupled' *corner columns*. The dial of the first is painted white, while the second is silvered with *engraved* arch and corner spandrels. The third clock is of Classical design which reflects a brief period of architectural style known as the *Greek Revival*, which may be seen in such buildings as the British Museum (1847) by *Sir Robert Smirke* (1780–1867) or *Henry Lonsdale Elmes'* (1814–49) St. George's Hall, Liverpool (1841), where the clock illustrated was made. The case has brass strip inlay and side carrying rings, but the top is Greek Revival in its flattened pedimental form, crowned by a cast and gilded 'pineapple' finial, exactly the same as the one on the 'balloon' clock.

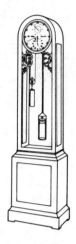

REGULATOR CLOCK
Thomas Brown, Maidstone, c.1850

MANTEL CLOCK, REGULATOR DIAL
Wray & Son, Birmingham, c.1840

The regulator clock (pp. 100, 117) came into its final phase towards the middle of the 19th century, its further development being concerned with electrically controlled devices which were taking their first, tentative steps about the same time (p. 147). The one shown here, signed by Brown of Maidstone, the retailing agent, is a good example of its kind, made in the London area by one of the Clerkenwell firms such as *John Smith & Sons*. With rounded top and fully glazed, severely plain case the only concession to ornament is the pair of carved and scrolled frets beneath the dial. Such clocks are sturdily built, the back board of the case being over 1 in. thick to give rigidity. The movement, with its regulator-type dial (p. 117), is a high precision timepiece only, employing a *jewelled dead-beat escapement*, heavy *mercurial pendulum* and *maintaining power* of the Harrison type, to avoid losing precious seconds while the clock was wound. In some regulators of this kind there are two small doors at the top of the clock for easy access to the movement.

The *winding square* of the Brown regulator is between X and XI of the hour dial and the lay-out keeps the *brass-cased weight* clear of the pendulum. The clock runs for 8 days and a hole is left in the board at the bottom of the glazed section to allow the weight to descend the whole height of the case. The door is fitted with felt-covered rebates to filter the air as it flows in and out. The small Birmingham clock has a regulator dial but is powered by a spring and is really a *mantel* clock. The pendulum of the tall regulator beats seconds but this clock beats half seconds with its much shorter pendulum. A *pin wheel* escapement is fitted which, although controlled by a half-second pendulum, allows the escape wheel to move at second intervals, registering the seconds correctly on the upper dial. Although a precision clock, its spring drive and uncompensated pendulum would not allow it to keep such precise time as the tall case regulator.

MARINE CHRONOMETER
P. P. Barraud, London, c.1835

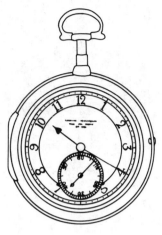

DECK WATCH
Thomas Earnshaw, London, c.1810

The *marine chronometer* above, made about 1835, had achieved the final style of movement and case which it has kept until the present day. Chronometers are spring driven, mostly of 2-day duration, with *fusee* and *maintaining power, centre wheel, third, fourth* and *escape wheels* and *spring detent escapement, balance* controlled for temperature and a *helical balance spring*. The *bezel* is screwed in place, holding the glass cover securely down. The clock is swung in its *gimbals* to wind it from underneath. The stout mahogany *carrying case* with brass *side handles*, external in this example but recessed into the case side later in the century, contains two gimbal rings to keep the clock level at sea, a lock for holding the gimbals firm when required and a slot for the key. The cover locked to prevent interference with this vital navigational aid, but the top of the lid has a subsidiary cover over a glass screen, to allow the chronometer to be consulted without unlocking the case.

Many firms, including *P. P. Barraud* who took into partnership *William Howells* and *George Jamison* who had previously worked for *Thomas Mudge junior* (pp. 116, 130), manufactured and retailed chronometers in the 19th century. The best known are *Thomas Mercer* of London and St. Albans, *Charles Frodsham, Morris Tobias, J. F. Cole, Victor Kullberg, McCabe & Son, Robert Molyneux, Edward John Dent* (in partnership with John Arnold until 1840), *Edward Thomas Loseby* and *Litherland, Davies & Co.* of Liverpool. Allied to chronometers were pocket watches, sometimes called *deck watches* of which the one illustrated is by *Thomas Earnshaw* (p. 116) of earlier date than the chronometer, and fitted with his '*sugar tong*' compensation curb, acting on the balance spring to correct for changes of temperature. The enamelled dial of the watch illustrates Earnshaw's use of radiating Arabic numerals; Arabic figures began to be used on watch·dials towards the end of the 18th century and frequently in the early 19th, a fashion inspired by French watches.

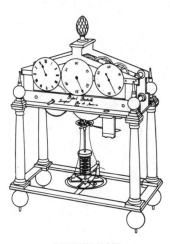

SKELETON CLOCK
Robert Roskell, Liverpool, c.1820–5

SKELETON CLOCK
William Mayo, Manchester, c.1840

The Greek Revival (p. 131) clock by *Robert Roskell* of Liverpool is of *skeleton* form, the entire movement being visible and protected from dust by a glass cover. Powered by spring and fusee, the *lever escapement* is clearly seen below; this is a type devised by *George Savage* (?–1855), a native of Huddersfield, and known as the *Savage two pin*, controlled by a helical, chronometer-type balance spring. The time is shown with hours on the left dial, minutes in the centre and seconds on the right. Another famous maker of skeleton clocks was *James Condliff* who also employed the helical spring with a lever escapement (Plate VI, 19), and the fascination of such clocks is that they expose mechanisms which are normally hidden in domestic clocks. The Victorian characteristic of wishing to understand, to know how and why, coinciding with the beginnings of universal education and a new-found admiration for the machine, is symbolised by skeleton clocks, though they owe their inspiration to French 18th century predecessors.

The skeleton clock enjoyed wide popularity throughout the 19th century, though later examples are perhaps somewhat spoiled by the elaborate decoration of their pierced openwork frames. Often un-named, and when signed carrying only the name of the retailer, they were made by such firms as *W. F. Evans* of Birmingham, *John Smith & Sons* of Clerkenwell, *William Haycock* of Ashbourne, Derbyshire and doubtless many others. The clock shown here, beneath its parabolic glass dome or 'shade', dates from about 1840 and although signed W. Mayo, Manchester, is clearly from the firm of *James Edwards* of Stourbridge, Worcestershire. Its cleanly scrolled lines look well when compared with the elaborate Gothic style which we see on p. 135 and even the spring barrel is pierced to reveal the coils of the mainspring within. Skeleton clocks have become very collectable today and sometimes have elaborate striking on bells, with *gongs* for the hours inside the wooden bases beneath.

MOVEMENT OF A WATCH WITH A SKELETON FRAME
Joseph Finney, Liverpool, 1812–13

ILLUSTRATION OF A GOTHIC SKELETON CLOCK
From the 1865 catalogue of John Smith & Sons,
Clerkenwell

The skeleton watch shown here is by *Joseph Finney* of Liverpool (p. 127). Externally the watch is plain, but the back of the case has an internal glazed cover and the movement can be fully examined in all its details including the mainspring inside the spring barrel. Owing to its peculiar construction the traditional English balance cock could not be used and the Continental *bridge cock* holds the upper balance pivot, with diamond endstone in a blued steel *collet*. The escapement of this watch is a type of verge with two co-axial escape wheels, the balance staff pallet acting between them. This type of construction appears to have been confined mainly to Lancashire makers, particularly from the town which gives it its name, the *Ormskirk verge*. It was first devised by *Peter Debaufre* in 1704 (p. 116) and is also known as the *club-footed verge*. The movement of this watch was possibly made about 1770, under French influence, but the dial and case can be dated by the hall mark to 1812–13.

The Gothic skeleton clock is from the catalogue of *John Smith & Sons* of Clerkenwell, published in 1865. It is typical of a host of Gothic designs vaguely copying the profiles and elevations of Gothic churches, with pinnacles, crockets, spires, pointed arches and quatre-foil piercing. As it is a simple timekeeper, the bell at the top is struck only once at each hour, the bell hammer tail being lifted by a pin on the minute wheel and the hammer, when released, striking the bell under the action of a spring. Though typical of the fashion for Gothic design, these clocks suffer from being extremely difficult to read, as the hands are lost against a background of intricate detail. Perhaps we should think of them as Victorian furnishing items, in company with the dried flowers, shells, stuffed birds and lustres, housed underneath glass domes; these were indispensable items of the Victorian interior, matching the general confusion of the furnishing fashions of the time.

CARRIAGE CLOCK
J. & A. Jump, London, c.1830–40

CARRIAGE CLOCK
Charles Frodsham, London, c. 1850–60

It is difficult to trace the exact ancestry of carriage clocks because clocks for travelling, with handles to carry them and special carrying cases, were made in England from the 17th century onwards. In design they owe something to the French 'pendules d'officier', adapted for military use in Napoleonic times, and most carriage clocks are of French manufacture, called by them pendules de voyage (p. 180). With this French ancestry one might think of them as the adaptation of the 'four glass' mantel clock to the needs of the traveller, with a watch-type escapement which would not be affected by movement, of small size and weight and with a handle for carrying. They were generally contained in a case of wood or leather. In spite of the countless thousands made in France, particularly during the last quarter of the 19th century and into the present, fine carriage clocks were made in England by the London trade. Two such are illustrated here, both by prominent makers.

The escapements of carriage clocks are placed on a horizontal platform at the top of the clock, seen through a glazed aperture. In most examples a door at the back gives access for winding, an exception being the Frodsham here, and sometimes they incorporate striking and repeat-work on bells, gongs or both, and sometimes alarms. The clock by the firm of *Joseph Jump*, who was articled in 1827 to *Benjamin Lewis Vulliamy*, shows a strong French influence in the Breguet-type hands (p. 181) and a Greek Revival quality in its proportions and style. The clock from the firm of *Charles Frodsham* (?–1871) has something of the revived Rococo, another style in vogue in the '50s and '60s. Wooden cases are rare in carriage clocks; most have brass frames, either lacquered or gilded according to quality, and like the skeleton clocks their movements can be seen through the glazed sides and back. Mostly rectangular, they are sometimes elaborately engraved on the outside casework and on the backplate of the movement.

IMITATION OAK GOTHIC TIMEPIECE
Exhibited 1851

CARVED WOODEN CLOCK
Bennett, London, exhibited 1851

The *Great Exhibition of 1851* saw the display of a wide range of clocks and watches, and four are illustrated from the official catalogue, two on this and two on the following page. It is important to remember, when considering these designs, that they were shown in a prestigious exhibition and should therefore be regarded as masterpieces of their kind and in that sense rather special. We can learn, however, what was admired at that time and the attitudes of our Victorian forbears. One point stands out very clearly indeed, that the originality and *design of the case* for a clock was the most important consideration, whatever the quality of the movement inside. In this way the Victorians were emulating the French, whose clocks, albeit often of fine quality, provided in many ways an excuse for the cabinet-maker and the sculptor (Ch. 9). Whatever we might think about Victorian taste and attitudes, they were to affect profoundly the approach to domestic clock design, from the mid-19th century onwards.

The 'Gothic' timepiece is so extraordinary and ill-proportioned to our eyes that it seems impossible that it should have been selected for the exhibition; its use of Gothic motifs could not be more incredibly deployed nor more structurally misunderstood, and its description as 'in imitation oak' must have infuriated such Gothic purists as John Ruskin. Mr. Bennett's carved wooden 'Elizabethan/ Jacobean' effort, described in the catalogue as showing 'some bold carving, executed with considerable taste . . .' is also conceived with the same misplaced historical zeal, and these are only two of a range of styles for domestic furniture from Byzantine to Gothic and Renaissance to Baroque, with a heavy admixture of Victorian Rococo! It is significant that the movements are never even mentioned, for the clockmaker was regarded as an artisan, not an artist, and the engineer deemed inferior to the architect. This is another example of the Victorian paradox, for the skeleton clocks we have seen show a completely reversed approach.

PARIAN CLOCK CASE
Charles Meigh & Son, Hanley, Staffs. exhibited
1851

METAL CLOCK CASE
G. R. & Henry Elkington, Birmingham, exhibited
1851

Ceramic materials had rarely been used for clock cases before the 19th century except for decorative details such as porcelain panels or figures on French clocks, or an occasional Wedgwood jasperware case in the Neo-Classical taste. The clock shown here, however, from the Crystal Palace in 1851, was made by *Charles Meigh & Son* of the Old Hall Works, Hanley, Staffordshire Potteries. The style of the case is mentioned in the catalogue as '. . . executed in statuary porcelain, copied, we believe, with some alterations from a French model'. It is more than likely that the clock movement itself was of French manufacture, for the English trade was absorbing large numbers of these standard and well-made clocks to put in English cases. The 'statuary porcelain' referred to is a type of porcelain known as '*Parian*', a hard, white, unglazed material much used in Victorian times for ornamental figures displayed, as the clock would have been, under a glass dome to keep it clean.

The metal-cased clock exhibited by the firm of *G. R. and Henry Elkington* of Birmingham is a different matter, for it is of considerable artistic merit and shows a technical innovation in clock case manufacture which developed in the 19th century. The process for making metal cases like this was known as *electrotyping*, a method using electrolytic deposits inside a mould from an original clay or wax model. The two Elkingtons had taken out a series of patents as early as 1836, 1837 and 1840 for *electro-plating* and *electro-gilding* and developed electrotyping at the same time. G. R. Elkington said about his discoveries 'This is one of those instances where Science, in her most exalted form, stoops to the aid of her sisters, Art and Manufacture . . .' and goes on '. . . the labour of the Sculptor, the skill of the Engraver, of the Modeller . . . may be in a few hours copied and multiplied with rigid accuracy and precision.' The original model for the clock was by John Bell.

CERAMIC CLOCK CASE
Doulton & Co., Lambeth, *c.*1875

WOODEN CLOCK CASE WITH PORCELAIN PLAQUES
Howell & James, London, *c.*1875

Both clocks shown here use ceramics in the construction of their cases. The first was made entirely of *pottery* and is from a model manufactured by the firm of *Doulton & Co.*, Lambeth, London, about 1875. This company produced several architectural cases constructed from moulds by casting techniques, the various parts being luted together before firing and glazing. The winged 'putti' or cherubs on each side of the case are from models designed by one of Doulton's most famous modellers, *George Tinworth* (1843–1913), who joined the company in 1866 after studying at the Lambeth School of Art. The case is coated with coloured glazes in ochre, blue, green and purple, the design reminding us of the heavy, Germanic style found in much late 19th century furniture. The clock itself is of German origin, for large numbers of mass-produced German movements were imported into England at this time. It is held in the case by metal rings and the numerals on the dial are Arabic. (Plate VIII, 23.)

Arabic numerals became increasingly popular on European clocks of the late 19th century, with a variety of designs used for the dial centres. Sometimes of *printed* or *painted* porcelain, and sometimes of thin, machine-stamped bràss sheet, the dials are instantly recognisable as dating from about 1870 to about 1910. The clock above, with high-pitched 'roof' ornamented as though tiled, is reminiscent again of German architecture and the case is constructed from ebonised wood with panels of blue and white porcelain to match the blue, white and gilded porcelain dial. This clock was designed by *Henry* and *Lewis F. Day* and made by the firm of *Howell and James* for sale to a discerning client, but with an imported movement. *Lewis F. Day* (1845–1910) was one of the great pioneers of industrial design, a contemporary of *William Morris* (1834–96) and yet unlike him in that instead of dreaming of the mediaeval world, he preferred to look *forward* to the world of 'machinery, steam-power and electricity' to quote his own words of 1882.

POTTERY WATCH STAND
Dixon, Austin & Co., Sunderland, c.1820

POTTERY 'FLATBACK' AS AN IMITATION CLOCK
Staffordshire, c.1865

Before leaving the link between ceramics and clocks, two more examples may be seen, the first an early 19th century *watch stand*, and the second is not a clock at all, merely an imitation but nevertheless of interest in the context of the 1860s. The watch stand is made in glazed earthenware, or *pearlware* as it is called, with orange, blue and sage-green painting under the glaze in a manner known as Prattware. It was made at the Garrison Pottery of *Dixon, Austin & Co.*, Sunderland, between 1820 and 1826, and is a stand in which a pocket watch could be placed at the end of a working day. The 'grandfather clock' on which it is modelled is in the proportion of the ones on pp. 128 and 129. Wooden watch stands with metal hooks or hinged, upright backs for the watch to lean against were imported from Switzerland in very large quantities later in the century to suit the same purpose.

The *imitation* clock perhaps hardly deserves a place in a book of this kind, yet with its gold painted dial it was made in many styles for the cottage mantelpiece or sideboard shelf. The example here dates from about 1865 and represents the preacher John Wesley in his pulpit, a figure very popular in the midlands and north of England, with the spread of Wesleyan Methodism. Here the Gothic tabernacle, introducing the relevant ecclesiastical note, is mixed with Rococo scrollwork on the base, and with the winged cherubs forms a primitive composition of humour and charm, the word 'Wesley' itself being in ornamental 'fairground' lettering style. With no modelling whatsoever on the reverse these Staffordshire ornaments are often called 'flatbacks'. They were never intended really to imitate clocks, but they added colour, warmth and character to the kitchen or parlour, and perhaps the stationary but salutary dial, linked with the preacher's admonishing hand, was a useful reminder of the passing of that precious commodity, time.

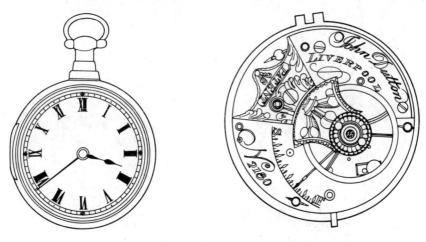

DIAL AND MOVEMENT OF A RACK LEVER WATCH
John Dutton, Liverpool, 1808–9

In dealing with watches we must return to the early years of the 19th century, to take up the story where it was left in Ch. 6. Some hint has been given of the precision work being done by the famous horologists (p. 116), of the introduction of the *cylinder escapement* (p. 122) and the *detent escapement* for chronometers and accurate watches (p. 133). Another form of horizontal escapement was devised in the 18th century known as the *duplex* (p. 42), perfected by *Pierre le Roy* in France and introduced into England in 1782 by *Thomas Tyrer*. The *lever escapement*, which is basic to all our spring wound watches today, was first made by *Thomas Mudge* about 1770 as an attempt to free the oscillations of the balance from continual interference by the escapement, and after much development this came to be used as the standard escapement for 19th century English watches. The *verge*, however, continued to be made until well into the century because of its simplicity of construction and reliability.

Meanwhile the *rack lever escapement* came into being, invented and patented in 1791 by *Peter Litherland* (1756–1804) who was born in Warrington and established a Liverpool business lasting into the 1870s. To some extent his work was based on that of *Jean Hautefeuille* (1647–1724), who had devised an early form of it in 1722. The watch shown above, signed *John Dutton* (working 1780 to 1829) of Liverpool, cased in 1808, is of the rack lever type, typical of many produced by Lancashire makers. The rack lever escapement has a curved, toothed *rack* on the inner end of the lever, engaging with a *pinion* on the balance staff. As the lever moves backwards and forwards, releasing the teeth of the escape wheel, the rack is both controlled by and gives impulse to the balance. For this reason the balance is *never* detached, but the escapement gives good service and is at least as accurate as a verge (p. 42). The shape of the balance cock is characteristic of rack lever watches.

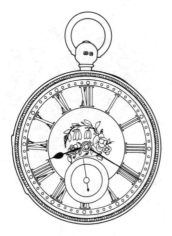 

DIAL AND BACK OF CASE OF AN ENGLISH SILVER WATCH
Unsigned, 1862–3

Numerous types of lever escapement were devised during the later years of the 18th century. Many, however, were of an experimental nature and as far as England is concerned it was the *detached lever escapement* of *Edward Massey* (1772–1852) of Coventry, which he introduced in 1815 which was to become the basis for all those used in English watches throughout the 19th century, except for the detent and duplex in precision work (Plate VIII, 25). One characteristic of the English lever is that it employed an escape wheel with what are known as 'ratchet' or *pointed teeth*, giving impulse only to the *pallets* of the lever, unlike the *club-toothed* escape wheel introduced by *Abraham Louis Breguet* and *Jean Moise Pouzait* and used on the Continent from the 1780s, where the impulse is divided between the pallets and the teeth of the wheel. Edward Massey is also to be credited with an early type of *keyless winding*, achieved by 'pumping' the pendant up and down with the thumb, patented in 1814.

The watch above is a typical English silver pocket watch of the mid 19th century (1862), employing the English lever escapement, the movement being hinged in the case and protected by a brass dust cover. It shows a variant of dial design in metal which takes us back, in spirit, to the 17th century (pp. 101–104), though the actual design is quite different. The raised *gold* numerals are *soldered* to the *silver* dial, which had previously been *engine-turned* with fine concentric circles on the chapter ring and radiating lines in the centre. A spray of leaves and flowers is engraved by hand at the centre of the dial, in true Victorian style, and the blued steel hands contrast well with the silver ground. The back of the case, which springs open on its hinge to give access for winding, is also engine-turned, with overlapping eccentric circles except for the Rococo shield and garter at the centre. This watch is almost $2\frac{1}{4}$ in. in diameter.

o (*above*). Pillar and scroll shelf clock, veneered case, painted lass tablet, wooden strap-frame movement, off-centre endulum; printed label of Seth Thomas, Connecticut, U.S.A., 1822–3. *Kenneth D. Roberts, Fitzwilliam, N.H.* 21 (*above ght*). Time Globe, manufactured by Juvet & Co., Canajoharie, ew York, U.S.A. The movement is inside the globe and the al at the top. The clock is wound by the tail of the arrow. verall height 35 in., *c.* 1880. *City Museum, Sheffield.* e (*right*). Orrery clock, month striking movement, spring detent scapement, the orrery showing relative positions of the sun, oon and earth throughout the year including annual calendar, ay of the week on the dial. Case of gilded bronze with four gures representing the seasons. Signed Raingo Frères à Paris, 1825. *City Museum, Sheffield.*

PLATE VIII

23 (*above left*). Mantel clock in a pottery case by the Della Robbia Pottery Company Ltd., Birkenhead, *c.* 1900. The movement is a conventional French timepiece. *City of Liverpool Museums.* 24 (*above*). Mantel clock in a silvered Britannia metal stand; Swiss movement signed Janin et Delarue, Geneva, *c.* 1900. *Faculty of Art and Design Galleries, Manchester Polytechnic.* 25a (*far left*). Silver pocket watch, English lever escapement with steel balance; signed Hornby, Liverpool. Hallmarked 1837–8. 25b (*left*). Gold pocket watch, English lever escapement with compensated balance; signed Chas. Lupton, Liverpool. Hallmarked 1853–4. *Private collection.* 26a (*below left*). Movement of a pocket watch; Elgin National Watch Company, U.S.A. 26b (*below centre*). Movement of a pocket watch; Lancashire Watch Company Ltd., Prescot, England. 26c (*below right*). Pocket watch, Lancashire Watch Company Ltd., Prescot, England. *Private collection.*

DIAL AND MOVEMENT OF AN ENGLISH LEVER WATCH
J. Preston & Co., Bolton, movement from
Wycherley's factory, Prescot, Lancashire, 1889–90

From at least as early as the beginning of the 18th century the Lancashire watchmakers, centred on Prescot near Liverpool, were making *rough movements* or *ébauches* for *finishing* in London and Liverpool and by the 19th century in other places, the most important being Coventry. The records of one of the many Prescot movement makers, Isaac Hunt & Co., show that this small workshop supplied movements of various grades to over four hundred different watchmaking firms from 1874 to 1896, at a time when the trade was in decline. The watch shown here, its case hall-marked at Chester in 1889–90, bears the signature of the Bolton retailer, but its movement was made by the firm of *John Wycherley* (1817–91) of Prescot, a pioneer in the making of standardised watch parts which could be interchanged and made to a standard gauge. Until almost the end of the century the Lancashire makers used their own special gauges, with consequent damage to their international trade.

Like the one on p. 142 this watch is a typical English lever, with late form of engraved balance cock, regulator index and gold balance. The enamelled dial is in three parts, chapter ring, centre and seconds dial, and as the centre and seconds are below the outer ring it is known as a *sunken dial*. The movement has its top plate *pinned* to the pillars, a tradition going back as early as watches were made. Other examples of about the same date are of *three-quarter plate* construction with *screws* to hold the plate in place, a method used in watchmaking ever since. Whereas the watch illustrated uses the balance traditionally *outside* the plate, the newer type has the balance recessed, the balance cock now being screwed to the pillar plate (cf. p. 166). This evolution is important as it helped in the problem of making watches thinner, and with the fusee beginning to disappear about the same time it heralds the style of watch movement used today.

ENGLISH DIAL CLOCK
Parkinson & Frodsham,
London, *c*.1825

ENGLISH TRUNK DIAL CLOCK
Prescot, Lancashire, *c*.1900

MARINE CLOCK
Prescot, Lancashire, *c*.1900

Many public buildings in the growing towns of the 19th century were provided with clocks known as *English dial*, manufactured in tens of thousands by firms in London, the midlands and the north. The earliest dial clocks date back to the 18th century and are in the continuing tradition of the tavern clock (p. 121), though the early ones, fitted with the short bob pendulum and verge, did not require a trunk below. With the early 19th century more popular use of the anchor escapement and pendulums longer than the height of the movement, a trunk was often fitted, sometimes with a glazed front door. The first dial clock shown has a silvered brass dial, its escapement being of the *platform* type as used in carriage clocks (p. 136), with a slot below XII for adjustment of the regulator. This London-made clock is otherwise quite conventional, with mahogany case, brass bezel and the whole front removable from the box at the back and held on to it with round wooden pegs.

The *trunk dial* clock made in Lancashire about 1900 illustrates the conservative tradition of these simple but dignified clocks. It was more cheaply made than the London clock of about 1825, with its *painted sheet zinc* dial, though many qualities of finish and casework were available, with double-dials, back or front winding, crown or plate glass fronts, fusees with chain, gut or wire, oak, walnut or mahogany cases, maintaining power and non-magnetic platform lever escapements if required—a useful alternative for generator rooms in power stations or ships. Another name sometimes used for these clocks is the English *'round head'*, and though once neglected because so common and plentiful, they are now creating a revival of interest. The brass-cased *marine clock* has always been something of a collectors' item and has much in common with the dial clock, being used in ship's saloons, dining rooms or on the bridge. As a sea-going clock it was invariably fitted with a lever type escapement and is usually smaller than the land-based dial.

ST. MARK'S CHURCH
Worsley, Sir George Gilbert Scott, 1846

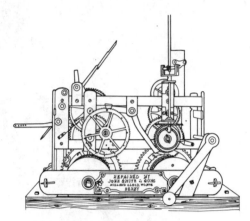

TURRET CLOCK
St. Mark's Church, Worsley, c.1840

Though not subject to changes of fashion, the construction of the *turret clock* evolved during the 19th century, making use of new techniques and new methods of lay-out. The clock shown here is from the first half of the 19th century, and is of the *chair frame* type, in that the wrought-iron frame, *bolted* together at the corners and *pegged* on the barrel bar, is roughly shaped like a chair, because the winding barrels are extended to allow for longer winding and running, while the arbors of the wheel trains above are conveniently short. With striking on the left and going on the right, the clock has steel arbors and pinions running in *brass bushed pivot holes*, a *pin-wheel escapement*, and drives four dials through the bevel gears to a four-way gear above (not shown). The lower bevel is also the *setting dial* and the diagonal arm at the front, on the right, is the gravity operated *maintaining power lever*, which must be lifted into action before the clock can be wound.

St. Mark's Church, Worsley, near Man-chester, was chosen partly because it is a good example of Sir George Gilbert Scott's Gothic Revival architectural style (1846) (p. 131), and also because the clock is of the chair frame structure. This clock was not originally made for the church, however, but was installed in the Duke of Bridgewater's works yard at Worsley in the 1840s, near the western terminus of the Bridgewater Canal. The workmen in the yard used to complain that although they could hear the clock strike twelve, they often missed the single stroke at one o'clock, after their dinner hour! To remedy this unsatisfactory situation the Duke had the clock altered to strike *thirteen* at one o'clock, and even though the movement was not placed in the parish church until 1946 its striking was left unaltered and it *still* strikes thirteen at one. This peculiar tradition was continued in another local clock on the Bridgewater Estate Offices, erected in near-by Walkden in 1867.

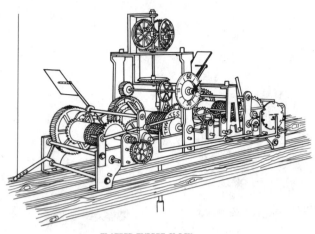

FLATBED TURRET CLOCK
Thwaites & Reed, Clerkenwell, *c.*1880

The tradition of building turret clocks from wrought-iron strips ended with the mid-19th century chair frame lay-out. A more convenient form was by this time taking its place—the *cast-iron flat bed* frame, consisting of a cast-iron base to which bars òf wrought iron are bolted carrying the pivot holes for the arbors of the wheel trains, now arranged in a *horizontal* position. There are advantages in this arrangement, the most important being that any faulty part could be removed from the frame with minimum disturbance to the rest of the clock. When the clock needed re-bushing, i.e. replacing the worn brass pivot holes, it was easier to do this by removing the short bars which contained them and working on the bench, than to work on the clock frame *in situ*. This form of construction might be compared with the *bar construction* of watches (shown in the American watch of 1907 on p. 167), a type of arrangement first introduced in France in 1770.

The example here is from an engraving of the clock installed by the London firm of *Thwaites and Reed* in the Knightsbridge Barracks, Kensington (1878–9). It has the going train in the centre, quarter striking on the right and hour striking on the left. The escapement is almost entirely hidden behind the barrel of the going train great wheel in the centre of the clock. The escapement was of the kind very widely used for turret work after its invention by *Edmund Beckett Denison* (1816–1901), otherwise known as *Lord Grimthorpe*, for his use in the great clock at Westminster built by the firm of E. J. Dent. Known as the *double three-legged gravity escapement* (p. 27), its principal virtue was that the impulse delivered to the pendulum was always quite independent of that normally transmitted through the train wheels of a clock in a conventional anchor escapement, the impulse being given by the action of two pivoted arms, lifted by the train but impulsing by the force of gravity.

ELECTRIC CLOCK WITH AN 'EARTH BATTERY'
Alexander Bain, c.1845

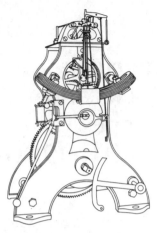

MASTER CLOCK
Sir Charles Wheatstone, c.1870

While the effects of magnetism had been observed in ancient times and some knowledge of the behaviour of electric currents had been obtained during the first half of the 18th century, it was not discovered until the early 19th century that electric currents, flowing through coils, could produce magnetic fields. This property of electricity made possible the first electric telegraph invented by *Sir Charles Wheatstone* (1802–75) in 1837, and in 1840 *Alexander Bain* (1810–77) was conducting experiments to drive clocks by electrically induced magnets. In 1843 he patented his first electric clock. Powered by Bain's newly-discovered 'earth battery' the current is supplied alternately to two coils on each side of a magnetised bar on the pendulum bob, thus giving regular impulses to keep the pendulum swinging. The sliding contacts half way up the pendulum rod deliver current alternately to the coils, and the 'clock' itself is moved forward, at each double swing of the pendulum, by a simple ratchet and pawl mechanism.

Although there are problems to this system, Alexander Bain was a man ahead of his time and the first to produce a working electric clock. At first encouraged by Wheatstone, difficulties soon arose as Wheatstone was working on similar problems himself. Bain's ideas had been leading him to solve the problem of simultaneously transmitting time from one place to another, in which he succeeded in 1846, for the *transmission of time* was perhaps the most important application of electrical power in these early years. By 1870 the British Telegraph Manufacturing Company was making clocks designed by Wheatstone to do just this; the one we see here is an ordinary weight-driven clock, the one-second pendulum having attached to it a coil swinging over a pair of horseshoe magnets. As the current is *induced* in the coils at each swing, the pendulum in effect becomes a dynamo generating alternating current which could be used to drive the dials of a series of clocks throughout a building, with this clock, therefore, becoming the 'master'.

8
American Clocks and Watches c. 1780 to 1900

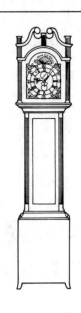

LONG CASE OR 'TALL' CLOCK
Daniel Burnap, East Windsor, Connecticut,
*c.*1785–90

The settlers of the 17th and early 18th centuries in North America took with them the clocks and watches they had used at home, or if sufficiently wealthy ordered them to be shipped from European makers. By about 1750, however, clockmaking had begun in the eastern seaboard area of the six New England states, New Hampshire, Vermont, Maine, Massachusetts, Rhode Island and Connecticut, as well as in certain parts of the vast area from New York and Pennsylvania to Virginia and the Carolinas. With a thinly dispersed population the demand was at first relatively small, most clockmakers combining their trade with furniture-making, tool-making or blacksmithing. In the 19th century, to meet the needs of the vastly expanded population in the east, new industrial techniques came into being to produce enormous numbers of cheap but reliable clocks, notably in Connecticut but also in Massachusetts. The American contribution to domestic clockmaking is of outstanding importance, both in solving old problems by new methods, and using old materials in new and unconventional ways.

Not too much is known about many of the humble American clockmakers of the early period, but the workshop and tools of three generations of the *Dominy family* of craftsmen from East Hampton, Long Island, New York, who combined clock-making with furniture-making from 1770 to 1868 may be studied at the Henry Francis du Pont Museum at Winterthur, Delaware, and the records and some of the clocks of *Daniel Burnap* (1759–1838), a fine maker of East Windsor, Connecticut, are preserved in the Connecticut Historical Society Museum at Hartford (see Bibliography). Daniel Burnap had been apprenticed to the English-born *Thomas Harland* (1735–1807) who settled in Norwich, Connecticut, and Burnap made many fine brass-movement clocks like the one shown here, its outline and proportions being of English long case style (p. 110) but of more simple lines, without the detailing of English quality cases of the time. Scarcity of both established craftsmen and expensive materials gave early American clocks an austere, primitive, yet attractive quality.

148

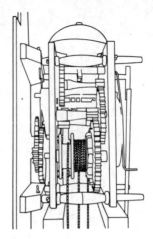

LONG CASE CLOCK AND WOODEN MOVEMENT
Alexander T. Willard, Ashby, Mass. *c.*1815

The clockmaking trade in the American colonies broadly developed in two areas, the more *southerly and westerly* following the line of the Delaware River and extending south to the Carolinas. Philadelphia was the centre for the fashionable trade, where fine furniture and clocks, such as those made by *David Rittenhouse* (1732–96), were made. The *New England school*, centred upon Boston, was to develop during the 19th century with the making of mass-produced clocks, though the early makers in that area were faced with the same problems as their southern neighbours. A shortage of clients amongst the settlers made full-time clockmaking hazardous, except in the larger towns; materials such as brass, iron and steel were short, tools had to be imported from Europe and vast distances had to be traversed with raw materials and finished goods. It is therefore not surprising to find that specialised parts such as completed dials were *imported* for the American makers, and complete clocks too for fitting in American-made cases.

The resourcefulness of early American clockmakers is illustrated in this clock, signed by *Alexander T. Willard* (1774–1850) of Ashby, Massachusetts. Its movement, apart from the escape wheel, pallets and a few other minor parts, is made entirely of *wood*, with wheels, pinions and arbors turned on the wood-lathe and fitted with steel pivots running in holes drilled in the *wooden plates*. Even the dial is of wood, painted on the front. The 30-hour movement has *divided barrels*; as the weight runs down from one half the cord for the *pull-winding* coils round the other, to be ready for winding again. This technique was used from time to time in 17th century Europe and the tradition for making wooden clocks with oak and maple plates no doubt came from southern Germany. The arched hood with triple spires is based on European lines except for the American type of cresting. When brass movements were made, superfluous parts of the plates were often cut away, to save precious brass.

BANJO CLOCK
Aaron Willard, Boston, Mass. *c*.1810

GALLERY CLOCK
Simon Willard, Roxbury, Mass. *c*.1810

The history of the American long case clock still presents many difficulties, one of the main problems being to assess just how much of the clock movement was American-made and whether or not the dials and hands were imported, for the early clockmakers must certainly have found it cheaper and more convenient to order such parts from abroad. The clocks above, however, by *Simon and Aaron Willard*, illustrate a clock type which, in the *banjo case* at least, is pure American, though the *gallery clock* shows a good deal of French influence, of the Empire period (p. 176). *Simon Willard* (1753–1848) was born in Grafton, Massachusetts and moved to Roxbury, a suburb of Boston, about 1778, where he set up his clock-making business. After experimenting with the production of inexpensive clocks, as did his brother *Aaron Willard*, he patented his banjo clock in 1802, introducing what has since become perhaps the most collectable of American clocks—a style of case much copied by Willard's contemporaries in spite of the patent.

The banjo clock contains a simple rectangular movement, housed in the circular top; the long *neck* or trunk accommodates the heavy *weight* and pendulum rod, and the square box below allows the pendulum bob to swing in front, kept separate from the weight by a thin metal sheet. The glazed panels, or *glass tablets*, are back-painted with pretty linear designs and flowers. The curved *brass frets* on each side give a splendid 'line' to the handsome proportions of the case. Sumptuously decorated banjo clocks with circular boxes at the base are often known as *girandoles*. Simon Willard's name will always be associated with the banjo and he is remembered too for the clocks he made for the U.S. government, one of which was designed to fit a case of pure French Empire taste made by the sculptor *Carlo Franzoni* in 1819 for the Capitol, Washington. He also patented in 1822 a mantel clock in the form of a *lighthouse*, with a movement similar to that of the banjo.

LYRE CLOCK
Aaron Willard, Boston, Mass. c.1820

SQUARE BOX BANJO CLOCK
Howard & Davis, Boston, Mass. c.1841

Simon Willard's brother, *Aaron Willard* (1757–1844) appears to have been the more determined of the two to make a commercial success of clockmaking, and in the early 1790s he set up a clock factory on a narrow strip of land at that time joining Boston with the mainland, known as the Neck. He retired a wealthy man in 1823, and the new production methods and reduction in costs which his factory made possible were to affect 19th century clockmaking in America. One model which he introduced in Boston, a variant of the banjo type, is the *lyre clock* seen here, similar in form to the banjo but with carved curving sides and a pendant-shaped bracket below. The features of this particular style remind us of the Greek Revival in English architecture of the early 19th century, a form at the time most popular in banks, churches and similar public buildings in the U.S.A. The heavily carved lyre has a French appearance too, especially in the foliate finial, and indicates that America was to enter on a period of widely derived styles of clock case design.

Aaron Willard's only son, *Aaron Willard Jnr.* (1783–1864) took over his father's business in 1823 and one of his apprentices was *Edward Howard* (1813–1904) (pp. 162, 164, 167). One of Howard's fellow apprentices was *David P. Davis*, whom he got to know well, and after a brief period in the firm of Henry Plimpton, a manufacturer of coin balances, he entered into partnership with David P. Davis and *Luther Stephenson* to form the firm of *Stephenson, Howard & Davis*, manufacturing balances, church clocks, regulators and Willard-type timepieces. The firm was later known as *Howard & Davis*, and so firmly implanted had the banjo type become that Howard continued to make them, as in the one shown here, with black back-painted *glass tablets* and *gold lining*. This square-box example, which might have been somewhat altered from its original form, was followed by Howard clocks with *curved sides* to the pendulum box; the Breguet-type hands are an indication of a date early in the 1840s.

  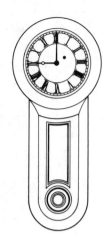

CLOCKS FROM THE HOWARD WATCH AND CLOCK
COMPANY, ROXBURY, MASS.
c.1870

a. Figure 8 timepiece   b. Marble dial clock   c. 'Keyhole' case clock

In 1857 David P. Davis left the firm and Edward Howard carried on the manufacture of clocks and watches at Roxbury under the name of the *Howard Watch & Clock Co.* Although Edward Howard himself retired in 1882 the firm is still continuing in business, though now only making turret clocks in the name of Howard Clock Products, Inc., since 1934. The watch-making venture which Howard & Davis undertook with *Aaron L. Dennison* (1812–95) between 1854 and 1857 at Waltham, under the name of the *Boston Watch Co.* belongs to later pages (164–5). The three clocks here from Edward Howard's factory in Roxbury are illustrated from the firm's 1874 catalogue and they serve to show the continuing development of what had begun with the Willard type banjo, for all three are *wall clocks* with the same basic kind of weight-driven movement, though the cases have evolved in different ways. Interesting too is the fact that the banjo case was still manufactured in the 20th century.

The *figure 8 timepiece*, of polished black walnut, was extremely well made in Howard's cabinet-making department. The glazed neck has a black ground with gold lining, as has the circular base, within which the swinging pendulum bob 'blinks' like an eye. The large *marble* clock, 3 ft. 6 in. high with a dial diameter of 2 ft., was advertised as suitable for public halls or buildings. The heavy marble dial, about 1 in. thick, is screwed to the long wooden box behind, which holds the movement and pendulum, the numerals and minute circle being painted on to the marble and completely unglazed. The *keyhole* design clock, has a cherry wood case, glass-fronted trunk and wooden bezel. All the movements are of 8-day duration and may be thought of as the American equivalent of the English *dial clock* (p. 144), and like them are seen with retailers' names upon the dials, not the name of the manufacturer. Unlike many American clocks of the period they were not exported in large numbers and are not often seen in England.

WALL-BRACKET CLOCK
Simon Willard, Grafton, Mass. *c.*1775–80

SHELF CLOCK
Aaron Willard, Roxbury, Mass. *c.*1815

To return to the 18th century and Simon Willard (p. 150) we look at the American Massachusetts tradition of the *bracket* or *mantel* clock, known better in America as the *shelf clock*. The one by Simon Willard is strictly a *wall-bracket* clock, for the case stands on a wall-mounted bracket, with space inside it for pendulum and weights —a spring-driven clock is rare to find in America until the 1840s. This particular clock, with phases of the moon, has a *kidney-shaped dial*, echoing the *balloon case* clock (p. 130) which is partly French inspired; the inward scrolling 'feet', in continuing the lines of the dial, also echo European taste, but in a much more simple vein, with American scrolled *fret* to crown the design. A simple timepiece designed in this way, resting on a hollow bracket for weights and pendulum is almost, if not entirely, unknown in Europe. It was also constructed with a base to stand on a level surface, known as the Massachusetts *shelf* or *half clock*.

In this Aaron Willard example the clock and bracket are designed as one unit, to stand on a shelf and therefore known as a *true* shelf clock. Early 19th century influence may be seen in the Arabic numerals on the dial and the Empire style cast brass 'lion's paw' feet. Characteristic also is the glazed case door and front of the base, both elaborately back-painted with stencilled leaves and flowers, an oval *cartouche* in the upper door with the name 'Aaron Willard, Roxbury'. In the painting on the bottom glass tablet are two young girls with a birdcage in a garden; the style of their dresses and hair alone would help to date this clock. Banjo clocks, shelf clocks and the *pillar and scroll* are the most distinctive of American designs, made when the hand-craft tradition was coming to an end but before the onset of industrial production. At the same time *miniature* long case or 'tall' clocks were occasionally made, known as *dwarf* clocks and reaching about 4 ft. high.

PILLAR AND SCROLL CLOCK
Eli and Samuel Terry, Plymouth, Connecticut,
*c.*1825

'WHALES TAIL' PILLAR AND SCROLL CLOCK
Samuel Terry, Plymouth, Connecticut, *c.*1828

The *pillar and scroll* shelf clock, driven by weights descending down the sides, shows an American form of mantel clock unique to that country, and though never made directly for export was the ancestor of clocks which came to Europe in their thousands. With slender and elegant *side pillars,* bevelled *veneering,* *maker's labels* pasted inside, *back-painted tablets,* simple fret-cut *bracket feet* and *skirt,* the crowning glory is the *scrolled pediment* and *finials* of the first example, and the imaginative *'whales tail' scrolling* of the second. The key figure in the development of these clocks was *Eli Terry* (1772–1852) who was born at East Windsor, Connecticut, becoming apprenticed to Daniel Burnap (p. 148), who taught him the making of tall clocks, both with expensive brass movements and with much cheaper wooden ones (p. 149). In the early 1790s Eli Terry left East Windsor and moved to Northbury, now called Plymouth, a few miles north of Waterbury, where he started to make wooden movements.

By 1806, his business flourishing, Terry moved to an old water-mill which he turned into a water-powered factory for making wooden clock movements. Having contracted with Edward and Levi Porter of Waterbury to supply them with four thousand tall clock wooden movements, he completed the deal between 1807 and 1809. In 1810 he sold the plant to *Seth Thomas* (1774–1859), (pp. 161, 162, 163) and *Silas Hoadley* (1786–1870) and by the end of 1812 he acquired another site on the Naugatuck River to make wooden or brass movement shelf clocks, obtaining a patent in 1816. The earliest of these had *strap-frame* movements in a rectangular box, called a *box-case,* and by 1818 Eli, with his younger brother *Samuel,* was making wooden clocks with brass escapement wheels *outside* the dial, known as *'outside escapement'* followed by the *'outside-inside escapement',* i.e. outside the front movement plate but behind the dial. Terry made a wide range of pillar and scroll variants, both 30-hour and 8-day, copied by numerous makers (Plate VII, 20).

BRONZED LOOKING-GLASS CLOCK
Jerome & Darrow, Bristol, Conn. *c.*1830

EMPIRE STYLE CLOCK WITH GILDED COLUMNS
Jerome & Darrow, Bristol, Conn. *c.*1830

The next man of stature in American clockmaking was *Chauncey Jerome* (1793–1868), who originally made cases for Terry's shelf clocks in 1816. Leaving Terry he went into business himself, moving to Bristol, Connecticut, in 1821, and by 1827 had formed a partnership with *Elijah Darrow*, known as *Jerome & Darrow*. Manufacturing shelf clocks of the 8-day type, and by 1827 the *bronzed looking-glass clock* (though not the originator of these as sometimes stated), Jerome incorporated ivory or brass bushes for the pivots in his wooden movement plates in the 1820s. By the late 1830s Chauncey Jerome was completely absorbed with his production of cheap, 30-hour *brass movements* which were easier to make and more reliable than wood. Although wood continued to be used for some movements until the late 1840s Chauncey Jerome's cheap brass ones, designed by his brother *Noble Jerome*, laid the foundation for the future Connecticut clock industry.

The two clocks here are both by Jerome & Darrow of Bristol, Connecticut, and retain the proportions of the Empire style. The term *bronzed* refers to the cheap bronze powders used for *stencilling* designs on the top splats and sometimes on the columns, in place of the more expensive gold leaf used earlier. The term *looking-glass* was used until about the end of the 19th century, when clocks of this sort began to be called *mirror clocks*. The Empire clock, with its heavy gilded half-columns shows a decline both in proportion and quality when compared with the scroll and pillar clocks, and sometimes such clocks were of 'three-deck' design. The half-columns, like those on the so-called 'Vienna regulators' (p. 186) were made from lathe-turned pillars sawn down the middle, glued on to the case and lavishly gilded. Though we are seeing a cheapening and lowering of standards, clocks of this kind were filling a genuine need; although inexpensive they were reliable and attractive.

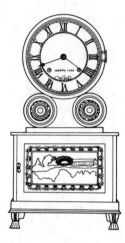

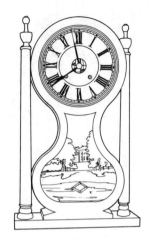

EMPIRE STYLE WAGON-SPRING SHELF CLOCK
Joseph Ives, Brooklyn, New York, c.1825–30

'HOUR GLASS' SHELF CLOCK
Joseph Ives, Plainville, Farmington, Conn. c.1840

Joseph Ives (1782–1862) also started in the wooden movement business, at Forestville on the opposite side of Bristol from Plymouth, in 1811. One feature of the tall clock movements made though not invented by Ives is the *roller pinion*, a type of *lantern pinion* (p. 21) in which the 'leaves' are rollers, designed to reduce friction and transmit power smoothly. In 1812 Ives sold the Forestville site and moved into North Village, Bristol, which he sold in 1818 moving to South Village. In the same year he applied for a patent for a *metal* movement clock to be cased in a tall, narrow *looking-glass case*, which was granted in 1822. Ives moved to Brooklyn, but was back in Bristol by 1830, having made while away 8-day brass clock movements powered by cantilever-operated springs, i.e. cantilevers tensioned by a *wagon-leaf spring* across the bottom of the case. The first clock is an example, the spring being in the wide part of the base with one half operating the striking and the other the going train.

The movements of these clocks were of strip brass frames, riveted together and pinned to the pillars, using roller-type metal pinions. Ives made rapid advances in making brass and steel movements, wrought brass being available in Waterbury. Blanking presses, gear cutters and other specialised machines formed the basis of his mass-production techniques. Empire style cases and three-decker cases were used to house the clocks and the eventual development was the Joseph Ives rectangular *O.G. style case* (p. 159). About 1839 Ives moved to Plainville, east of Bristol, and between 1839 and 1842 made the *hour-glass clock* in which the power was provided by *coiled springs and fusees*, though arranged differently from the English pattern. A little earlier Ives had introduced a coiled spring power unit to fit to conventional wooden clock movements. Whereas a single bell had been the normal form of striking before, in clocks by Ives the *coiled wire gong* was coming into use, later to be universal in cheap American clocks.

'ACORN' SHELF CLOCK
Forestville Manufacturing Company, Bristol, Conn.
c.1845

TWIN FINIAL, SHARP GOTHIC WAGON-SPRING CLOCK
Birge & Fuller, Bristol, Conn. c.1845

A number of manufacturers in Connecticut were experimenting with and making brass movement clocks, made possible by the introduction of brass rolling mills at Waterbury. By the 1830s three firms in Bristol were producing 8-day brass movements, one being the *Forestville Manufacturing Company* of *J. C. Brown* (1807–72), the firm which made the *acorn clock* shown here, a much-illustrated though rather rare type of spring and fusee-driven clock made about 1845. The two springs were mounted in a wooden block inside the wide curving base, with long cords to the great wheel barrels of the movement, the pendulum swinging in front. This attractive clock was only one type of the long tradition of Connecticut clock-making in the early days of the strip brass movement. A smaller version of the 'acorn' type was marketed by J. C. Brown in 1848, without the side stalks and with fusee spring barrels placed just below and to left and right of the movement, the wide base unoccupied except for the pendulum.

By the 1840s the Connecticut makers were producing thousands of clocks and were nothing if not original in developing their product. As the Gothic taste had become so popular in England (pp. 112, 131), so the Gothic phase became implanted in America, one result being the *sharp Gothic clock*, aptly called because of its pointed gable and pinnacles. Somehow the Romantic era of Gothic sprang to life in the United States about 1835 to 1840, perhaps as a reaction to the Greek or Roman architectural style formerly thought ideal for the new Republic. Hardly understood from a structural point of view, American Gothic was but surface decoration on the vernacular style, a kind of 'carpenter Gothic' where the motifs were mixed with clapboard structures to produce buildings of wonderful charm. So the Gothic case was but a container for the 8-day brass movement, in this example powered by a wagon spring in the base, from *Birge & Fuller* (1844–8) of Bristol, Connecticut.

SHARP GOTHIC FUSEE SHELF CLOCK
Smith & Goodrich, Bristol, Conn. c.1850

ROUND GOTHIC 'RIPPLED' CLOCK
J. C. Brown, Bristol, Conn. c.1850

The sharp Gothic clock shown here is by the firm of *Samuel B. Smith and Chauncey Goodrich* of Bristol, Connecticut, working between 1848 and 1856 and formerly partners with J. C. Brown of the Forestville Manufacturing Company. K. D. Roberts (see Bibliography) gives statistics for this and many other firms. The capital invested in the enterprise was $25,000, employing thirty hands and retailing clocks to the annual value of $60,000. In so doing the company consumed an annual average of 20 tons of brass, 300,000 ft. of timber and mahogany to the value of $2,500. This represented an output of about 30,000 clocks in the year 1849–50, the total number of clocks from eleven Bristol firms in that year being 187,500. In 1854 Braithwaite Poole of Liverpool wrote: 'American clocks are imported from the United States by almost every vessel, in small boxes containing dozens or half dozens . . . the number of boxes brought to Liverpool last year amounted to upwards of 8,000, and the clocks 60,000, weight 300 tons, value £30,000.'

This trade continued unabated through the rest of the century and few working-class homes in England were without an American timepiece, with a gradual but disastrous effect on English clockmaking, while the same thing happened in watch-making too (pp. 164–7). The *'rippled'* *Gothic clock* from the firm of J. C. Brown was another design used also by the Bristol firm of *Brewster and Ingrahams* (p. 160) containing an 8-day brass movement, the rippled effect on the arch, bezel and door frame being produced by *pressing* the wood. This was done either between dies or through engraved rollers, both methods being capable of turning out large quantities of moulding at very low cost, used not only on clocks but also on furniture and mirror frames for the popular market. Another change may be noticed in the frosted glass treatment of the lower case door, with laurel-leaf designs mechanically produced by stencil etching, in contrast with the attractive coloured back painting of earlier days.

O.G. STYLE WEIGHT-DRIVEN CLOCK
Ansonia Clock Company, Brooklyn, New York,
c.1880-90

SPRING-DRIVEN MANTEL CLOCK
William L. Gilbert Clock Company,
Winchester, Conn. c.1880

Most manufacturers of the brass movement clocks of Connecticut were located in Bristol and nearby towns; these included the Litchfield Manufacturing Company, the New Haven Clock Company and the Waterbury Clock Company. The clocks illustrated here are from the *Ansonia Clock Company*, established at Ansonia, near Derby between 1851 and 1878, and the *William L. Gilbert Clock Company* of Winchester. The Ansonia clock, made when the firm had moved to Brooklyn, New York (1879–c.1930), is one of the ubiquitous O.G. clocks, so-called because the moulding round the case is of ogee section, i.e. a continuous curve part concave part convex. The movement is of 30-hour brass type, made about 1880 or later, and in form it is still a shelf clock though quite convenient for hanging on a wall. The clock is powered by weights hidden on both sides of the case interior, and as in all these American clocks the painted dial is *fixed to the case* and not to the movement.

Gradual cheapening of these popular American clocks is illustrated by the decorated glass panel of the Ansonia clock. Whereas in the shelf clock by Aaron Willard (p. 153) or the early pillar and scroll clock (p. 154) the glass panels are *painted*, in the Ansonia panel the designs are *transferred*, the blossoms and birds done first in stencilled gold and the cupid in the cartouche printed from a *transfer* or *decal*, leaving the blue and white backgrounds to be painted quickly by hand. The mantel or shelf clock from the William L. Gilbert Company is decorated with a *lithographic transfer*, another popular mass-production technique. The Gilbert clock is also spring-driven and therefore somewhat smaller in height than the Ansonia. Although so cheaply made it is astonishing how long many of these clocks have lasted and will perform quite well, with sloppy pivots, worn pinions and having had hardly any maintenance. William L. Gilbert (1806–90) was very successful in his clock business; the firm which bears his name lasted from 1866 to 1934.

 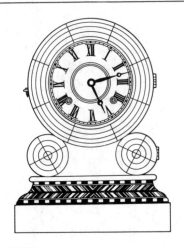

SPRING–DRIVEN MANTEL CLOCKS,
ELIAS INGRAHAM & COMPANY, BRISTOL, CONN. *c.*1880

Venetian No. 3 pattern   Grecian Mosaic pattern

Elias Ingraham (1805–85) was originally apprenticed to the cabinet-making trade and his major contribution to American clockmaking was his designing of new cases. It is said that he was responsible for the original 'round Gothic' and 'sharp Gothic' cases, in 1841 and 1844 respectively, though these styles became widely used by many makers. A newspaper account, discovered by K. D. Roberts, tells how Ingraham purchased the factory of one Josiah Davis, where clocks and cases were made in parts to be shipped to Macon in Georgia and assembled there. The southern states had raised licensing fees so high for manufactured goods that it amounted to prohibition for the 'Yankee clock peddlers'; goods made in Georgia, however, could be sold without licence and the northerners therefore sent men there to complete clocks from the parts and thus avoid the fees. Ingraham was in partnership with his brother Andrew and Elisha C. Brewster as *Brewster & Ingrahams* from 1843 until 1852, with *Epaphroditus Peck* (1811–57) as European agent.

Between 1847 and 1850, Brewster & Ingrahams made a brass clock movement powered by springs set in cast-iron cups, fixed directly to the great wheel arbors, without fusees, then finally without spring retainers at all, the forerunner of cheap brass clocks today. Following a number of setbacks from 1852, *Elias Ingraham & Company* was established in Bristol in 1859, Elias continuing to design new cases such as those shown here. Both are striking mantel clocks with similar spring-driven movements of 30-hour or 8-day duration, pendulum controlled. Their names give some idea of the variety of styles which Ingraham used, others in his catalogue being Ricarda, Crystal, Huron, Dakota, Arctic, Britannia, Baltic, Idaho, Empire and various forms of Doric, Ionic, Grecian and Venetian. About 1880 polished black walnut cases were made by Ingraham to compete with black marble cases imported from France.

OFFICE CALENDAR CLOCK
Seth Thomas Clock Company, Plymouth Hollow,
Conn. *c.*1880

PARLOUR CALENDAR CLOCK
Seth Thomas Clock Company, Plymouth Hollow,
Conn. *c.*1880

Seth Thomas (1785–1859) of Wolcott, Connecticut, came to Plymouth with Silas Hoadley to work for Eli Terry and subsequently bought the business in 1810 (p. 154). Seth Thomas was a good businessman, an entrepreneur who took advantage of the possibilities, but who did not seek to improve or change things unless forced to do so by competition. After three years with Hoadley, Thomas set out on his own and obtained the rights from Eli Terry to make the pillar and scroll, with wooden movements, which he continued in the split column models after about 1830 and ceased to make about 1844, having obtained from Chauncey Jerome information for making the new brass movements, which he began in 1842. At Plymouth Hollow he formed the *Seth Thomas Clock Company* in 1853, after establishing rolling mills there for brass, copper and other metals the year before. Seth Thomas clocks achieved high reputation in their day and the firm still continues, though now incorporated as part of the General Time Corporation. (Plate VII, 20.)

Two *calendar clocks* shown here were made by the Seth Thomas Clock Company from the 1860s to the mid 1880s, the one on the left being designed for the office, but that on the right as a 'parlour' clock. To avoid complications both are weight-driven timepieces only, with calendar mechanisms arranged in the lower part of the case. The calendar work is controlled by rods from the movement, the day in the left aperture and the month in the right being actuated automatically, and arranged on horizontal barrels which turn backwards when changing. The calendars are fully *perpetual*, the various lengths of the months being accounted for including the 29th day of February every Leap Year. It is likely that these clocks, made by several firms including the Ithaca Company of New York and mostly displaying the calendar on a separate lower dial, were the American answer to the French perpetual calendar clocks of the 19th century, and they have a pleasing, business-like air.

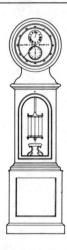

REGULATOR CLOCK
Howard Watch & Clock Company, Roxbury,
Massachusetts, c.1870

DOMESTIC REGULATOR CLOCK
Seth Thomas Clock Company, Plymouth Hollow,
Conn. c.1870

Edward Howard's early career has already been mentioned (pp. 151, 152) in connection with his clock factory at Roxbury, and this Boston, Massachusetts, firm made good quality clocks, carrying out the founder's wishes for reliability and durability. The Howard clocks should not be compared with the cheap, mass-produced products of Connecticut as they were mostly for a different market, which is not to condemn the Connecticut clocks, made to fill a different need. Howard's movements, with traditional brass plates, pillars and wheel trains have long given good service and an example of his very high quality clocks, illustrated here, is a *regulator* (compare p. 132), retailing in 1874 at $525.00. Controlled by a *mercurial pendulum*, the mercury is in four bottles instead of the single glass bottle of Graham type (pp. 28, 100), for in temperature changes the mercury in the slender bottles responds more quickly than in a single, wide one. The mahogany case, of extremely simple and elegant Classical design, matches its dignified purpose.

The clock shown here from the Thomas factory, of about 1870, is not correctly a regulator in spite of the name on the trunk, but simply a good quality domestic or office clock. It is curious that this kind of clock should have acquired the name regulator, for although often fitted with a good escapement, its wooden pendulum, mode of construction and striking train could never allow it to perform with the accuracy of the real thing, though the timekeeping could be good by domestic standards. It is more than likely that the name originated to *suggest* the quality and performance of a real regulator, and perhaps because of the influence of the 'Vienna regulators' from Austria and Germany, with which they were competing. The Vienna regulator style was, in fact, copied in America by the Howard Watch & Clock Company and others, sometimes in extremely elaborate cases (p. 186). The twelve-sided shape of this Seth Thomas clock is similar to that of the calendar clock from the same firm (p. 161).

TOWER CLOCK AND STAND
Seth Thomas Clock Company, Thomaston, Conn.
*c.*1874

TWO DIAL STREET CLOCK
Seth Thomas Clock Company, Thomaston, Conn.
*c.*1875

The construction of *tower* or *turret* clocks in the 18th and early 19th centuries followed the European tradition, though turret clocks with *wooden movements* were made, such as the one now preserved at the American Clock and Watch Museum in Bristol, Connecticut. This was made by *Samuel Terry* (1774–1853) brother of Eli Terry (p. 154), and given to the Congregational Church in Bristol in 1832, where it kept time until about 1923. By the second half of the 19th century, however, industrial capacity made possible the casting of large components for turret clock frames, such as the one shown here from Seth Thomas's clock factory at Thomaston, near Plymouth, Connecticut, about 1874. This clock is a timekeeper only, the *pendulum crutch* hanging in front of the *setting dial*, with the 50-lb. iron bob for the 4-ft. pendulum shown lying below, complete with winding handle and four-way gearing to transmit the action of the clock to four tower dials, each dial having its own motion work.

The *stencilled gold flower sprays* and *lining* on the turret clock add that touch of decoration which late 19th century makers felt necessary to give 'finish' to their products. The Seth Thomas Clock Company bought out the firm of *A. S. Hotchkiss & Company*, manufacturers of turret clocks between 1865 and 1868, *Andrew S. Hotchkiss* remaining on the staff for the tower clock work. The New York agents for Seth Thomas (and other Connecticut clockmakers) was the *American Clock Company*, seen inscribed on the *street clock* with two dials facing up and down the street on a cast-iron column of heavy Classical design. The movement for this street clock would be housed in a building alongside, with its power to the dials transmitted under the sidewalk and up the column through sets of bevel gears. The sidewalk clock was a pure American style, equated in England by many clocks supported on brackets outside building façades, or erected in ornamental towers at important street crossings.

MOVEMENT OF A WATCH
Luther Goddard, Shrewsbury, Mass. *c*.1815

WATCH MOVEMENT
Howard & Davis, Waltham, Mass. *c*.1855

In America in the 18th century, watch-making was practically non-existent, such watches as do appear with American names probably having been made up from English ébauches. Similarly watch cases, a very specialised manufacture, were frequently imported and many early 'American' watches occur in English hall-marked cases. After 1800, however, with the importation of large numbers of English watches, impetus was given to the American trade coinciding with mechanical and metallurgical developments in Connecticut. Perhaps the first Connecticut maker was *Thomas Harland* (1735–1807), a clockmaker who is known to have had a watch factory which produced about 200 movements in 1802. The embargo on trade by both Britain and America from 1806 to 1814 stimulated *Luther Goddard* (1762–1842) to start a small factory in Shrewsbury, Massachusetts, but in appearance those watches which survive are so similar to English ones that it is hard to believe that they were not made from English ébauches (p. 141).

The real beginnings of the American watchmaking story are concerned with the meeting of Edward Howard and Aaron L. Dennison (p. 152) and their partnership about 1851, first known as the *American Horologe Company*, then the *Warren Manufacturing Company*, becoming the *Boston Watch Company* in 1854. These beginnings took place in the *Howard & Davis* factory at Roxbury but space being insufficient they moved to a site at Waltham in 1853 where a series of problems held up production, forcing bankruptcy in 1858 and sale of the assets to *Tracey & Baker*, a Philadelphia watch-case making firm. The watch movement above shows how closely they followed the English tradition at this stage, the narrow, straight-sided balance cock being exactly similar to contemporary English ones, with full-plate movement and large 'Liverpool' type jewels set in separate *chatons*. The *difference* was that Howard and Dennison were making their movements on a standardised basis and using as much automatic machinery as possible.

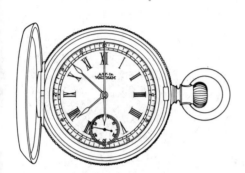

CENTRE SECONDS CHRONOGRAPH
American Watch Company, Waltham, Mass. c.1885

'B. W. RAYMOND' WATCH MOVEMENT
Elgin National Watch Company, Illinois,
introduced 1867

The introduction of automatic machinery by Howard and Dennison was the turning point of Anglo-American trade, for whereas previously England had exported large quantities of hand-made watches to America, from the middle of the century onwards the tide was to turn and new American factories, organised on a large scale and making standardised watch parts by machinery, sent ever increasing numbers of watches to England. This was eventually to ruin the English trade except for high quality work (pp. 130, 143). Two or three attempts were made in England to introduce American methods, but all were more or less abortive, the longest lasting being the *Lancashire Watch Company* (1889–1910), established in Prescot using American-made machinery and production methods, but hamstrung by deep-rooted prejudices against the new ideas. The designs of some of the movements made by this factory are almost indistinguishable from those produced in U.S.A. (Plate VIII, 26.)

The history of the American watch factories is a confusion of many firms starting enthusiastically and becoming bankrupt or changing hands after a few years, or even before the actual production of watches had begun. Two of those which were successful, however, were the *American Watch Company*, which became the *American Waltham Watch Company* in 1885 and which had its beginnings in the move to Waltham by Howard and Dennison, and the *Elgin National Watch Company* near Chicago, Illinois (see Bibliography). The first watch illustrated is a Waltham centre-seconds *chronograph* in a hunter case of about 1885, while the second shows the movement of a watch from Elgin of about 1869, of conventional English full-plate lay-out, but including an American device known as a *patent* or *safety pinion*, in which the centre wheel pinion is *screwed* to its arbor and which would come undone and prevent further damage if the mainspring broke.

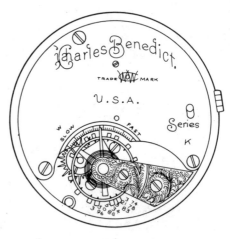

ROTARY WATCH
Waterbury Watch Company, Waterbury,
Connecticut, c.1885

'CHARLES BENEDICT' WATCH MOVEMENT
Waterbury Watch Company, Connecticut, c.1892

The Elgin National Watch Company began to manufacture in 1864 and finished production of men's watches in 1964. The Waltham factory under various names began about 1850, if we take into account the *American Horologe Company* of Howard, Davis and Dennison, and manufactured watches until 1957; the name still exists in a retailing agency. Many American firms introduced new ideas, such as the *Auburndale Watch Company* of Auburndale, Massachusetts, where *Jason R. Hopkins* attempted to put into production his patent for a 'rotary' watch about 1875, designed to sell at 50¢. The idea was that the movement would revolve inside the case once each hour, carrying the minute hand with it. Controlled by a straight-line lever escapement and of simple construction, the idea was excellent for it is possible to compensate in this way for positional errors, although the Auburndale watch itself was too cheap and rough to benefit from this refinement. The venture was a failure but the idea was revived a few years later, at Waterbury.

The *Waterbury Watch Company* came into being in 1878 when *D. A. Buck* persuaded the Waterbury manufacturer *Charles Benedict* to invest in the production of a rotary watch to his design of only fifty-eight parts, counting every last screw and the case. Like the Auburndale, the movement rotated once an hour, but to save wheelwork it was powered by a spring about 9 ft. long which took an incredibly long time to wind. The early movements were *skeletonised* (p. 135) and could be seen through the open dial, but about 1885 a new model of conventional arrangement was introduced, the rotary model also being in production until 1891. These watches were cheap at $3.50 and all employed a form of the *duplex* escapement; the illustration above shows the movement of a model called the *Charles Benedict* (about 1892) with three-quarter plate movement and separate balance cock. In 1898 the firm became known as the *New England Watch Company*, this in turn being taken over by *Robert H. Ingersoll & Brothers* in 1914.

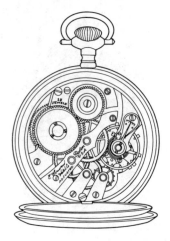
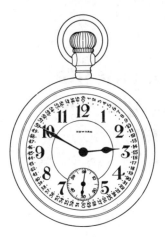

RAILROAD WATCH MOVEMENT AND DIAL
E. Howard Watch Company, Waltham, Mass.
*c.*1910

After the failure of Howard and Dennison's enterprise for making watches at Waltham in 1858, Edward Howard returned to Roxbury where his clock factory was still in production, and revived the *Boston Watch Company* which he had started in 1854, though the name was now changed to *E. Howard & Company*; Aaron L. Dennison interested himself in other ventures and eventually started a watch-case making business in Birmingham, England. The watches Howard produced were of very fine make, for unlike the Connecticut firms who were bringing down costs in both clocks and watches, Howard pursued the ideals of quality and reliability as he did in his clocks. He introduced new features such as transmission of the power from the winding ratchet with the spring in a stationary barrel, and he was the first to introduce the 'fast train' in which the balance vibrates 18,000 times an hour instead of the more usual 14,000 count. Howard retired in 1882 but his business continued until 1903, the year before he died.

In 1903 the Howard company came under the control of the *Keystone Watch Case Company* of Philadelphia, and it continued manufacture under the name of the *E. Howard Watch Company* in Waltham, though the movements were marked Boston which is a few miles away. The watch illustrated was called the *Railroad Watch* and has the unusual feature of minute numbering. Precision-built, this bar-movement watch is superbly finished and was available in 1907 in 16-size with 19 jewels, hunting or open face, described as *adjusted to five positions*. This means that the watch was timed in five separate positions, pendant up, left and right, face up and face down, in order to achieve the best possible mean in rating the balance. There were many other American firms producing fine quality watches, such as the *Hamilton Watch Company* which acquired the Howard name rights in 1931 and which is still manufacturing in Lancaster, Pennsylvania, but almost all were overtaken by the Swiss wristlet watch industry after the First World War.

9
Continental Europe and Japan c.1675 to 1900

Clockmaking during the early Renaissance owed its primary evolution to France, Germany and northern Italy and it was not until the second half of the 17th century that England began to play a conspicuous part. From about 1650 national styles began to develop where previously the style was of international character (pp. 77, 87), and the most important of the Continental countries was France. France and other European countries developed clock and watch styles which were far more elaborate, as to casework, than their English counterparts. In France particularly, a clock was often judged by its impact as a work of art or fine furniture rather than for its mechanical properties. This is not to say that 18th century French clock mechanisms were not of high quality, for many of the world's finest horologists were French, but in France the casework gave opportunities for the artist, sculptor, cabinet-maker, gilder, bronze caster and others such as never occurred in England, where decoration was restrained, at least until the 19th century. (Plates V, 14, 15.)

The development of French clocks and watches was influenced by the patronage of royalty and the aristocracy, which happened on only a moderate scale in England. The French 'Horologers du Roi' were privileged clock and watchmakers who worked under the protection of the court and did not have to struggle and compete, in the commercial sense, as did the English. Other trades, too, received support from court circles and thus Diderot's vast *Encyclopédie, ou Dictionnaire des Sciences, des Arts et des Métiers*, including a section on horology, could be published for a wealthy clientele between 1751 and 1780, while nothing of this sort appeared in England until the following century. The collections of the *Conservatoire des Arts et Métiers* in Paris contain superb clocks, watches and tools, confiscated from their aristocratic owners after the French Revolution (1792–95); the Revolution dealt a heavy blow to the French clockmaking trade, from which it recovered in the 19th century under very different circumstances.

PENDULE LOUIS XIV
Jean Godde (l'aîné), Paris, c.1710

DIAL AND MOVEMENT OF A WATCH
Pierre Gaudron, Paris, c.1700

The *'pendule religieuse'* is so called because its severe and sombre lines resemble types of religious structures. Made during the reign of Louis XIV (1643–1715), its counterparts in England were the early pendulum clocks of the 1660s (pp. 90, 91), though in this mantel clock we already see the French love of intricate decoration in the *tortoiseshell veneer* and *silver and brass inlay*. The gilded *swag and scrolls* beneath the chapter ring, mounted on a velvet background, herald a French feature which persisted through the 18th century. Typically French on the clock above, of about 1710, is the use of *separate enamel plaques* or *cartouches* for the individual numerals of the dial, enamelled in black in early examples but often done in blue at a later date. Another feature is the gilded bronze *campane* or *lambrequin* appearing to hang over the edge of the plinth; extra gilded mounts may be seen in the *caryatid corbels* on each side of the dial and formalised *acanthus leaves* on the 'inverted bell' top.

French watches of the period used the same separate plaques for the hour numerals and should be compared with English contemporaries (pp. 104, 105). Although it has a balance spring, this watch retains the early feature of a single, blued-steel hand, the hour and half-hour divisions being indicated by separate enamel plaques, though here placed close together to form a complete ring. The balance cock on the back of the movement is a *bridge cock*, unlike English ones in that it is attached by two screws, one at each side. The symmetrical design of the pierced engraving should be compared with the designs of *Boulle* work on the following page, for here in simplified form we see the essential ingredients of this lavish French Renaissance style. In similar spirit is the symmetrical cartouche below the dial of the clock on this page, its pair of 'putti' or cherubs holding an owl on the left, for night, and a cock to represent day on the right.

DETAIL OF BOULLE MARQUETRY OF THE FIRST AND
SECOND PART

Long case clocks in France were rare, though often a clock may be seen standing either on a pedestal or on a wall bracket. The *pedestal*, sometimes called a *socle*, was designed in keeping with the style of the clock and ornamented with *gilded mounts*, *marquetry veneering* and a large *lambrequin*. The clock shown here has characteristics of the end of the Louis XIV period— outward scrolling feet and a sculptured figure at the top, sometimes seen on the finest English clocks by Tompion and others. The clock is clearly becoming important as a *piece of furniture* and French clock cases were made by the foremost cabinet-makers, or *ébénistes*. Amongst the cabinet-makers of the day the most important was *Charles-André Boulle* (1642– 1732) who had workshops in the Louvre in Paris and who developed a superb type of marquetry, known as *Boulle-work*, though he did not invent it.

Marquetry and parquetry on English clock cases have already been described (pp. 92, 94), but not until the early years of the 19th century do we see metal (brass) used as an inlay with veneering (p. 131). Boulle produced rich designs in *brass, pewter and tortoiseshell*, applied to undulating surfaces, producing the finest effects when used with shell as the background, shown in the diagram here as black, though used also in a reversed way as in the diagram with a white ground. The designs are defined as the 'first part' and 'second part'; like English veneering the sheets of metal and shell were laminated, cut with a fine saw, the parts sorted out and then glued, under heavy pressure, to the case. When the glue was hard and dry the surface was polished and the metal parts were often *engraved* to add richness and quality to the ornament, especially for leaves, flower petals, birds, figures and folded drapery. Sometimes stained *horn* in blue or green was used instead of tortoiseshell (p. 172).

CARTEL RÉGENCE
Mynuel, Paris, c.1710

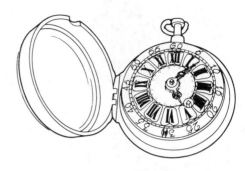

WATCH SIGNED MYNUEL
Paris, c.1710

The Regency of the Duc d'Orleans, known as *La Régence* (1715–23), came between the death of Louis XIV and the beginning of the reign of Louis XV. It was a period which witnessed a change in style from the architectural forms of the Louis XIV 'pendule religieuse'. The case of the clock above, still symmetrical in form but composed entirely of curving lines, shows the change to restless, flowing shapes which developed at length into the Rococo style, only the bracket of this clock having the discipline of the earlier period. The clock is from the workshop of a fine Parisian maker who always signed his products '*Mynuel*' and who was working between about 1693 and 1750. The dial is covered by a hinged circular bezel and the enamel plaques of the numerals now surround a *central enamel plaque* which has replaced the embossed or engraved metal centre of older style. Dials of this kind with a central enamel plaque are often called the *thirteen-piece dial*.

In clocks of the Regency period *repeat striking* began to be used and *repeating watches* were made too, such as the one shown here, also by Mynuel. As with English watches, the repeat-work is operated by pressing the pendant (p. 105), but the dial is quite different from English versions for although of enamel the numerals are surrounded by fine lines, as though divided into plaques like the clock dials, and the surface is *raised in relief* under the numerals, again to simulate the separate enamel plaques. The *hands* are pierced and scrolled, a feature which does appear on English watches sometimes under the influence of Rococo, and the Mynuel watch shows *winding through the dial*, a rather unattractive feature which is common in French work. On the *bridge-cock* of the movement is screwed a key-hole shaped *flat steel coqueret*, a form of 'shock absorber' to act as the end bearing of the upper balance wheel pivot and to protect it from breakage in the event of a sudden shock.

CARTEL LOUIS XV AND BRACKET
Louis Montjoye, Paris, c.1750

CARTEL LOUIS XV AND BRACKET
Jean Louis Bouchet, Paris, c.1760

With the beginning of the reign of Louis XV (1723–74) the *Rococo style*, which had already begun to evolve in the Regency period, came to full flower in extravagances of asymmetrical convolutions, scrolls, curves, flowers and shell shapes—a richness rarely seen in England though it had its effect (p. 108). In this connection three designers should be noted for their work in furniture generally, *Charles Cressent* (1685–1768), *Juste-Aurèle Meissonier* (1695–1750) and *Gilles Marie Oppenordt* (1672–1742). This Rococo style was a French invention, the name derived from the French word 'rocaille', an original creation quite unrelated to past styles and as an abstract art form having incomparable charm. When applied to clocks it is a *furnishing style* only, for the clock inside had by this time become of standard design, with circular plates containing two straightforward though well-made wheel trains, the striking invariably of the *count-wheel* type, and power supplied from *going barrels*, not the spring barrel and fusee almost always used in England.

The clocks shown here are sometimes known as *cartel clocks*, though this term is usually used for those which *hang* on the wall (p. 173). That signed by *Louis Montjoye*, a master clockmaker from 1748 to 1789, has a case covered with *green-stained horn* behind the gilded brass scrolls, while that by *Jean Louis Bouchet*, working in Paris from 1762 to 1789 and 'horologer du Roi', is in a case of blue *vernis Martin*, a type of lacquer named after *Robert Martin* (1706–65) and his brothers who developed its use. The case is also signed by a fine *ébéniste*, *B. Lieutaud*, as was often done on quality furniture. In the first, which is somewhat earlier, the *thirteen piece* dial of enamel plaques is used, with an extra twelve plaques for the minutes; the second dial is also of thirteen parts, but here they are segments of the circle fitting closely together and pointing the way to the *complete* enamel dial which became almost universal later.

PENDULE LOUIS XV IN A PORCELAIN CASE
Ladouceur, Paris, c.1745

CARTEL LOUIS XV
Estienne le Noir, Paris, c.1740

While ceramic materials were rarely used for clocks in England before the 19th century (p. 138), the small circular movements of French clocks were entirely suitable for use in *porcelain* cases, as with the example here, combined with *ormolu* or gilded brass mounts. Three features are of particular interest, the porcelain case, the Chinese figure and the plain, one-piece enamel dial. The case was made at *Chantilly*, other clock cases in this material being made at St. Cloud, Vincennes, Paris and Mennecy. The reclining Chinaman illustrates the vogue for 'chinoiserie' which was so much part of the Rococo tradition, his body and the globe being hollow to accommodate the pendulum of the clock. The gilded mounts are Rococo asymmetrical scrolls, the *gilding* being produced by coating the brass with an *amalgam* of gold and mercury, the pieces then being heated to drive the mercury away leaving gold combined with the surface of the brass, later to be burnished. This method is known as *mercurial* or *fire-gilding*.

The name *cartel* appears to be derived from the Italian '*cartella*' or bracket, a term applied to almost any object fixed to the wall and thus also used for the clock on the previous page, or for this hanging clock known in France as the '*pendule à cartel*'. These were sometimes carved in wood, smoothed with *gesso* (a type of plaster) and gilded, and English versions do appear from time to time to harmonise with Chippendale furnishings. More often they were made of cast brass or a base metal such as lead or zinc. The one here is signed by a famous French maker *Estienne le Noir*. The '*sunburst*' *rays* on the top left-hand side are an early example of a feature which became popular later on *lyre clocks* in the reign of Louis XVI. The 'rays' surround a female mask on these later clocks and are known as '*rayons Louis XVI*', persisting in French design until well into the 19th century (pp. 176, 183 and Plate V, 14).

RÉGULATEUR LOUIS XV
Casemaker B. Lieutaud, Paris, c.1770

The true, scientific regulator did not evolve in France until later (p. 179), but the name is applied to long case clocks under Louis XV. Many new devices and ideas were introduced into clocks by such makers as *Julien le Roy* (1686–1759), who devised a compensated pendulum in 1738 and improved the verge escapement by means of a screw-adjusted potence; his son *Pierre le Roy* (1717–85), the greatest French horologist of all, applied temperature compensation to the balance wheel of watches and made a detent escapement for chronometers; *Jean André Lepaute* (1720–87) devised a special form of pin-wheel escapement; the brothers *Jean Baptiste* and *Nicolas Charles Dutertre* (1715–93) were also of this number. In 1741 *Antoine Thiout* the elder (1692–1767) published his book *Traité de l'Horlogerie, mécanique et pratique*, indispensable for the study of French clock mechanisms and tools.

The '*régulateur*' here is very different from the English long case clock of about the same date (p. 112). The outward-curving, swelling form of the trunk of the clock is often called '*bombé*' and in this case it has some function in allowing space for the swing of the pendulum. The clock case is stamped by the maker *B. Lieutaud* (p. 172). Other important *ébénistes* were *Charles-Claude Saunier, Charles Cressent, J. H. Riesener* and *J. Jollain*. Of these *J. H. Riesener* (1734–1806) was to become more important under Louis XVI, in particular for his much more sober Neo-Classical designs. The *ébénistes* relied on veneering of the finest quality, sometimes patterning the background with geometric designs, though in this example the veneering is simply quartered. Timber such as walnut and rosewood were used to cover large areas, while details were finished in mahogany, sycamore, apple, olive and tulipwood, their natural colours contrasting well with the *ormolu* mounts.

PENDULE LOUIS XVI
Pierre Henry, Paris, c.1775

PENDULE LOUIS XVI
Jean Baptiste Lepaute, Paris, c.1785

Under Louis XVI (1774–89) many of the Rococo features which we have seen under Louis XV survived, but changes in style had been taking place from the middle of the century—indeed the *style Louis XVI* often refers to the period from about 1750 to 1790, longer than the actual reign of the king which ended with the Revolution. The restless convolutions of Rococo began to give way to quieter, more gentle forms; symmetry returned to design and the elegant and slender proportions which were contemporary with the English Neo-Classical style appeared in France, showing the same influences at work in both countries (pp. 118, 119). New 'cool' materials such as marble or biscuit (i.e. unglazed) porcelain began to be used and the classical *urn* or *vase* appeared with other decorative features derived from Greek and Roman architecture. Another fashion which appeared under Louis XVI and continued in the *Directoire* (1795–9) and *Empire* (1800–30) periods was the sculptural use of both human and animal figures (pp. 176, 178).

While the essential form of the bracket clock continued in England until well into the 19th century, in France the bracket or cartel clock gradually declined, to be replaced by the almost universal *mantel* clock, its symmetrical design looking well above the centre of a fireplace and called a '*pendule de cheminée*', often accompanied by matching *candlesticks*, *girandoles* or *vases*. The supporting lion of the clock above is a sculpture in bronze, made when Italian bronzes of the Renaissance were being widely collected, studied and copied, and the other clock here, of symmetrical design, is a three-dimensional group in gilded bronze mounted on a base of marble, itself inset with a gilded bas-relief entitled 'love clasping friendship'. The pair of sphinxes, derived from a new interest in Egyptian art and archaeology, may be paralleled with the Wedgwood and Adam English versions of Neo-Classical and Etruscan patterns, though the full flowering of Egyptian taste was more strongly felt in France after Napoleon's conquest of Egypt in 1798.

PENDULE LOUIS XVI
Case attributed to E. M. Falconnet, Paris, c.1785

PENDULE LOUIS XVI
Paris, c.1785

This sculptured 'Toilet of Venus', in careful pose, is expressive of the spirit of Neo-Classical art such as may also be seen in the work of the Italian *Antonio Canova* (1757–1822), the Englishman *John Flaxman* (1755–1826), an artist who worked for Wedgwood in Rome, or the French painter *Jacques Louis David* (1748–1825). The composition of the group in this 'statuary' case is attributed to the sculptor *Etienne Maurice Falconnet* (1716–91) who amongst his many successes was appointed Director of Sculpture at the Sèvres porcelain factory and was commissioned to model an equestrian figure of Peter the Great at St. Petersberg. The clock itself is hardly noticeable, ingeniously arranged to give the time on the edge of the revolving table, with minutes above and hours below, the time indicated by the pointing finger of cupid who is otherwise indifferent to the scene. This may be called a *revolving dial clock*, with its movement hidden in the base and very much 'à la mode'. (Plate V, 13.)

This revolving clock belongs to the superb collections bequeathed to the English nation by Sir Richard and Lady Wallace in 1897 and which may be seen at Hertford House, Manchester Square, London. The '*column clock*' of about the same date is another French style where gilded mounts are combined with marble in Classical symmetry. Of *theatrical* appearance, the pendulum bob, swinging in centre 'stage', is designed as a 'sunburst' with star-like rays spreading from the *central mask head* (Plate V, 14). Greek *caryatids* and *bronzed Egyptian sphinxes* flank the plain white, one-piece enamel dial and an Austrian eagle crowns the design. The column clock was particularly popular just before the Revolution. The base or plinth with adjustable feet, like that of the 'Toilet of Venus' clock, is a good indication of the date and period, though care must be taken not to confuse this style with that of the period of Charles X (1814–30), superficially similar but usually deeper.

DIAL AND BACK OF A WATCH
Jean Antoine Lépine, Paris, c.1785

In addition to the great French horologists already mentioned (p. 174), there are others. *Robert Robin* (1742–1809), a fine maker to the king and later to the Republic, devised a watch escapement known by his name and used by Breguet; *Antide Janvier* (1751–1835) made fine planetary clocks of superb construction; Swiss-born *Ferdinand Berthoud* (1727–1807) is famous for his work on escapements, precision clocks and marine chronometers including his invention of a spring detent escapement, probably independently of Earnshaw (p. 179); *Frédéric Japy* (1749–1813) was the first watchmaker to manufacture ébauches by machine tools in 1776 and founder of the firm of Japy-Frères (pp. 143, 165); and *Jean Antoine Lépine* (1720–1814) will always be remembered for the introduction of the *Lépine calibre* about 1770 in which the top plate of a watch was replaced by *bars* to hold the individual pivots, and who also used the *hanging barrel*, i.e. a spring barrel supported at one end of its arbor only, thus helping to reduce the thickness of the watch.

The watch shown here is a highly decorative example from the firm of Lépine, made about 1785 and sumptuously elaborate with its jewelled filigree cover to the movement top plate, dial jewelled at the half-hour marks, jewelled hands and double-glazed (front and back) decorative case. This watch has a conventional verge movement and, like the clocks we have seen, is more important for the way its casework reflects the taste of the period than for its timekeeping properties. The jewels are *paste* or imitation diamonds, but their extravagant use and the insertion of an oval enamelled *miniature* in the back, amongst the filigree, gives the watch a particularly French look that rarely found favour in England. In many French watches *enamelling* was used extensively for the exterior of the case, comprising pictorial scenes copied from the work of court painters such as *Francois Boucher* (1703–70) and during the Revolutionary period many dials were enamelled with symbols or emblems of 'love', 'hope' 'liberty' and 'justice'. (Plate V, 16a.)

PENDULE DIRECTOIRE
c.1797

PENDULE EMPIRE
Basile Charles le Roy, Paris, c.1810

The short period of the *Directory* (1795–9) saw a return to the making of fine clocks after the upheavals of the Revolution, in a style following directly from the Neo-Classical phase of Louis XVI. The military exploits of Napoleon in Italy in 1795 and his conquest of Egypt in 1798 stimulated public interest in the art of the past and the clock above is almost entirely in the 'Grecian' style, the table and chair being minute replicas of the furnishing designs of the period; the whole group, including the lady with her Greek-style dress and hair arrangement is in *gilded* or *patinated bronze*, set on a *marble base*. The figure of a lady at a table, desk or musical instrument was a popular theme for these superlative cases (Plates V, 15, VII, 22), sometimes re-creating the setting of an entire room or library interior. Clock movements, however, were standardised as industrial production was encouraged by the new government to strengthen trade against English and Swiss imports.

Patination of bronze is a technique in which the surface is artificially darkened by oxidation to contrast with gilded bronze; it is done both by chemical and heat action, various colours and finishes being possible. The *pedestal* clock above is crowned by a Grecian lamp like the one on the table of the other clock, surmounted by a flying cupid. *Anthemion* or *honeysuckle* decorate the front and side, copied from Greek buildings and used extensively on all kinds of furniture of the period. The clock measures about 18 in. high, intended for a bedroom or small apartment. It was made by the firm of *Basile Charles Le Roy*, who was official clockmaker to the Emperor Napoleon. The style is known as *Empire* and is reckoned, for furnishing, from about 1800 to about 1830, though this period embraces the era of the Consulate and the reigns of Napoleon (1804–15), Louis XVIII (1815–24) and Charles X (1824–30). It had considerable influence on both English and American clocks (pp. 130, 150).

RÉGULATEUR LOUIS XVI
Ferdinand Berthoud,
Paris, c.1775–80

RÉGULATEUR EMPIRE
c.1805

By the late years of Louis XVI and in the Empire period very fine *regulators* were made. The two clocks here show clearly the change in style between Louis XVI and the Empire period. The first regulator is by *Ferdinand Berthoud*, utilising the *gridiron pendulum* and showing the *equation of time* and the dates of the months. This is also a striking clock, the method of striking following the French tradition of a single stroke on the bell at the half hour and normal striking at the hour. In clocks of this kind Berthoud experimented widely to 'detach' the pendulum, as far as possible, from interference by the action of the escapement, and the French makers generally did not adopt the recoil anchor or Graham-type dead beat as was universally done in England. Various forms of *pin-wheel escapement* were used in France following the introduction of the principle in 1741 by *Amant*, who worked in Paris from about 1730 to 1749.

The Empire style regulator is a good example of the *true* regulator, made by various emminent men in France early in the 19th century. Like the English ones, but of very different proportions, the case is severely plain, a particular characteristic being the square top with overhanging *cyma-recta cornice* and plain rectangular plinth which occasionally has a central moulded panel. Also characteristic of French regulators are the very large and complex gridiron pendulums, comprising up to nine rods of alternating brass and steel to effect temperature compensation, the action of changes of temperature being indicated, in this example, by a pointer and scale mounted above the pendulum bob. This pendulum bob is of normal 'dished' shape, but many in regulators or ordinary clocks are flat-sided with angular, chamfered edges. The dial, as befits the case, is plain and the time is indicated as in a conventional clock.

PENDULE DE VOYAGE
Abraham Louis Breguet, Paris, c.1810

PENDULE DE VOYAGE
Jean Paul Garnier, Paris, c.1835

The *carriage clock* is perhaps the best known type of French clock in England, being made throughout the 19th century, many thousands especially for the English market (p. 136). The first 'pendule de voyage' shown is from the workshop of *Abraham Louis Breguet* (1747–1823) and is now in the Musée des Arts Décoratifs in Paris. The dial shows conventional hours, minutes and seconds; phases of the moon; alarm indicator on the middle, right-hand dial; 'up and down' dial at the bottom left (showing the state of winding of the mainspring); regulation dial at the bottom right; day, date, month, year and temperature indicators below the main dial; strike/silent above left and strike/silent quarter-striking above right. This magnificent mechanism is contained in an Empire style case of gilded metal, with Grecian motifs above and below (compare p. 178), pilaster columns at each side and a moulded carrying handle above the glass-covered escapement platform. Glass panels reveal the movement at the sides and back.

A. L. Breguet was born in Switzerland in 1747. As a young man it is thought he studied in Paris with Ferdinand Berthoud and others. His outstanding abilities caused him to be introduced to, and gain the favour of, the royal family. After his marriage he set up house and workshops at No. 39 Quai de l'Horloge in the Île de la Cité in Paris, and founded what became one of the most famous watch and clock-making firms of France, with the highest possible international reputation. Breguet first marketed an automatic (*perpétuelle*) watch in 1780, improved the cylinder escapement soon after 1790, introduced a *perpetual calendar* in 1795 and made many other devices of which the most astonishing is the *pendule sympathique* between 1805 and 1810 (p. 181). The carriage clock by *Jean Paul Garnier* (1801–69) dates from about 1835 and shows in the style of its hands the beginning of the Gothic revival. The clock has repeat-striking and the small dial is for an alarm.

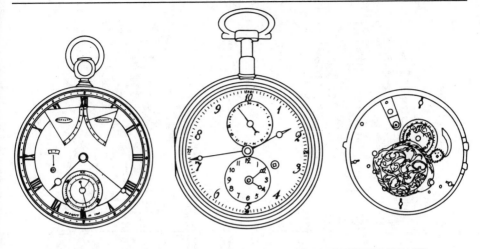

COMPLICATED WATCH
Abraham Louis Breguet, Paris, c.1795

FRENCH WATCH WITH A REVOLUTIONARY DIAL, AND
MOVEMENT
c.1792

Breguet was well-known for work of considerable complication. The first watch shown here is self-winding, quarter-repeating, indicates date and month, the equation of time and mainspring 'up and down'. Breguet gave his name to the characteristic style of hands, sometimes called 'moon' hands, which are normally of blued steel on a white enamel dial, but gold when on an engine-turned silver dial. Breguet made seven *'pendules sympathiques'*, consisting of a 'parent' clock fitted with a special cradle to take a watch. Every night the watch is wound and placed in this receptacle and the clock automatically sets it to time at midnight and adjusts the regulator according to the previous day's error. Later versions in which the watch had temperature compensation did not alter the regulator but set the watch to time and wound it! Breguet also made *montres à tact* which could be used to tell the time in darkness by feeling the position of a strong hand on the outside of the case against 'touch pieces'.

The unsigned watch above is an example of the French Revolutionary dial of *ten hours*, with a calendar for a *thirty day* month and an auxiliary dial showing normal, twelve hour time. A decree was issued in 1793, during the Revolution, that clocks and watches should show *decimal time*, related to the new Revolutionary calendar. The day would be ten hours long, with one hundred minutes for each hour. The calendar would continue to have twelve months: 1. *Vendemaire* (vintage) 2. *Brumaire* (foggy) 3. *Frimaire* (sleety) 4. *Nivose* (snowy) 5. *Pluviose* (rainy) 6. *Ventose* (windy) 7. *Germinal* (budding) 8. *Floreal* (flowery) 9. *Prairial* (meadow) 10. *Messidor* (harvest) 11. *Thermidor* (hot) 12. *Fructidor* (fruit) beginning on September 22nd 1791. Each month had thirty days, giving a year of 360 days, the five extra ones being used for National festivals and the extra Leap Year day being the Festival of the Revolution. These ideas were never fully implemented, but a few watches and clocks remain incorporating Revolutionary dials.

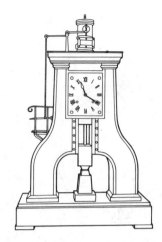

MANTEL CLOCK OF BLACK MARBLE
French, retailed in Berlin, c.1865

CLOCK IN THE FORM OF A STEAM HAMMER
French movement, c.1890

French clock design in the 19th century suffered the same sort of decline as happened in England, Gothic influences in the first half of the century giving way to a confusion of styles based on great periods of the past. Clocks were manufactured as cheaply as possible and although case styles declined, good quality movements continued to be made in standardised sizes and mostly circular. Made for export as well as for home use, French clocks spread throughout Europe in an astonishing variety of cases, often marked on the dial with the name of the retailer, as with the black marble clock shown here signed with a *Berlin* name. Many of similar form are to be found in England with the '*brocot*' pin-wheel escapement (p. 26), invented by *Achille Brocot* (1817–78) in Paris, the 'D' section pallets being of ruby, visible on the *front* of the dial, below XII. It was this type of clock against which Ingrahams of America were competing in making black walnut cases about 1880 (p. 160).

The brocot escapement is often found in 19th century clocks with a *brocot suspension* mechanism whereby the clock can be regulated from the front of the dial above XII; a screw fitting, turned by a watch key, alters the effective length of the suspension spring at the back. With the 19th century desire for novelty, French clocks were made to fit a curious assortment of cases representing steam-engines, locomotives, even wine-presses. They illustrate a vogue before and immediately after 1900 which might be interpreted as the complete breakdown of sympathy between the case designer and movement-maker. The one shown here represents a steam-hammer invented by *James Nasmyth* (1808–90). The 'U' shape pendulum swings inside the hollow legs of the case, controlling through levers a conventional brocot escapement, while at the same time counterbalancing the hammer which rises up and down with the action of the clock. Of polished brass and black patinated iron, the clock was retailed in London about the time of Nasmyth's death.

DIAL OF A MORBIER CLOCK
Early 19th century

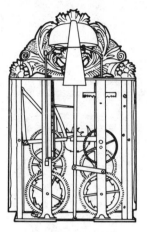

MOVEMENT OF A MORBIER CLOCK

Before finally leaving French clock manufacture there is one type of *provincial* French design which should be mentioned, the *Morbier* clock. These were sold very cheaply, and made in large numbers. They were produced in the Morbier district of eastern France, near the town of Morez in the Jura mountains, close to the Swiss border. Like so many 19th century clocks their dials are signed by numerous retailers, particularly in central and eastern France, and they were made with very few modifications from the end of the 18th century until the early years of the 20th. Until the later years they were fitted with an *inverted verge* escapement, the pallet arbor linked horizontally to a long pendulum, mostly hanging in front of the movement, behind the dial, but sometimes at the back. Elaborate examples have quarter-striking on two extra bells and alarms are fitted on some, operating either on the hour bell or on an extra bell in quarter-striking specimens. Very late versions were made with a conventional anchor escapement.

One peculiarity of these clocks is their mode of striking, the *rack* being arranged in a vertical position, falling directly on to the *snail* when tripped. A system of levers and *gathering pallet* return the rack while completing the striking, an ingenious arrangement allowing the clock to strike once at the half hour, as was normal French practice. The striking is also *double* at each hour, i.e. the clock strikes *again* about two minutes after the hour, not unknown in earlier clocks. Dials are of white enamel, held in place by a thin pressed brass mount which rises above the frame to conceal the bell, its upper part being made in a variety of designs. Sometimes these clocks are housed in large and rather ungainly cases, though often they simply hang on the wall, with side doors to keep out the dust. The movement, with its vertical framework, is similar to much earlier lantern-type clocks from which it was undoubtedly derived (p. 89).

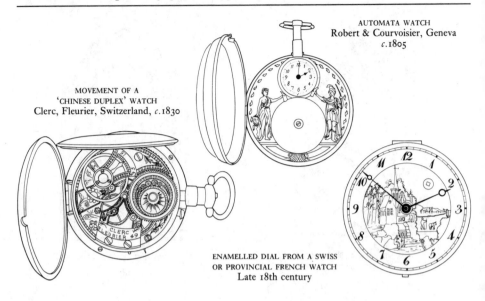

AUTOMATA WATCH
Robert & Courvoisier, Geneva
c.1805

MOVEMENT OF A
'CHINESE DUPLEX' WATCH
Clerc, Fleurier, Switzerland, c.1830

ENAMELLED DIAL FROM A SWISS
OR PROVINCIAL FRENCH WATCH
Late 18th century

Switzerland has a history of watchmaking dating back to the 16th century. The town of *Geneva* on the French border early became an important commercial centre and it was here that Swiss watchmaking began. Early Swiss watches followed the pattern of France and Germany and the isolated 'cantons' of Switzerland were ideal for the development of a seasonal cottage industry specialising in making parts to be finished in such centres as *Neuchâtel*, *Le Locle* and *La Chaux-de-Fonds*. Specialised machinery was first used in Switzerland at Geneva in 1804. By 1840 *Vacheron & Constantin* were using machinery, to be followed by *Patek Philippe & Cie.*, to the detriment of the English trade. The Swiss combined with Americans in a few experimental ventures in the second half of the 19th century, e.g. the *Tremont Watch Company* under Aaron L. Dennison had wheel trains, balances and escapements made in Zurich to be fitted to plates, barrels and other parts made in Boston, the resulting watches being retailed in 1865.

Three Swiss watches are illustrated here, the first known as the *Chinese duplex*, containing a type of duplex escapement which made possible the use of a *sweep second hand*. These elaborate movements were made in the 1830s and 1840s, particularly in the region of *Fleurier*, and were exported in large numbers to the Far East. The second watch with *automata* dial was made in Geneva very early in the 19th century, its two figures appearing to strike the bell at the hours and quarters when the 'repeat' is operated, though in fact two *gongs* are struck inside. The third example is of a Swiss enamelled dial of which the movement may be seen on p. 39. Italicised Arabic nùmerals follow the style which began in France towards the end of the 18th century (pp. 133, 181) and the centre of the dial is decorated with a scene of a watermill, in greens, reds, yellows, blues and browns, to the detriment, perhaps, of seeing the Breguet-type hands. (Plate V, 16b.)

MANTEL CLOCK OF THE BIEDERMEIER STYLE
Vienna, *c.*1835

RACK CLOCK
Jacob Bentele, Saltzburg, *c.*1775

Clockmaking in *Austria* began in Vienna and Innsbruck during the 16th century, but the trade started seriously in Vienna during the first half of the 18th, though it was always somewhat overshadowed by its neighbours in Germany and Switzerland. By 1789 a colony of Genevan clockmakers had settled in Vienna and had influenced the establishment of the Austrian work. The style of clocks made at this time was largely French inspired, but this was combined with the much heavier manner of the *German Baroque.* The clock above is like a French column clock (p. 176) in general form, but its coupled columns with exaggerated *entasis*, heavy base with frontal *serpentine curve* and its almost equally heavy superstructure owe as much to German as to French influence. The paintings are also not characteristic of French work. The lower painting has *automata* figures which move when the clock strikes and this painted panel, with flanking columns, had some effect on the style of 'Empire' clocks made in America (p. 155).

The style of Austrian clocks of the period about 1815 to 1848 is known as *Biedermeier.* This name is given to furnishing and decoration of a clear, simple and unpretentious manner. The word is derived from the combined names of two fictitious German Philistines, Biedermann and Bummelmeier. The *rack clock* of about 1775 has something of the decorative style of French Rococo, but the arrangement is quite unlike anything from France at the time. The clock is powered by its own weight as it slowly descends a vertical toothed rack operating on a pinion of the great wheel arbor inside. The verge escapement has a short bob pendulum which swings *in front of* the dial, an Austrian feature used on the small, popular '*Zappler*' clocks of the early 19th century, the pendulum swinging extremely fast. Conversions of early 16th century south German 'tabernacle' clocks from verge and balance often adopted a front-hanging pendulum which obscured the dial but clearly showed if the clock was going.

REGULATOR
Philipp Happacher, Vienna, c.1825

'VIENNA' REGULATOR
Southern Germany, late 19th century

True *Vienna regulators* are of superb construction and finish. The one shown here was made in Vienna and marked on the dial *Philipp Happacher*, recorded by Baillie (see Bibliography) as a master clockmaker in 1818. These early regulators, with *jewelled anchor pallets* and *escape wheel pivots*, micrometer adjustments for *depthing*, screws to adjust *endshake*, *undercut pinions* and the highest quality steelwork, should not be confused with the cheaper, mass-produced 'regulators' made in Silesia and in the Black Forest area. The true Vienna regulator is housed in a simple but elegant case of ebony with inlaid stringing of a lighter wood; the pendulum rod is of pine and a trace of Empire styling is seen in the curved pendant base. The dial is plain white enamel with a recessed sub-dial for the *true* seconds hand—true in this example for in many of the so-called Vienna regulators the 'seconds' hand does not register seconds, for the pendulum is *less* than the necessary 39.14 in.

The 'Vienna' regulators which were factory produced in Germany were exported in enormous quantities during the second half of the 19th century and until after the First World War. Their cases can be rather ugly and over-ornate, particularly in the smaller versions. They are either weight-driven, like this one, or spring-driven, the hour and half hour striking on a wire *gong* fastened to the backboard of the case. The enamel dials are usually of two parts, the centre part sunken to accommodate the seconds (?—see opposite) hand. The example here has a wooden rod pendulum, though many used the gridiron type and some have an imitation gridiron. Not all the German 'Vienna' regulators were of cheap quality, for the firms of *Winterhalter and Hoffmeier* of Neustadt and *Gustav Becker* (1819–85) of Freiburg in Silesia made many good quality clocks. The manufacturers *Gebr. Junghaus Uhrenfabrik*, founded in 1861 at Schramberg, exported vast quantities of the cheaper variety to numerous European agents and many are still in use in Britain.

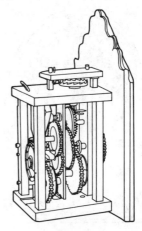

MANTEL CLOCK IN A PORCELAIN CASE
Meissen, c.1745–50

WOODEN MOVEMENT OF A BLACK FOREST CLOCK
Mid 18th century

The finest period of German clockmaking was undoubtedly the Renaissance, in the Bavarian area centred on such towns as Augsburg (Ch. 4). In the 18th century, southern Germany remained predominantly Catholic and in Bavaria particularly there was a widespread flowering of Baroque and Rococo architectural styles, even more elaborate than in France. For a relatively brief period this Rococo influence affected the design of clock cases until the emergence of Neo-Classicism about 1765. The clock above is an example of German Rococo and it has a case made of porcelain, a material perfectly suited to the style. The modelling of this clock case was by *Johann Friedrich Eberlein* who assisted the modeller *J. J. Kaendler* at the Meissen factory in Saxony, where the first true European porcelain was produced about 1710. Several of the other German porcelain-making factories such as Höchst (1750), Berlin (1751), and Frankenthal (1755), as well as producing tablewares and ornamental figures, made porcelain clock cases in the Rococo manner.

In complete contrast to the dilletante quality of German Rococo porcelain cases, a clockmaking industry was growing in the Black Forest area during the 18th century of a much more primitive and peasant character. This was the production of wooden clocks, where all the principal parts were of wood except for the escape wheel, pallets and, in the example above, the lantern pinions. This clock is fitted with a horizontal verge attached to a short pendulum, not seen in the drawing for it is hanging, in German fashion, in front of the dial. This tradition of building clocks from the most easily available material dates from the 17th century; the use of *verge and foliot* in this remote area continued in wooden clocks until well into the 18th century and often the weights were simply rounded stones tied to the ropes. The wooden dials were painted with flowers, birds, animals or figures in which one can see a link with the mediaeval tradition (p. 71).

WOODEN PAINTED DIAL FROM A CUCKOO CLOCK
Black Forest, *c*.1770

CARVED WOODEN CUCKOO CLOCK
Switzerland, *c*.1900

The *cuckoo clock* has often been disparaged by serious clock historians, or simply ignored, and yet like many of the cheap and popular clocks made in 19th century America (Ch. 8) it has held a place of affection in many homes and has a lineage dating back two hundred years. The example of a cuckoo clock dial above dates from about 1770; its painting is not unlike much English painted-dial work, and perhaps the style of English painted dials was derived from the areas of south Germany and the central European countries, perhaps in common with the formalised painting of roses and castles on English canal barges. In a somewhat later clock, the frame is of wood but the wheelwork is brass. The *carved* cuckoo is supported on a swinging stand, ready to sweep forward at the hour and half hour, his 'song' emitted from two small pipes with miniature bellows inside the case, one on each side, with slots opposite the vents to allow the sound to escape.

As the 19th century progressed the making of these wooden clocks changed from a peasant to a factory industry, in both the Black Forest area of Germany and in Switzerland. The '*hunting lodge*' or '*chalet*' style, such as the one shown here, did not come into fashion until after 1850 and by this time the movements were completely of brass and steel, mass-produced in standardised sizes and not unlike the brass movements of the American trade. Elaborately carved with birds, animals, sometimes human figures and forest foliage surrounding the basic mountain chalet or log cabin, the dials carry numerals of German Gothic design and the weights are moulded in the form of pine cones. Some of the most elaborate and often very large cuckoo clocks, along with barometers, were made just before and after 1900, and were very fashionable indeed in English Edwardian interiors. These clocks were strong and had undoubted character, though horologically unimportant.

BRACKET CLOCK
Johannes van Ceulen, The Hague, c.1685

LONG CASE CLOCK
Cornelis Uijterveer, Rotterdam, c.1705

The Dutch clock shown here is not unlike the *pendule religieuse* (p. 169), with its cartouche of the figure of 'Time' apparently supporting the dial and both set in front of a background of black velvet; the style of the case is also similar in proportion though it differs in many details. One characteristic of this type of 17th century Dutch clock is that the movement is fixed to the dial, which in turn is *hinged* to the case, so that the whole movement and dial will hinge outwards when the door front is opened, rather like the hinged movements of watches. As we have seen earlier (p. 90) it is to Holland that we look for the introduction of the *pendulum* into clocks and the *balance spring* into watches (p. 102), but the *evolution* of these devices in terms of subsequent refinement was taken up by England, and from this point onwards the national styles diverged, though *Dutch cabinet-making* contributed much to English work until the beginning of the 18th century.

The Dutch long case clock of the early 18th century is similar to English examples, especially in the *break-arch* hood. Distinctive Dutch features include the projecting scrolls at each corner of the base, the 'C' and 'S' scrolls at the top and bottom of the trunk door, triangular apertures for calendar work on dials and *arcaded minute rings*, sometimes used in England too (p. 114). Another Dutch innovation was a striking system in which the *hour* is struck at the *preceding half hour* on a high pitched bell and the hour itself on a low one. *Joseph Knibb* may have got his idea for *Roman striking* from Holland. In this a high pitched bell is used for the numeral I and low for V; the strokes are thus—one high and one low for IV, one low for V, one low and two high for VII, two low for X and so forth. Knibb reduced the number of strokes for striking every twelve hours from 78 to 30.

ZAANDAM CLOCK
Dutch, c.1740

STAARTKLOK
Dutch, late 18th century

FRIESLAND CLOCK
Dutch, 18th century

From the closing years of the 17th century three distinct types of Dutch clock begin to evolve, the *Zaandam*, *Staartklok* and *Friesland* types. The *Zaandam*, made in the area of that name north of Amsterdam, is in effect a hooded lantern clock, the movement being of posted type set inside a wooden case of architectural style, with cast metal *frets* above the sides and front. The escapement is arranged like a 'balance wheel' lantern clock, with a vertical escape wheel and verge, from the top of which a horizontal rod with a vertical piece at the rear engages with the pendulum, the latter being suspended from the backboard of the clock. This back, or wall-board, is in fact a bracket, on the table of which the clock stands. *Pear-shaped weights* on *rope lines* and *two bell quarter striking* are characteristic of the style. This type and the Friesland example are known as '*Stoeljeskloks*' because their construction incorporates a form of small stool supporting the movement on the projecting wall bracket.

The *Staartklok* is also a wall-mounted clock but is different from the Zaandam in that an *anchor escapement* is used and the pendulum swings in the *hollow case* of the backboard, its bob appearing either behind a pierced ornamental *grille* or a *glazed aperture*. Its hood is more like the top of a long case or bracket clock and the cylindrical *brass weights* hang on *chains*, not ropes. The staartklok was first made in the mid 18th century and it was exported in large numbers. The decorative *Friesland* clock has a lantern-type movement with iron plates above and below, connected by turned brass pillars; the escapement is almost the same as the Zaandam but the horizontal wire at the top of the verge communicates *directly* with a slot in the pendulum rod, instead of having a vertical downward projection. There are carved and painted *mermaids* on the back-board sides, cast lead and gilded frets, including the front of the canopy, and mermaid frets on each side of the dial.

PRINT BY KORYUSAI
Japanese, c.1770

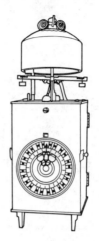

LANTERN CLOCK
Japanese, 18th century

The earliest contact of the West with Japan was in 1542 when Portuguese travellers landed on Tanegashima at the southern tip of Kyushu. Jesuit missionaries landed at Kagoshima on Kyushu seven years later, bringing with them European Christianity and goods including arms and clocks with which the Japanese were fascinated. During the following period of about ninety years Spaniards, Dutchmen and Portuguese imported more western clocks and other artefacts, as well as establishing Christian missions, and the Japanese themselves set up clockmaking centres in Tokyo, Nagoya, Kyoto, Osaka and Nagasaki. An abrupt end came with the Japanese expulsion first of the Spaniards in 1624, the massacre, it is said, of 40,000 converted Japanese Christians and the expulsion of the remaining Portuguese in 1638. Apart from contacts with the Dutch, restricted to the port of Nagasaki, the doors of Japan were closed to Europeans from this time until 1854 when official treaties were negotiated between Japan and Britain and the U.S.A.

The Japanese divided their days into two parts, sunset to sunrise and sunrise to sunset, each part having *six equal divisions*. These divisions varied as the length of day and night varied and this problem was solved as far as their clocks were concerned either by *altering the rate* for the daily and nightly periods, or by *altering the division of the 'hours'* on the dial. Above we see an 18th century Japanese lantern clock in which 24 *moveable* plates, representing the hours and half hours, can be adjusted for their changing length and the *whole dial revolves* against a fixed pointer. Beneath the bell the foliot is seen quite clearly with no hiding frets as in European lantern clocks. Adjustments to dials were usually made about once a fortnight. In the drawing from a Japanese print by *Koryusai*, a girl is hoisted on the shoulders of her companion *to alter the weights on the foliot* in order to change the rate of the clock for the night hours.

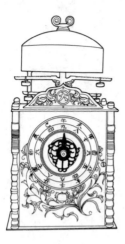

LANTERN CLOCK ON A STAND
With detail of dial, bell and double foliot,
Japanese, c.1750

In Japanese timekeeping the twelve hours are numbered 9, 8, 7, 6, 5, 4, 9, 8, 7, 6, 5, 4, known respectively as Rat, Ox, Tiger, Hare, Dragon, Snake, Horse, Sheep, Monkey, Cock, Dog, Wild Boar. 9 was a mystical number and to obtain the above notation the six daily and nightly hours 1, 2, 3, 4, 5, 6, were multiplied by 9, e.g. $1 \times 9 = 9$; $2 \times 9 = 18$; $3 \times 9 = 27$ etc., the second figures of the resulting table being the numbers actually used. Mid-day and midnight were placed at the top and bottom of the twelve hour dial at the *invariable* hour of 9, while the hours of sunset and sunrise were marked 6 at each side and moved up or down according to the adjustment required when using an adjustable dial. In the clock above without an adjustable dial, regulation is made on a *pair* of foliots to change the *rate*, the upper one working in the day and the lower at night, the verges and foliots working alternately on two co-axially mounted escape wheels, automatically changed.

Japanese lantern clocks were made either to hang on the wall, or to be supported on a stand with space below to accommodate the weights. Many of the earlier lantern clocks had simple and entirely unadorned stands of a square, pyramidal shape, the clock itself standing up to an average of 3–5 ft. from the ground. The clock shown here is supported on a stand of mulberry wood in perfect harmony and proportion with the clock and combining a glazed cover to keep out the dust. When Japan was opened again to European visitors and trade in the 1850s, designers and artists were profoundly affected by the 'discovery' of Japanese art and standards of design. Just as the Japanese wood-block prints influenced the French Post-Impressionist painters and Japanese design had a part to play in the evolution of Art Nouveau (p. 199), so the influence of Japanese architectural proportion and style may be seen in the furniture and clocks of the late 19th and early 20th centuries (p. 200).

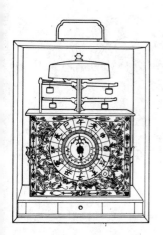

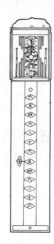

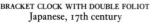

BRACKET CLOCK WITH DOUBLE FOLIOT
Japanese, 17th century

BRACKET CLOCK WITH BALANCE
Japanese, 18th century

PILLAR CLOCK
Japanese, 19th century

In Japanese clocks hours were struck on the bell in *diminishing* number as they progressed; half hour striking was of *one* blow for the half hour following an odd hour and *two* blows following an even one. Alarms were also fitted as on the *bracket clock* above, a peg being inserted into one of the holes in the *lower* or *night* half of the dial to trip a detent and release the alarm as the pointer moved round (compare p. 69). The clock is spring-driven with two foliots, contained in a well-proportioned wooden case with a drawer in the base to hold the winding key. Its black lacquered dial is fixed. The second bracket clock has a *revolving* dial with fixed pointer and adjustable hours. Below the bell a *balance wheel* is used instead of a foliot, controlled by a *balance spring*, the latter being protected by a shallow brass cylinder underneath. Above the dial are two calendar apertures relating to days and months in a 60-year cycle.

Pillar clocks were made in Japan from about 1830. The principle used was to measure the *rate of descent* of the driving weight as the balance-controlled movement at the top allowed it to fall. A pointer on the weight projects through a central slot in the case, indicating the time against a series of *moveable* markers or plates which could be altered for the changing lengths of the hours. There are *thirteen* such plates to measure out the *twelve* spaces of the hours and the clock would stop when the weight reached the bottom. It would be re-wound exactly at mid-day when time could best be checked by a sundial. The pillar clock could not accommodate striking work except when it was combined with a lantern clock, which occasionally happened. Japanese clocks are rarely marked with makers' names or places and are difficult to date accurately. The old forms of clock were abandoned when Japan adopted the western method of timekeeping and calendar in 1873.

10
Modern Clocks and Watches c. 1900 to the present day

THE EUREKA CLOCK
c.1906

The closing decade of the 19th century and the first twenty years or so of the 20th were to see technological developments which have revolutionised our lives, such as the invention of the motor car, the aeroplane, and the beginnings of radio broadcasting leading ultimately to television. Completely new ideas have been applied to the making of clocks and watches too, and although today we are still dependent on spring-driven timepieces which are the end product of several centuries of development, it is likely that by the end of the 20th century spring powered clocks and watches could well be obsolete. With the progress of electronic engineering the traditional use of wheels and pinions and mechanical escapements is giving way to complex electronic circuitry which functions far more accurately and in many ways more conveniently. As movements change the outward appearance of our clocks and watches is changing too, and the so-called 'digital dial' is becoming increasingly popular for the public clock and the personal wristlet watch.

An early example of an electrically controlled clock is the *Eureka Clock* which was invented by *T. B. Powers* and the *Kutnow brothers* in America in 1906 and made by the *Eureka Clock Company Limited*. As early electric clocks had worked on the principle of an electromagnetically impulsed pendulum (p. 147) so the Eureka clock employed the same idea but with a large *balance* instead of a pendulum, to make the clock more easily portable, the balance being controlled by a conventional, though very large balance spring. On the arm of the balance *coils* are mounted which, when energised, create a magnetic field which attracts one side of the balance to a magnetised armature in the base of the clock; on the return oscillation the contacts on the balance staff reverse the current and impulse is given in the opposite direction. The battery is contained in the wooden base and the motion work for the hands is moved forward at each swing of the balance through a pawl and ratchet mechanism.

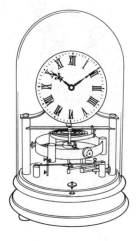

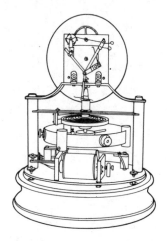

FRONT AND BACK OF ELECTRIC CLOCK
T. J. Murday, *c.*1910

In spite of the *timing screws* (p. 44) and the *split balance* of the Eureka clock, the disadvantages of the balance as a regulator were still present, with the added disadvantage that as the voltage of the battery varied so did the impulse to the balance. For this reason the Eureka clock had achieved no advance on a conventional clock driven by a spring through wheels and pinions, though this cannot be said for Murday's clock illustrated here. This clock was first patented by *Thomas John Murday* working in Brighton, Sussex, in 1910, and is different from the Eureka clock in that the balance is mounted horizontally instead of vertically, and the electro-magnet for delivering impulse to the balance is fitted to the base of the clock instead of on the balance arm. Like the Eureka the balance is 5 in. in diameter, the period of oscillation being about 4 seconds. Both these clocks were housed under glass domes with their movements fully exposed like 19th century skeleton clocks (pp. 134, 135).

The important difference between the Eureka and Murday's clock is that whereas the former receives impulse at every oscillation, the latter only receives it when the natural vibration of the balance has fallen below a given arc. In this way the balance is *free of interference* for a good deal of the time (pp. 27, 41), the length of the period between impulsing depending on the state of the battery and therefore the power of the impulse. This action is achieved by a method similar in principle to the *Hipp toggle*, described on p. 196, and the Murday clock is thus very much better than the Eureka in spite of the disadvantages of using a mechanical balance which has no compensation for temperature changes. The revolution of the motion work on the Murday clock is achieved by a reciprocating mechanism on the back of the dial which, using a ratchet wheel and pair of pawls, converts the alternating movements of the balance to direct forward drive to the minute and hour hands.

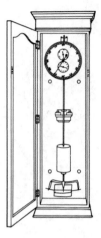

DIAGRAM OF HIPP'S TOGGLE
1842

ELECTRIC REGULATOR
P. A. Bentley, Leicester, c.1910

The principle used by Murday was first devised by *Matthaus Hipp* (1813–93) in 1834 and made by him in Würtemberg in 1842 for pendulum clocks. This system was arranged to give impulse only when the amplitude of swing of a pendulum fell below a certain level. It is known as *Hipp's butterfly*, or *Hipp's toggle*. The principle is illustrated above. The pendulum is free to swing from side to side; about the middle of the rod a *toggle* is pivoted, which rides backwards and forwards over a notched block just below it, with a trailing action. As the amplitude of swing of the pendulum gradually falls away, a point is reached where the toggle, instead of riding over the block, *engages with the notch* in the block, forcing it downwards as it passes. As the block descends a contact is made to an electric circuit which energises the electromagnet below the pendulum and attracts the magnet on the lower end of the pendulum, giving it impulse and increasing the arc of vibration again.

To drive a clock with this pendulum a mechanical system of wheels and pinions is advanced forwards at each beat by means of a pawl and ratchet wheel, the pawl being fitted to a lever which is lifted at each beat of the pendulum. Another important type of electro-magnetically controlled pendulum clock was that of *Percival A. Bentley* of Leicester, first patented in 1910. In principle it has something in common with that of Alexander Bain (p. 147), particularly in its system of contacting by means of a *sliding bar* on the pendulum rod and the *earth battery*, but Bentley apparently had no knowledge of Bain's work. One important difference, however, is that whereas Bain used a make-and-break slide, Bentley's contacts were provided through small wheels with an arrangement that the current could be *reversed* to reduce the arc of the pendulum vibration if it should become excessive. Bentley's clocks were retailed in several patterns all over the world and were made by his *Earth Driven Clock Company* in Leicester.

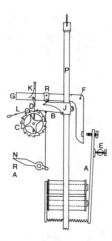

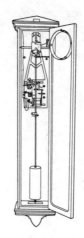

DIAGRAM OF THE SYNCHRONOME REMONTOIRE
*c.*1907

SLAVE MOVEMENT FOR THE SHORTT FREE
PENDULUM CLOCK
*c.*1922

The last and nearest to perfect form of *free* pendulum was the Shortt Free Pendulum Clock, developed by *William Hamilton Shortt* (1882–1971) and *F. Hope-Jones* between the years 1921 and 1924. Its beginning was a form of pendulum impulsed every half minute, devised by F. Hope-Jones and *Sir Henry Cunynghame* in 1907 and known as a *synchronome remontoire*. As it swings, a pendulum (P) rotates the wheel (C) by means of a gathering hook (B) at every alternate swing. On (C) a vane (D) unlocks a catch (K) at each complete revolution every half minute. When this happens the gravity arm (G) falls and, being pivoted at (F), gives impulse with the pallet (R) on the inclined plane of the plate (J) which is attached to the pendulum. At this point the lower end of (G) makes contact with the armature (A), completes an electric circuit which energises the coils causing the electro-magnets to attract (A) and in so doing to re-set the gravity arm (G) until the next unlocking.

This beautiful system was incorporated by the *Synchronome Company Limited* in the Shortt Free Pendulum Clock, first installed at the Edinburgh Observatory in 1921. A *master* free pendulum is employed swinging in a vacuum, kept closely to one temperature and mounted as firmly as possible. The free pendulum is impulsed in the middle of its swing every half minute from a *slave clock* of synchronome remontoire design which is *corrected* as required from the master. The slave is regulated to go fractionally more slowly than the master and when it falls behind the latter a device advances it sufficiently to bring it to the correct time to give its impulse. Thus the slave imparts impulse to the master at half minute intervals but is itself governed by it! This system worked so accurately that its error was measurable in terms of one or two thousandths of a second fast or slow each day. The Shortt Free Pendulum Clock was used as the standard at Greenwich Observatory from 1925 until 1942.

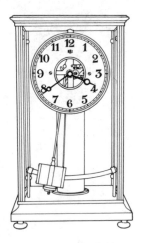

ELECTRIC MANTEL CLOCK
M. Favre Bulle, c.1920

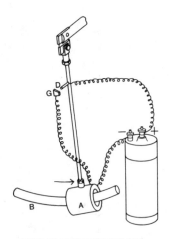

DIAGRAM OF THE BULLE CLOCK

F. Hope-Jones and Sir Henry Cunyng-hame owed some credit to *R. J. Rudd* (1844–1930) of Croydon, who in 1898 first applied the idea of a free pendulum and slave clock, using his own design of synchroniser. Unfortunately his ideas, although published in the *Horological Journal* in 1899 were entirely overlooked by the horological world until the introduction of the Shortt free pendulum. The principal astronomical observatories by about 1910 had adopted an *electrically operated remontoire* to provide impulses to a type of *dead beat* escapement devised by *Sigmund Riefler* of Munich in 1893, in which the impulse was delivered to the pendulum suspension spring, the whole apparatus being contained in an airtight cylinder to maintain constant air pressure since the use of electric power gave no need to provide access for winding. These specialised clocks marked the beginning of a new era. The clock shown here was invented by *M. Favre Bulle* about 1920 and its action is somewhat reminiscent of Bentley's regulator (p. 196) but in a domestic form.

The *bar magnet* (B) along which the *solenoid* or *coil* (A) moves at each swing of the pendulum, has a north-seeking pole at the centre and south poles at each end. As the pendulum swings contacts (G) and (D) are closed at every *alternate* swing and (A) is energised and attracted to the centre of the magnet (B). As the solenoid (A) swings over the magnet a current is *induced in it* in *opposition* to that of the cell, thus as the pendulum swings more quickly in response to the impulses it receives, the impulses are reduced in strength by the action of the induced current acting in opposition. The cell is of the Leclanché type in which a positive rod of carbon is surrounded by manganese dioxide and carbon in a porous vessel, in turn surrounded by a solution of sal-ammoniac in a glass jar. This is contained in a cylinder and motion to the dial is supplied by a pawl and ratchet mechanism.

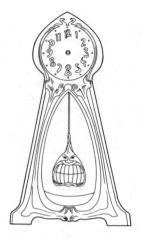

FRENCH 'PENDULETTE'
In Art Nouveau case, c.1900

SILVER CLOCK CASE
W. H. Haseler & Son, Birmingham, 1913

The electrical devices described in pp. 194–8 show something of the pioneering efforts in horological science at the end of the 19th century and the beginning of the 20th. Traditional methods of timekeeping, however, retained the upper hand and many clocks and watches of the 20th century should be judged by the style and design of their casework rather than for their mechanisms. Both the clocks illustrated here are interesting as examples of progressive styles of design fashionable at the beginning of this century and the French one illustrates the influence of *Art Nouveau*. This curious artistic style spread throughout Europe and America in the 1890s, characterised by flowing and writhing 'whip lash' lines and highly stylised naturalistic forms. Amongst the most important designers who created or contributed to Art Nouveau were the architect *Victor Horta* (1861–1947), illustrator *Aubrey Beardsley* (1872–1898), poster designer *Alphonse Mucha* (1860–1939), glassmaker *Louis Comfort Tiffany* (1848–1933) and jewellery designer *René Jules Lalique* (1860–1945).

Art Nouveau influence may be seen in the 'pendulette' of about 1900 in the design of the numerals on the dial, the grimacing face of the pendulum bob and the flowing lines of the case (Plate VIII, 24). The other clock, made in England in 1913 is a clean and elegant example of hand-craftsmanship from the silversmithing firm of W. H. Haseler & Son. By the time this was made the effects of Art Nouveau were largely dying away, but designers were left in a kind of aesthetic vacuum, not accepting the pure functionalism of the machine wherein form is dictated by materials and purpose, and at the same time not wishing to rely on the styles of the past and yet finding it impossible to disregard them altogether. The clock here has a vaguely 'Egyptian' quality and is somewhat self-conscious. It contains a standard French movement of no particular merit and instead of the usual chapters the dial reads FESTINA LENTE—'make haste slowly'.

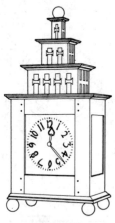

CLOCK CASE
C. F. A. Voysey, 1906

LONG CASE CLOCK
G. G. Elmslie, 1912

Charles F. Annesley Voysey (1857–1941) was an architect and designer and member of the Art Workers' Guild founded in 1884. Like many other designers he was concerned to maintain hand craftsmanship in an age increasingly involved in mass production; he believed in traditional ideas and, like the great inspirer of the *Arts and Crafts* movement *William Morris* (1834–96), he was not yet ready to come to terms with the machine. Voysey's hand-made clock case of 1906 illustrates his position perfectly. In ebony and oak, with pegged joints, its design shows a link with the past though it is in no way a copy. The pagoda-like top recalls 18th century oriental influence and the ball feet suggest late 17th century tradition. The dial shows an attempt to produce a modern solution to an old problem; the numerals are derived from the calligraphic lettering which was enjoying a revival through the work of *Edward Johnston*, and the style of the hands shows an attempt to modernise the classical proportions.

Long case clocks of this time are rare and a fine example here is from the designs of *George Grant Elmslie* in 1912. It was specifically made for a house at Riverside, Illinois, also designed by Elmslie who was working for the American architect *Louis Sullivan* (1856–1924). Again a quality of 'modernism' is present, combined with elements of tradition such as brass inlay in the mahogany case, like the early 19th century (p. 131), and overall proportions reminiscent of Japanese influence at the turn of the century (p. 192). The general design calls to mind the architecture of *Frank Lloyd Wright* (1869–1959) and the finials at the top belong to the age of the American skyscraper, in strange association with the pierced Celtic cross in the centre of the front which takes us back once more to the Arts and Crafts movement of the 19th century.

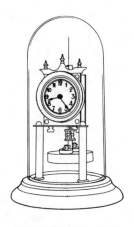

'GRAVITY' CLOCK
*c.*1920

TORSION PENDULUM CLOCK
*c.*1910–20

DIGITAL OR TICKET CLOCK
*c.*1920

The clock cases by Voysey and Elmslie do not have much in common with the design of cheap clocks which were being produced in vast numbers for the majority of homes. The three clocks shown here may be regarded as a more popular type of product. They were made in the 1920s and those which still survive are now attaining some degree of 'respectability' fifty years later. The *gravity clock* utilises its own weight to drive it, like the Austrian rack clock on p. 185; to wind the clock it is simply raised and the driving pinion engages with a rack on one of the two brass pillars. As the dial is glass, with the numerals applied inside, the movement can be seen with a type of *bar balance* controlling a tic-tac escapement (p. 27). The *torsion pendulum clock* is often called a *400-day clock* since it will run for over a year at each winding, the power being very slowly released as the torsion pendulum oscillates in a horizontal plane.

At the upper end of the fine, flat torsion spring a forked arm is linked with an anchor escapement. Torsion clocks have become increasingly popular and the one shown here is an early version, probably made between about 1910 and 1920. The flat disc of the pendulum has two weights which can be adjusted inwards or outwards to regulate the clock, and the *pediment* above the dial and *beading* round it are of Neo-Classical derivation found in much popular furniture of this period. The third clock, known as a *ticket clock* or *digital clock*, has a conventional clockwork movement in the base and the time is shown as the 'tickets' flick past as each minute elapses. This method of showing the time is now enjoying a revival though the digital dials of today are driven by electric movements (p. 210). The design of the case of this ticket clock owes a good deal to the carriage clock, many thousands of which were still being imported into England from France (pp. 136, 180).

MODERN METAL-CASED ALARM CLOCK

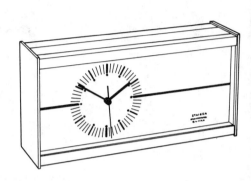

MODERN QUARTZ CRYSTAL CLOCK

With the increasing use of electric clocks and other complex technical equipment, many people feel a desire to hold on to reminders of an earlier age. A typical product of this is the metal-cased alarm clock of the 1960s and '70s, with its bell or bells on the top and its loud tick. The example shown here illustrates such a clock which, with its 'trendy' dial and lacquered brass case, is a product of the Carnaby Street tradition taken up by a large clock manufacturing concern. It has been designed to appeal to the young purchaser. Its appearance on the market is another facet in the change of taste which has made Victoriana or reproductions of Victoriana popular and which shows the effect on mass-produced products of 'Pop' art. There is a colourful quality about such clocks which should not be dismissed as ephemeral nonsense, for like the 'Mickey Mouse' watches of the 1930s they will one day be collected and studied, revealing much of our age.

In contrast is the comparatively expensive, elegantly cased, precision *quartz crystal clock*. The quartz crystal was first employed for timekeeping by *Warren A. Marrison* in the United States in 1929. Its action depends on the natural frequency of electrical oscillations from it, which can be amplified by valve or transistor circuits and electrically 'counted' to record the passage of time. The natural oscillation frequency is about 100,000 per second, which can be reduced to about 1,000 per second to provide a measurable unit for time recording. So constant is this frequency that with careful temperature control an accuracy of the order of one second's error in many years has been achieved. Quartz crystal clocks have now replaced the free pendulum in the world's observatories (p. 197). The quartz crystal clock shown here is a domestic or office version which has come into production during the last few years and which will perform with an error of less than one minute per year, powered by a 1.5 volt battery.

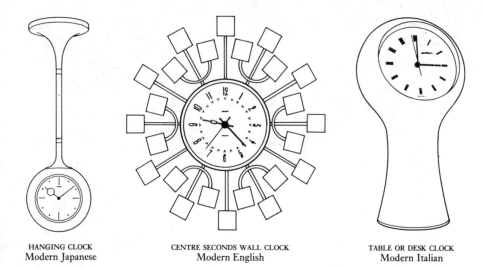

HANGING CLOCK
Modern Japanese

CENTRE SECONDS WALL CLOCK
Modern English

TABLE OR DESK CLOCK
Modern Italian

With the introduction of electric clock movements of various types, clock designers since the Second World War have developed new case styles using modern synthetic materials such as moulded plastics. Although Switzerland has dominated the horological market during the present century, rival concerns in Japan and Russia may well change the balance of the trade in the coming years, as has already happened with Japan in the fields of photographic equipment, radios and television. The three clocks illustrated show designs for electric clocks from Japan, England and Italy which may be taken as representative of many produced in recent years. The *hanging clock* makes use of a type of mounting previously used in public buildings such as offices, railway stations or banks since Victorian times, though then of completely different design. The English *wall-mounted clock* with central *sweep seconds hand* uses the traditional wood and polished brass to harmonise with the design of other furniture and fittings in a modern interior.

The black plastic-cased Italian *table* or *desk clock* designed by *Mangiarotti and Marassutti* in 1961 is perhaps the best and certainly the most subtle of the three shown here. Its rounded form is pleasant to handle as well as to look at and this approach to design owes a debt to the work of such modern sculptors as *Henry Moore* or *Barbara Hepworth*. The detailing of the dial should be particularly noted, as the two parallel lines which mark the hours gradually increase in thickness from I to XII and give a natural sense of clockwise direction. In addition they produce a pleasing and appropriate pattern of lines appearing to radiate from the centre in the same way as Roman numerals, but never entirely satisfactory with Arabic figures (pp. 199, 200, 201). The omission of minute marks on modern dials takes us back to the Mediaeval and early Renaissance periods when dials had no minute hands and clocks were not very accurate (pp. 68, 69, 71, 73).

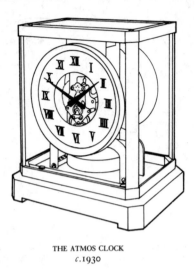

THE ATMOS CLOCK
c.1930

MODERN MODEL OF THE ATMOS CLOCK

Two of the nearest solutions ever found to the problem of *perpetual motion* are the *Atmos clock*, which is powered by the effects of changes in temperature and barometric pressure, and clocks driven by the action of light such as the one on p. 208. The idea of using changes in barometric pressure was first tried out by a London maker called *James Cox* (–d.1788) about 1760, in which the variations in the height of a column of mercury due to changes of atmospheric pressure were cleverly converted to rotary motion to provide power for a clock by the constant winding of a small weight. This idea, revived in 1913 by the Frenchman *J. E. Reutter*, produced the Atmos clock in which the principal factor is a *change of temperature* rather than atmospheric pressure, though the latter does contribute about 10% of the power. Whereas Cox's clock wound itself when the pressure was both rising and falling, the Atmos clock only winds itself when the temperature is falling.

The drawings of two versions of the Atmos clock illustrate one in which the movement can be fully seen, dating from the 1930s, and an elaborately cased version in production today in which only a part of the torsion pendulum can be seen below the dial. Mechanically the Atmos clock works by the same method as an aneroid barometer. A thin *hermetically sealed* aneroid type box acting like a pair of bellows is enveloped in a container of *ethyl chloride* which expands in rising temperatures and contracts as it cools. In the centre of these 'bellows' a *coiled spring* is put into compression as the temperature is raised, but on cooling it expands and conveys a winding action to the mainspring of the clock. This requires very little power as the mechanical part of the clock employs a *torsion pendulum escapement* system (p. 201) and a variation of 2°F between day and night temperatures will give the clock power for about 48 hours.

BACK OF A POCKET WATCH
New York Standard Watch Company, c.1910

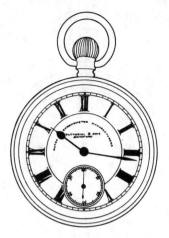

AMERICAN POCKET WATCH
With English retailer's name on the dial, c.1902

The years following the First World War were to mark the end of the long tradition of the pocket watch. As with most fashions older generations retain the customs of their younger days and the pocket watch has never entirely been superseded in spite of the ubiquitous wristlet watch of today (p. 208). The watches illustrated here are both American, the first drawing showing the back of a watch made by the *New York Standard Watch Company* which began operating in Jersey City, New Jersey, in 1885 and closed in 1929, coming under the control of the *Keystone Watch Case Company* in 1903. This firm had also absorbed, about the same time, the *Crescent Watch Case Company* which started in Chicago in 1882, moving to Brooklyn, New York in 1885. This 'Crescent' marked watch case has been chosen for illustration chiefly because of the elaborate engraving of the back and bezel. The date of the watch must be about 1910 and it has a full-plate movement with an external balance.

From the last quarter of the 19th century American pocket watches were often engraved with elaborate designs, scenes, railway engines, flowers, birds and animals. The watch on the right was made by the *American Waltham Watch Company* (p. 165) and housed in a case by the *Illinois Watch Case Company* of Elgin, Illinois, the dial being printed by the *retailing agents* Fattorini & Sons of Bradford, Yorkshire. While both watches shown have *keyless winding* their setting action for the hands is different, the Waltham being set by pulling the winding button outwards before turning, known as *stem-set*. The first watch has a lever which is hidden behind and kept in place by the bezel; when the front is opened and the lever pulled out the winding button can then be used to set the watch. The movement of the Waltham watch is in a frame of damascened nickel and from its serial number was made between 1902 and 1903. The escapement is a straight-line lever with a Breguet overcoil balance spring (pp. 43, 45).

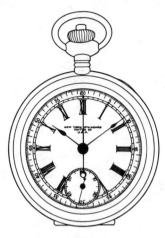

CENTRE SECONDS CHRONOGRAPH
New York Standard Watch Company, c.1910

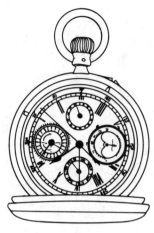

COMPLICATED REPEATER WATCH
Swiss movement, retailed in London, c.1895–1900

Shown here are two specialised pocket watches. The *fly-back chronograph* is a product of the New York Standard Watch Company (p. 205) and is not of particularly good quality but was made for the racing community and is appropriately engraved with a picture of a horse and jockey on the 'screw-on' back. On pressing the knob in the centre of the winding button a pinion engaging with the fourth wheel of the train drives a wheel on the arbor of the *centre seconds hand* which then begins to rotate until the knob is pressed again, disengaging the drive and causing the hand to stop. A third pressing of the knob causes the centre seconds hand to 'fly back' to zero so that timing can start again, the action being achieved by the use of a heart-shaped cam. This action in no way interferes with the normal going of the watch. The shape of the winding button and bow should be noted as typical of 20th century design (p. 48).

The second watch is also a *fly-back chronograph* but it has many other complications incorporated in it. The watch is of Swiss manufacture, retailed by Hunt and Roskell of London, and its dial contains chronograph indicators, perpetual calendar including the day of the week, phases of the moon, and the watch is also a *minute repeater* on gongs which surround the movement. If the watch should accidentally be allowed to stop the calendar work can be re-set using levers normally concealed when the bezel is closed. The watch case is of *hunter design* to protect the glass from damage and it is typical of many fine quality complicated Swiss pocket watches of the period just before and after 1900. Unfortunately many fine repeaters of this date were housed in rather thin gold cases which are easily dented during use. Unlike the early repeaters which were operated by pressing the pendant (p. 105) this type of watch has a *repeating slide* fitted to the edge of the case.

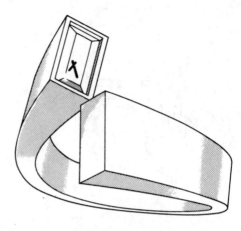

AUTOMATIC, CHRONOMETER QUALITY WRISTLET WATCH
1971

LADIES' DRESS WATCH IN GOLD
Designed 1970

The advantage of *automatic winding* produced by the movements of the wearer, apart from the owner never having to worry about winding it manually, is that the mainspring of the watch is always kept in a constant state of wind and the power applied to the wheel train is therefore constant. The winding is done by the oscillations of a pivoted weight inside the case which swings backwards and forwards as the wearer moves his arm, and in doing so it winds the mainspring as it swings. Although the idea dates back to the 1770s when it was first tried out by the Swiss maker *Abram-Louis Perrelet* (1729–1826) it was first applied to wristlet watches by *John Harwood* (1893–1964) in 1923. In Harwood's patent of 1926 the weight only wound the spring as it swung in one direction, but after the Second World War the Swiss industry developed the idea and designed movements in which the watch was wound as it swung in both directions.

The chronometer wristlet watch shown here is called *chronomatic* because it is of chronometer quality with automatic winding. This watch was introduced in 1971 and as a combined chronograph, calendar, navigator and automatic watch it has instant appeal for the man who wishes, or needs, to have complicated information built into a watch of high standard. There is an appeal in this kind of watch which has little to do with the requirements of ordinary timekeeping and this may also be said of the ladies' wristlet watch shown with it, which is attractive as a piece of high class jewellery of magnificent sculptural form and quality and containing a high class movement. This watch was produced along with many other fine modern designs by a Swiss firm in 1970, its individual styling in satin-finished gold creating a highly expensive article. Watches like these may be thought of to some extent as prototypes of styles which eventually become available to the person of more modest means.

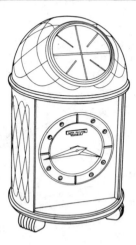

LIGHT CLOCK
Patek Philippe & Cie., Geneva

AUTOMATIC WRISTLET WATCH
Patek Philippe & Cie., Geneva

The clock and watch shown here come from the Swiss firm of *Patek Philippe & Cie*. The firm was started in Geneva in 1839 by the Polish *Count Antoine Norbert de Patek*, who in 1845 went into partnership with *Adrien Philippe* (1815–94) who was one of the early exponents of *stem winding*. In these watches the *hands were set* by pulling out the winding button, which continues as standard in most watches today. The *light clock* makes the same sort of use of natural power sources as the Atmos clock (p. 204) but in this case the source is *light*. Light falling on the glazed aperture in the domed cover activates a *photo-electric cell* which produces current sufficient to drive a small motor and wind the spring. Exposure to light for a period of four hours will provide power for the clock to run it for a whole day. When the mainspring is fully wound it has a reserve of power to last for three days in complete darkness.

Wristlet watches first came into use during the First World War when it was found that a watch strapped to the wrist was far more convenient in action than a pocket watch. Their development, however, has depended not just on their usefulness but also on the techniques of manufacture which have made possible miniaturisation of precision-made parts and high standards of reliability. In spite of the fact that they are in constant movement and in varying temperatures, often subject to shocks and vibrations, they can perform with an accuracy as good as, or much better than, many domestic clocks. The one shown here from Patek Philippe has been chosen from many different styles available of watertight, non-magnetic and automatic watches, as an example of a well-designed, clear, good quality product. In ladies' watches particularly a variety of case shapes such as square, oval or rectangular are produced, often designed as part of a bracelet rather than as a watch to which a strap has been fitted.

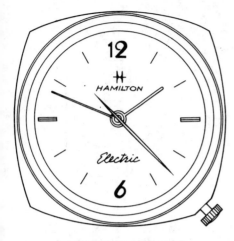

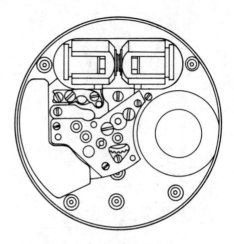

THE HAMILTON ELECTRIC WATCH
First introduced 1957

THE BULOVA ACCUTRON WATCH MOVEMENT
First introduced in 1960

Miniaturisation of electrical components and circuits has been responsible, since the Second World War, for the development of the electrically operated wristlet watch. The first electric watches appeared in 1952 in France and America and the first Swiss electric watch to be mass-produced was marketed by *Ébauches S.A.* from 1958. This development has posed a serious threat to the makers of conventional wheel train movements and it is more than likely that the traditional watch will slowly decline in the face of electronic progress. Tiny batteries such as the *mercury cell* can power small watches for over a year. These watches work on the principle of a more or less conventional balance oscillating in a magnetic field, the impulses being produced by current supplied to a coil on the balance, a contact system supplying the power as required. The balance is also a *motor* since it drives the motion work. The *Hamilton Watch Company* watch shown here used this system and was the first on the market in 1957.

In 1960 the world's first fully *electronic* watch was introduced called the *Accutron*, invented in Switzerland by *Max Hetzel* and manufactured by the *Bulova Watch Company* which was founded in America in 1875 by *Joseph Bulova*. In this watch the oscillating balance has finally disappeared after a history of some four hundred years (pp. 23, 73). The component replacing the balance is a *tuning fork* which vibrates at its natural rate of 360 times per second, the vibrations being produced by electrical means and counted by a miniature pawl and ratchet of great precision. Thus the vibrations are converted to rotary motion, providing excellent timekeeping and giving out a gentle hum instead of a tick. The Bulova Accutron is not quite the ultimate in wristlet watch history, for the *quartz crystal watch* from a Japanese firm has been on the market since late in 1969, while several Swiss firms and Bulova produced models in 1970. With their complex electronics they are remarkably accurate, with an error less than one minute a year.

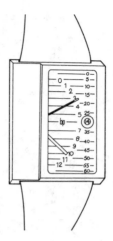

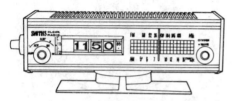

'DIGITAL' MAINS ELECTRIC CLOCK COMBINED WITH A
RADIO

WRISTLET WATCH WITH LINEAR READOUT DIAL

The so-called *digital dial* of the clock shown here illustrates a form of styling which has little to do with technical evolution, but reflects rather a change in ideas and outlook in our modern world of complicated scientific equipment and machinery. Whether or not the use of *figures only* will replace the conventional circular dial and hands is a matter for debate, but the well-known dial has the advantage of showing the time *diagrammatically*, so that at a glance the relationship of one part of the dial to another is automatically comprehended, whereas the digital dial requires a degree of reasoning or abstract thought before it is understood. On the other hand the digital system in clocks and watches is in complete accord with the use of the 24 hour time system as employed by railway and air line companies and as we become accustomed to change, what once seemed new and strange eventually becomes the acceptable norm.

Perhaps the French *linear readout* dial as an unusual application of the idea will be the most difficult to understand and accept, though its very rarity might well create interest and will certainly contribute to sales appeal. The minutes are read with the upper, white tipped hand on the vertical scale, and the hours by the white hand on the curved scale, each hand jumping back to the beginning after every twelve hours. The *date aperture* may be seen on the centre right. The digital dial on the radio cabinet is completely appropriate, for the design of the dial is right for this piece of 20th century household equipment, built from modern materials. Both the clock and the radio are supplied with mains power, the frequency of the mains supply guaranteeing the timekeeping of the clock as with all mains power clocks which are *synchronous motors* (p. 212). In this sense the generating station is the clock supplying the time to the equipment connected to it.

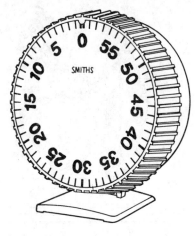

DOMESTIC ONE HOUR CLOCKWORK TIMER

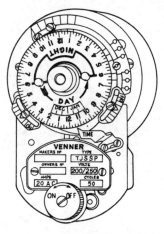

ELECTRIC AND CLOCKWORK TIME SWITCH FOR
DOMESTIC OR INDUSTRIAL USE

Interval timers have already been mentioned in the form of sand glasses and oil
clocks (p. 19) and the *fly-back chronograph*
is also an interval timer as well as a normal
watch (p. 206). The word 'chronograph' in
fact implies an instrument which records
its information graphically, the word being
derived from the Greek *khronos*—time and
graphos—written. The term chronograph
is applied generally to tape or drum
recording apparatus on which a pen traces
a record during observations of scientific
or industrial importance. The *interval
timer* illustrated is typical of many timers
for domestic use, and it can be set to
measure any interval of time up to an hour
by turning the pointer on its revolving
edge to the amount of time required. Many
such timers have conventional hands
which revolve anti-clockwise as the time
elapses, such as the ones used in photographic darkrooms, and most are spring-
powered with a simple lever escapement.
Clocks specially made to measure varying
intervals of time accurately are often
called *chronoscopes.*

Time switches are now considered essential
for modern living conditions, the most
common uses being for control of central
heating systems, street lighting, shop
window lighting, advertisement signs and
so forth. Control of electrical apparatus of
this kind may be done by an ordinary
synchronous motor clock but if there
should ever be any interruption to the
power supply the timing would be wrong
and be continuously so until re-set. For
this reason *clockwork* time switches are
usually used of which the mainsprings are
wound by electric motors intermittently,
or continuously through a slipping clutch.
The clock operates hand-set lever controls
to make and break electrical contacts at the
times required. The clocks used in factories
and known as *Time Recorders* are also
clockwork interval timers, for they automatically record the length of a man's
working day either on a roll of paper inside
the machine or directly on the workman's
card. Other instruments such as *barographs*
contain clockwork systems which record
time in relation to other factors.

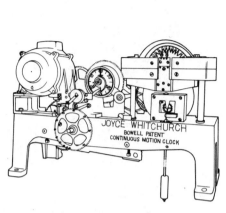

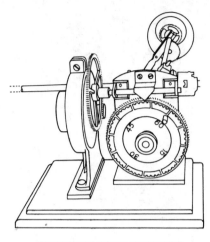

ELECTRIC 'CONTINUOUS MOTION' TURRET CLOCK
c.1920

SYNCHRONOUS MOTOR TURRET CLOCK

The system most commonly used for applying electric power to *existing* weight-driven turret clocks is to arrange for the weights to be re-wound electrically automatically at regular intervals, but otherwise to allow the clock to run normally. When the weight has dropped to a given point a small *counter-weight* rises to operate a switch causing an electric motor to wind up the driving weight. When wound sufficiently the driving weight then opens the switch and stops the motor. This method operates over a relatively small drop of the weight, but if there should be a power failure the clock will continue to go for a considerable time and will automatically re-wind when power is restored. An *endless chain* system, not unlike the *Huyghens endless chain* (p. 29) is used. Alternatively, the hands of the clock may be driven forwards at one minute or half minute intervals, the opening and closing of the circuit being controlled by a conventional pendulum as in the clock designed by *G. B. Bowell* which incorporates a synchronous switch.

The striking train of the Bowell *continuous motion clock* uses an ordinary geared down electric motor, the contacts being opened and closed by a detent acting on a *count wheel* of the type used on many conventional clocks. Although this kind of clock was introduced early in the present century and was still being advertised as late as the 1930s, it is clearly an electrical adaptation of the *flat bed frame* of the 19th century (p. 146) and combines its disadvantages of size, weight and exposure to dirt with electrical power. With the arrival of the *synchronous motor clock* in 1931, various small versions of which are now standard in every home and rely for their accuracy on the guaranteed average of 50 cycles per second A.C. supply, movements for turret clocks have become simple synchronous motors geared directly to the motion work, providing small, convenient, reliable (except during power cuts) and accurate machinery for driving the hands of dials on church towers, town halls and many other public buildings.

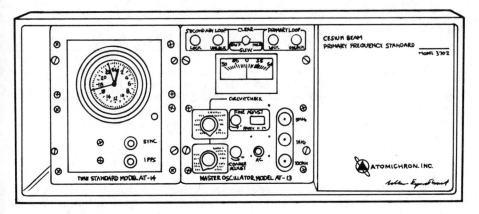

THE CAESIUM ATOMIC CLOCK
1970

Small, convenient, reliable, accurate—these are the adjectives which can be applied to so many of the electrical devices with which we now measure time and yet the romance, pleasure and sometimes disappointment which we may derive from older, conventional, mechanical clocks will be lost by their passing. In the sense that mechanical clocks have their faults, weaknesses and shortcomings they are like human beings and seem to have a life of their own which most of us, with a little care and trouble, can at least begin to understand. Not so, however, with the impersonal, highly complex and ingenious equipment which is illustrated here, the *caesium atomic clock* which was first developed in the 1950s and is now commercially available in the model above at about $16,000. The accuracy of the early models of the 1950s was measurable in terms of one second in three hundred years and at the National Physical Laboratory in Teddington, Middlesex, the equipment being used today is at least six times as accurate.

The caesium atomic clock works on the principle of counting the natural vibrations of caesium atoms by matching or tuning them to the frequency of an alternating field from a quartz crystal clock. Complex processes of this kind belong to the realms of highly specialised electronic engineering and physics which have made possible such developments of our age as computers and space travel. On a domestic scale, electronic devices are now available in the form of pocket-sized calculators which are rapidly replacing machines which worked on mechanical principles. This new technology instantaneously provides more accurate results and is more convenient to use. It is the use of such scientific equipment that is changing the pattern of human life. Mechanical clocks, for so long a part of our daily lives, are almost certain to disappear ultimately except for those which are cared for by people who find pleasure in what they have to tell about life in the past.

Select Bibliography

A. **General reading**
Baillie, G. H., *Clocks and Watches, An Historical Bibliography*, London, 1951
Baillie, G. H., *Watchmakers and Clockmakers of the World*, London, first published 1929; various later editions
Basserman-Jordan, Ernst von, *The Book of Old Clocks and Watches* (translated by H. Alan Lloyd), London, 1964
Britten, F. J., *Old Clocks and Watches and their Makers*, 1st edition, London, 1899; 6th edition available as a reprint, 1971; 7th edition by G. H. Baillie, C. Clutton and C. A. Ilbert, 1956; 8th edition revised and enlarged by C. Clutton
Camerer Cuss, T. P., *The Country Life Book of Watches*, London, 1967
Cescinsky, H. and Webster, M. R., *English Domestic Clocks*, London, 1913; available as a reprint, 1969
Cipolla, Carlo M., *Clocks and Culture*, London, 1967
Clutton, C. and Daniels, G., *Watches*, London, 1965
Cumhaill, P. W. (pseudonym), *Investing in Clocks and Watches*, London, 1967
Lloyd, H. Alan, *The Collector's Dictionary of Clocks*, London, 1964
Robertson, J. Drummond, *The Evolution of Clockwork*, London, 1931; reprinted 1972
Tait, Hugh, *Clocks in the British Museum*, London, 1968
Tardy, H. Lengelle, *La Pendule Française*, Paris, 1948–50; various reprintings in the 1960s. *Part 1: De l'Horloge Gothique à la Pendule Louis XV; Part 2: Du Louis XVI à nos Jours; Part 3: Provinces et Etranger*
Ward, F. A. B., *Time Measurement*, Descriptive catalogue of the Science Museum collection, London, 1966
Wright, Lawrence, *Clockwork Man*, London, 1968

B. **Specialised works**
Bird, Anthony, *English House Clocks 1600 to 1850*, Newton Abbot, 1973
Edwardes, Ernest L., *The Grandfather Clock*, Altrincham, 1949; New and enlarged edition, 1971
Edwardes, Ernest L., *Weight-driven Chamber Clocks of the Middle Ages and Renaissance*, Altrincham, 1965
Jaquet, Eugene and Chapuis, Alfred, *Technique and History of the Swiss Watch*, first published 1953; reprinted London, 1970
Lee, Ronald A., *The Knibb Family—Clockmakers*, Byfleet, Surrey, 1964
Lloyd, H. Alan, *Some Outstanding Clocks Over Seven Hundred Years 1250 to 1950*, London, 1958
Mody, N. H. N., *Japanese Clocks*, London, n.d.
Royer-Collard, F. B., *Skeleton Clocks*, London, 1969
Symonds, R. W., *Masterpieces of English Furniture and Clocks*, London, 1940
Symonds, R. W., *A History of English Clocks*, London, 1947
Symonds, R. W., *Thomas Tompion, his Life and Work*, London, 1951

C. **Precision clocks and electrical timekeeping**
Chamberlain, Paul M., *It's about Time*, London, 1964
Gould, Rupert T., *John Harrison and his Timekeepers*, London, 1958 (originally published in The Mariner's Mirror, 1935)

Gould, Rupert T., *The Marine Chronometer*, London, 1923 and 1960
Hope-Jones, F., *Electrical Timekeeping*, London, 1940
Jagger, Cedric, *Paul Philip Barraud 1750–1929*, London, 1968
Mercer, Vaudrey, *John Arnold & Son, Chronometer Makers 1762–1843*, London, 1972
Quill, Humphrey, *John Harrison, the Man who found Longitude*, London, 1966

D. **Mechanical information and manufacturing methods**
Ashton, T. S., *An Eighteenth Century Industrialist—Peter Stubs of Warrington 1756–1806*, Manchester, 1939
Britten, F. J., *The Watch and Clock Makers' Handbook*, London, 11th edition, 1915
Crom, Theodore R., *Horological Wheel Cutting Engines 1700 to 1900*, Gainesville, Florida, 1970
De Carle, Donald, *Practical Clock Repairing*, London, 1952
De Carle, Donald, *Practical Watch Repairing*, London, 3rd edition, 1969
Diderot et d'Alembert, *Horlogerie* from the 18th century *Encyclopédie, ou Dictionaire Raisonné des Sciences, des Arts et des Métiers*, reprinted Milan, 1971
Rees, Abraham, *Clocks, Watches and Chronometers* from *The Cyclopaedia; or Universal Dictionary of Arts, Sciences and Literature*, 1819–20, reprinted Newton Abbot, 1970
Smith, A. and Abbot, Henry G., *The Lancashire Watch Company, Prescot, Lancashire, England, 1889 to 1910*, Fitzwilliam, New Hampshire, 1973
White, Allen, *The Chain Makers—A History of the Watch Fusee Chain Industry*, Christchurch, 1967

E. **American Clock and Watchmaking**
Abbott, Henry G., *The Watch Factories of America*, Chicago, 1888, facsimile edition Exeter, New Hampshire, n.d.
Crossman, Charles S., *The Complete History of Watch Making in America*, 1885–1887, reprinted Exeter, New Hampshire, n.d.
Daniels, George, *English and American Watches*, London, 1967
Eckhardt, George H., *Pennsylvania Clocks and Clockmakers*, New York, 1955
Hooper, Penrose R., *Shop Records of Daniel Burnap, Clockmaker*, Hartford, Connecticut, 1958
Hummel, Charles, *With Hammer in Hand, The Dominy Craftsmen of East Hampton, New York*, Charlottesville, Virginia, 1968
Marsh, E. A., *Watches by Automatic Machinery at Waltham*, Chicago, 1896; reprinted Exeter, New Hampshire, 1968
Niebling, Warren H., *History of the American Watch Case*, Philadelphia, 1971
Palmer, Brooks, *The Book of American Clocks*, New York, 1928 and 1950
Palmer, Brooks, *A Treasury of American Clocks*, New York, 1967
Roberts, Kenneth D. (editor), *Elgin Reminiscences, Making Watches by Machinery 1869*, Bristol, Connecticut, 1971
Roberts, Kenneth D., *Eli Terry and the Connecticut Shelf Clock*, Bristol, Connecticut, 1973
Roberts, Kenneth D., *The Contributions of Joseph Ives to Connecticut Clock Technology*, Bristol, Connecticut, 1970
Thomson, Richard, *Antique American Clocks and Watches*, New York, 1968
Willard, John Ware, *Simon Willard and his Clocks*, New York, 1968

F. **Journals**
Antiquarian Horological Society, London, *Antiquarian Horology*, published quarterly. Special publications are also issued from time to time by this society
British Horological Institute, Newark, Notts., *Horological Journal*, published monthly
National Association of Watch and Clock Collectors Inc., Columbia, Pennsylvania, *Bulletin of the N.A.W.C.C.*, published six times yearly

Index